What Your Colleague

"This book is so incredibly practical and grounded in the hands-on implementation of the five practices! It takes the ideas of the earlier book, which focused more on the "what" of each practice, and looks closer at the when, why, and how that is so important for teachers in their planning. In each chapter, I found myself nodding in agreement as the authors described challenges in using the five practices and thoroughly enjoyed the opportunities to reflect on the practices in relation to my own planning and teaching."

Kristin Gray
Director of Elementary Curriculum and Professional Learning
Illustrative Mathematics

"This is a powerful and readable guide to shifting our elementary school mathematics instruction toward maximizing our students' learning. But it's the clarity and familiarity of the challenges we all face when trying to implement these five practices—and the practicality and detail of the guidance provided in each chapter to address these challenges—that set this book apart and make it so useful for professional growth."

Steve Leinwand
Researcher/Change Agent
American Institutes for Research
Washington, DC

"This book is packed with practical guidance, support, and actual footage of what it looks like to enact ambitious teaching through these practices. If there's a teacher or leader out there wondering how to ensure their classroom embraces ambitious teaching that is empowering and equitable, this is your guide. Read it. Practice it. Make it yours. There just isn't anything else out there pushing us to think and act as strategically in our math classrooms like this does."

Levi J. Patrick
Assistant Executive Director of Curriculum and Instruction
Oklahoma State Department of Education

"Peg Smith has done it again. Building on her previous work with Mary Kay Stein (2018), Smith and coauthors Miriam Sherin and Victoria Bill have taken the next step in supporting teachers to engage students in rich mathematics discussions. Filled with examples and insights, both in print and on video, this book allows teachers to 'see it in action,' make sense, and reflect on the challenges, and it provides support and guidance to implement the five practices in their own instruction. Perfect for teachers, teacher leaders, coaches, or others who support teachers in their instructional practices, this book literally connects theory to practice and provides honest and thoughtful reflections and guidance to work towards our ultimate goals—students' mathematics learning and agency."

Cynthia H. Callard
Professor and Executive Director
Center for Professional Development and Education Reform
Warner Graduate School of Education and Human Development
University of Rochester
Rochester, NY

"Every elementary school math teacher needs to understand the practices in this book and know how to use them effectively in the classroom. Use of these practices will empower elementary school students to understand mathematics and feel like they can do math!"

Lois A. Williams
Adjunct Professor, Mathematics Education Consultant, Author
Mary Baldwin University
Scottsville, VA

"This book is a comprehensive, ready-to-use, professional development plan inside a book's covers! Its components include student work, classroom video, features addressing challenges teachers face, as well as providing reflective opportunities to pause and consider. This amazing, must-have resource will truly engage elementary school mathematics teachers in 'doing' *The 5 Practices*."

Francis (Skip) Fennell
Professor of Education and Graduate and Professional Studies Emeritus
Project Director, Elementary Mathematics Specialists and Teacher Leaders Project
McDaniel College
Past President, Association of Mathematics Teacher Educators (AMTE)
Past President, National Council of Teachers of Mathematics (NCTM)

"This book takes *5 Practices for Orchestrating Productive Mathematics Discussions* to the next level as readers experience what these practices look like in real mathematics classrooms in Grades K–5. Readers will engage in analysis of videos and student work as they deepen their understanding of the five practices. The authors specifically address the challenges one might face in implementing the five practices in classrooms by providing recommendations and concrete examples to avoid these challenges."

Cathy Martin
Executive Director, Curriculum and Instruction
Denver Public Schools
Denver, CO

"The authors insightfully anticipate teachers' challenges and have designed a creative tool to support teacher learning. Their book is filled with highly practical reflective questions all tied to the five practices, enabling teachers to think for themselves. The result is a book that empowers elementary level teachers to determine the best ways to advance their own professional development to improve students' mathematical lives."

Ruth M. Heaton
Chief Executive Officer
Teachers Development Group
West Linn, OR

"As an elementary math teacher, nothing has helped me become more intentional and purposeful than the *5 Practices*. In a continued effort to move student thinking forward, I really appreciated how the authors walked us through specific K–5 examples because this will definitely help me improve my craft."

Graham Fletcher
Math Specialist
Atlanta, GA

"At Illustrative Mathematics we were looking for a framework that would enable us to embed in our curriculum ambitious but achievable goals for teacher practice. The five practices was the perfect fit: a memorable, learnable set of principles that could be used by novice and veteran teachers alike to get their students thinking and sharing their reasoning."

Bill McCallum
President, Illustrative Mathematics
University Distinguished Professor of Mathematics
University of Arizona

"Mathematical discourse is the heart of effective instruction, but is challenging to implement well. Finally, this book provides a step-by-step guide for bringing the five practices for orchestrating discourse—anticipating, monitoring, selecting, sequencing, and connecting—fully into classroom practice at the elementary level. Through video examples, tasks, and student work, the authors provide practical advice for engaging young students in powerful class discussions centered on their strategies and mathematical thinking. This book is an invaluable professional resource."

DeAnn Huinker
Professor, Mathematics Education
University of Wisconsin–Milwaukee
NCTM Board of Directors
Milwaukee, WI

"This book is a must for all elementary teachers who want to teach mathematics deeply and equitably, or as Smith, Bill, and Sherin write—ambitiously. From the first page, you are invited to take a deep dive into each of the *5 Practices* by unpacking the practice, considering the potential instructional challenges associated with the practice, and, through the use of videos, teacher responses, and student work, analyze the challenging and rewarding work of facilitating productive student discourse. Read this book, try what's suggested in your classroom, and watch ALL of your students truly shine as they demonstrate meaningful mathematical thinking and reasoning."

Beth Kobett
Associate Professor
Stevenson University School of Education
NCTM Board of Directors
Stevenson, MD

"*The Five Practices in Practice: Successfully Orchestrating Mathematics Discussions in Your Elementary Classroom* is THE tool for helping make ambitious elementary mathematics teaching a reality. It gives a rich, elementary lens to the original groundbreaking work through classroom examples, tasks, and accompanying videos. Simply put, it is a must-have for any mathematics teacher, coach, or administrator."

John SanGiovanni
Coordinator of Elementary Mathematics
Howard County Public School System
Howard County, MD

"I've been a fan of *5 Practices for Orchestrating Productive Mathematics Discussions* for a long time! In this practical, teacher-friendly follow-up to the popular resource, the authors provide educators with a roadmap to support facilitating productive mathematics discussions in their classrooms. In this new addition to the series, educators are treated to a comprehensive blueprint for implementing the five practices that includes scaffolds, realistic suggestions grounded by research, feedback and authentic data from practicing teachers, vignettes, grade-specific examples and opportunities to reflect on classroom practice, making this resource a valuable tool for elementary educators."

Latrenda Knighten
Elementary Mathematics Instructional Specialist
Baton Rouge, LA

The Five Practices in Practice
at a Glance

Candid quotes from
been-there teachers
illuminate the topic
of each chapter.

❝ While students are working
and I'm checking in with them, I'm
going to be thinking about how to
sequence the math and the kids.
I might have ideas, but I have to
wait and see what they do. I'll be
trying to see who's got something
that can help us make sense of
the math goals for today. ❞

—ANDREW STRONG, FIFTH-GRADE TEACHER

Pause and Consider moments invite teachers to reflect on and make connections to their own practice.

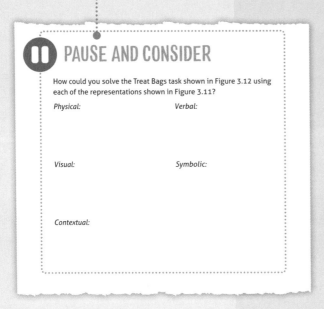

❚❚ PAUSE AND CONSIDER

How could you solve the Treat Bags task shown in Figure 3.12 using each of the representations shown in Figure 3.11?

Physical: *Verbal:*

Visual: *Symbolic:*

Contextual:

hat they have written or drawn. Using students' own ̶n often be helpful. Be aware that what you anticipated ̶do is not always what they end up doing. Asking students ̶ns about their work is an important way to uncover how ̶g about the task and their solution. As Ms. Tyus explained, ̶tegies outlined and I have my assessing questions. But ̶happen in the task. They might do different things." ̶ed this point, saying, "You never know what you're going ̶es" and that for him, the next step is "just to assess their ̶did you do this? Explain it to me." Assessing questions are ̶use they can help you uncover what students are doing, ̶that aligns with what you anticipated.

̶ng questions are most useful when they make students' ̶ in ways that can then help you move their thinking ̶ the lesson goals. You want to understand not only *what* ̶t *why* they did it. Understanding the reasons behind a ̶gy often provides the clues you need to help the student ̶position or move deeper into the task.

TEACHING TAKEAWAY

Look and listen *carefully*. Modify your planned assessing questions in real time based specifically on what students are doing and saying, rather than what you thought they would do or say.

Teaching Takeaways provide on-your-feet support for teachers, so they can jump into implementing the strategies discussed.

Video showcase panels highlight the rich film footage available for each topic and include related questions for consideration.

Analyzing the Work of Teaching 2.1

Launching a Task

Video Clip 2.1
In this activity, you will watch Video Clip 2.1 from Tara Tyus's first-grade class.

As you watch the clip, consider the following questions:

- What did the teacher do to help her students *get ready* to work on the Ms. Tyus's Markers task?

- What did the teacher learn about her students that indicated they were ready to engage in the task?

- Do you think the time spent in launching the task was time well spent?

 Videos may also be accessed at
resources.corwin.com/5practices-elementary

Illustrative vignettes and examples demonstrate real-world applications of the concepts discussed in each chapter.

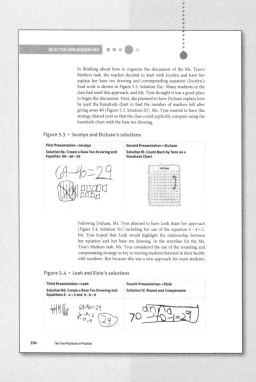

An in-depth **Linking the Five Practices to Your Own Instruction** feature helps teachers move even deeper into implementation, providing detailed support and additional reflective opportunities.

SELECTING AND SEQUENCING

In the next chapter, we explore the practice of connecting. Here, we will return to Ms. Tyus's lesson and consider what it takes to engage in this practice and the challenges it presents.

Linking the Five Practices to Your Own Instruction

SELECTING AND SEQUENCING

It is now time to reflect on the lesson you taught following Chapter 4, but this time through the lens of selecting and sequencing.

1. What solutions did you select for presentation during the whole group discussion?

   • Did the selected solutions help you address the mathematical ideas that you had targeted in the lesson? Are there other solutions that might have been more useful in meeting your goal?

   • How many solutions did you have students present? Did all of these contribute to better understanding of the mathematics to be learned? Did you conclude the discussion in the allotted time?

   • Which students were selected as presenters? Did you include any students who are not frequent presenters? Could you have?

2. How did you sequence the solutions?

   • Did the series of presentations add up to something? Was the storyline coherent?

   • Did you include any incomplete or incorrect solutions? Where in the sequence did they fit?

3. Based on your reading of this chapter and a deeper understanding of the practice of selecting and sequencing, would you do anything differently if you were going to teach this lesson again?

4. What lessons have you learned that you will draw on in the next lesson you plan and teach?

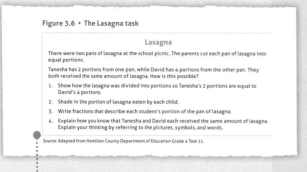

Figure 3.6 • The Lasagna task

Lasagna

There were two pans of lasagna at the school picnic. The parents cut each pan of lasagna into equal portions.

Tanesha has 2 portions from one pan, while David has 4 portions from the other pan. They both received the same amount of lasagna. How is this possible?

1. Show how the lasagna was divided into portions so Tanesha's 2 portions are equal to David's 4 portions.

2. Shade in the portion of lasagna eaten by each child.

3. Write fractions that describe each student's portion of the pan of lasagna.

4. Explain how you know that Tanesha and David each received the same amount of lasagna. Explain your thinking by referring to the pictures, symbols, and words.

Source: Adapted from Hamilton County Department of Education Grade 4 Task 11.

Clearly designed tasks promote mathematical reasoning and problem solving.

Figure 4.3 • Challenges associated with the practice of monitoring

CHALLENGE	DESCRIPTION
Trying to understand what students are thinking	Students do not always articulate their thinking clearly. It can be quite demanding for teachers, in the moment, to figure out what a student means or is trying to say. This requires teachers to listen carefully to what students are saying and to ask questions that help them better explain what they are thinking.
Keeping track of group progress—which groups you visited and what you left them to work on	As teachers are running from group to group, providing support, they need to be able to keep track of what each group is doing and what they left students to work on. Also, it is important for a teacher to return to a group in order to determine whether the advancing question given to them helped them make progress.
Involving all members of a group	All individuals in the group need to be challenged to answer assessing and advancing questions. For individuals to benefit from the thinking of their peers, they need to be held accountable for listening to and adding on, repeating and summarizing what others are saying.

Challenge and Description charts distill and demystify some of the common issues teachers encounter when teaching the concepts at hand.

What It Takes/Key Questions charts break down the critical components of the practice and explain what it takes to succeed and the questions you need to ask yourself to stay on track.

the components of this practice along with key questions to guide the process of monitoring.

Figure 4.1 • Key questions that support the practice of monitoring

WHAT IT TAKES	KEY QUESTIONS
Tracking student thinking	How will you keep track of students' responses during the lesson?
	How will you ensure that you check in with all students during the lesson?
Assessing student thinking	Are your assessing questions meeting students where they are?
	Are your assessing questions making student thinking visible?
Advancing student thinking	Are your advancing questions driven by your lesson goals?
	Are students able to pursue advancing questions on their own?
	Are your advancing questions helping students to progress?

THE 5 PRACTICES in Practice

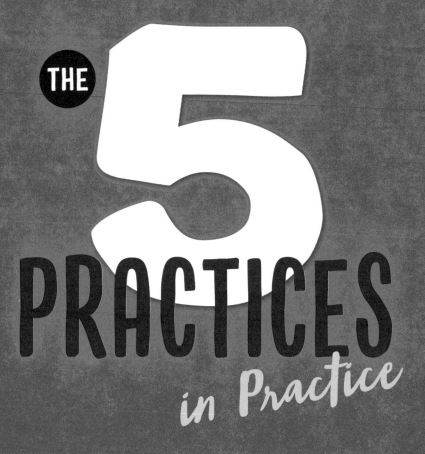

THE 5 PRACTICES

in Practice

Successfully Orchestrating Mathematics Discussions in

Your Elementary Classroom

Margaret (Peg) Smith • Victoria Bill
Miriam Gamoran Sherin • Foreword by Dan Meyer

A JOINT PUBLICATION

CORWIN Mathematics

NCTM

NATIONAL COUNCIL OF
TEACHERS OF MATHEMATICS

For information:

Corwin
A SAGE Company
2455 Teller Road
Thousand Oaks, California 91320
(800) 233–9936
www.corwin.com

SAGE Publications Ltd.
1 Oliver's Yard
55 City Road
London, EC1Y 1SP
United Kingdom

SAGE Publications India Pvt. Ltd.
B 1/I 1 Mohan Cooperative Industrial Area
Mathura Road, New Delhi 110 044
India

SAGE Publications Asia-Pacific Pte. Ltd.
18 Cross Street #10–10/11/12
China Square Central
Singapore 048423

ISBN: 978-1-5443-2113-4

Executive Editor, Mathematics: Erin Null
Associate Content
  Development Editor: Jessica Vidal
Production Editor: Tori Mirsadjadi
Copy Editor: Christina West
Typesetter: Integra
Proofreader: Scott Oney
Indexer: Will Ragsdale
Cover and Interior Designer: Gail Buschman
Marketing Manager: Margaret O'Connor

Printed in the United States of America.

This book is printed on acid-free paper.

19 20 21 22 23 10 9 8 7 6 5 4 3 2 1

Contents

CHAPTER 1   Introduction

CHAPTER 2   Setting Goals and Selecting Tasks

CHAPTER 3   Anticipating Student Responses

CHAPTER 4   Monitoring Student Work

CHAPTER 5   **Selecting and Sequencing Student Solutions**

CHAPTER 6   Connecting Student Solutions

CHAPTER 7   Looking Back and Looking Ahead

Visit the companion website at
http://resources.corwin.com/5practices-elementary
for downloadable resources.

List of Video Clips

Chapter 1

Video Clip 1.1: A District Engages in the Five Practices

Chapter 2

Video Clip 2.1: Launching a Task

Video Clip 2.2: Setting Goals and Selecting Tasks

Chapter 3

Video Clip 3.1: Anticipating Student Responses

Chapter 4

Video Clip 4.1: Assessing Student Thinking

Video Clip 4.2: Advancing Student Thinking—Part One

Video Clip 4.3: Advancing Student Thinking—Part Two

Video Clip 4.4: Determining What Students Are Thinking—Part One

Video Clip 4.5: Determining What Students Are Thinking—Part Two

Video Clip 4.6: Following Up With Students

Video Clip 4.7: Holding All Students Accountable

Video Clip 4.8: Monitoring Student Work

Chapter 5

Video Clip 5.1: Selecting and Sequencing Student Solutions

Chapter 6

Video Clip 6.1: Connecting Student Work to the Goals of the Lesson—Part One

Video Clip 6.2: Connecting Student Work to the Goals of the Lesson—Part Two

Video Clip 6.3: Connecting Student Work to the Goals of the Lesson—Part Three

Video Clip 6.4: Connecting Different Solutions to Each Other

Video Clip 6.5: Holding Students Accountable

Video Clip 6.6: Making Key Ideas Public

Video Clip 6.7: Connecting Student Responses

Note From the Publisher: The authors have provided video and web content throughout the book that is available to you through QR (quick response) codes. To read a QR code, you must have a smartphone or tablet with a camera. We recommend that you download a QR code reader app that is made specifically for your phone or tablet brand.

Videos may also be accessed at **resources.corwin.com/5practices-elementary**

Foreword

Why did you become a teacher?

Was it, as with many elementary teachers I've worked with, because you loved kids? Perhaps even at a young age you were an effective caregiver, and you knew how to care for more than just another person's tangible needs. You listened, and you made people feel *listened to*. You had an eye for a person's value and power. You understood where people were in their lives, and you understood how the right kind of question or observation could propel them to where they were going to *be*.

Spending a few decades helping people feel heard, helping them unleash and use their tremendous capacity—perhaps you thought that was a worthwhile way to spend what you thought would be the hours between 7 AM and 4 PM every day.

How do the demands of teaching mathematics affect your love for students?

Perhaps you *love* math and you're grateful for the opportunity to help students experience math as you have. Or perhaps you're fearful of math and you're able to relate to students who feel the same way. In either case, what I have learned in my work with math teachers is that it is impossible to separate your love for your students from your feelings about and knowledge of mathematics. Both sources of your energy—students and math—are vital. Neither source is renewable without the other. The teachers who struggle to love their students as people will struggle to help them learn mathematics. The teachers who struggle to love mathematics miss out on opportunities to express their love for their students as people.

If teachers draw their energy only from mathematics, for example, their students can become abstractions and interchangeable. They can convince themselves it's possible to influence *what students know* without care for *who they are*, that it's possible to treat their *knowledge* as deficient and in need of fixing without risking negative consequences for their *identity*. But students know better. Most of them know what it feels like when the adults in the room position themselves as all-knowing and the students in the room as all-unknowing. Your love for and understanding of mathematics are no help at all when students have decided you care less about them than about numbers and operations.

On the other hand, if teachers draw their energy only from students, then the day's mathematics can become interchangeable with any other day's. Some days, it may feel like an act of care to skip students past mathematics they find frustrating or to skip mathematics altogether. But the math that teachers skip one day is foundational for the math another day or another year. Students will have to pay down their frustration later, only then with compound interest. Your love and care for students cannot protect them from the frustration that is often fundamental to learning.

What is needed, of course, is love for students *and* mathematics. I could share with you any number of maxims and slogans that testify to that truth. I could perhaps convince some of you to believe me. But still that would not answer the key question: How?

My answer: anticipate, monitor, select, sequence, and connect.

Those actions, initially proposed by Smith and Stein in 2011, and ably illustrated in this book with classroom videos, teacher testimony, and student work samples, support a teacher's love for students and a teacher's love for math in ways that make both math and students matter.

For teachers who are motivated by a love of students, those five practices invite the teacher to learn more mathematics. The more math teachers know, the easier it is for them to find value in the ways their students think. Their mathematical knowledge enables them to monitor that thinking less for *correctness* and more for *interest*. Would presenting this student's thinking provoke an *interesting* conversation with the class, whether the circled answer is correct or not? A teacher's mathematical knowledge enables her to connect one student's interesting idea to another's. Her math knowledge helps her connect student thinking together and illustrate for the students the enormous value in their ideas.

And if you are also motivated by a love of mathematics, and want students to love mathematics as well, those five practices offer a way to connect your students as people to the math they produce. Students are not a blank screen onto which teachers can project and trace out their own knowledge. Meaning is *made* by the student. It isn't *transferred* by the teacher. The more teachers love and want to protect interesting mathematical ideas, the more they should want to know the meaning students are making of those ideas. Those five practices have helped me connect student ideas to canonical mathematical ideas, helping students see the value of both.

Neither a love of students nor a love of mathematics can sustain the work of math education on its own. We work with *math students*, a composite of their mathematical ideas and their identities as people. The five practices for orchestrating productive mathematical discussions, and these ideas for putting those practices into practice, offer the actions that can develop and sustain the belief that both math and students matter.

You might think your path into teaching emanated from a love of mathematics or from a love of students. But it's the same path. It's a wider path than you might have thought, one that offers passage to more people and more ideas than you originally thought possible. This book will help you and your students learn to walk it.

—Dan Meyer
Chief Academic Officer, Desmos

Preface

In 2001, a group of researchers at the University of Pittsburgh launched the ASTEROID (A Study of Teacher Education: Research on Instructional Design) project funded by the National Science Foundation. The project investigated what mathematics teachers learned from participation in practice-based teacher education courses—courses that used cognitively demanding mathematical tasks, narrative cases, and student work as a focus of critique, inquiry, and investigation (Smith, 2001). Mary Kay Stein and I (Peg) were co-principal investigators on the project and I was the course instructor.

The first course, taught in the summer of 2002, focused on proportional reasoning. The goals of the course were both to enhance teachers' own ability to reason proportionally and to enhance their capacity to teach proportional reasoning. The students in the course were 14 elementary and three secondary teachers, some of whom had just completed their Master of Arts in Teaching degree and others who were working on Master's of Education degrees. In order to investigate what teachers learned and how our instruction supported or inhibited learning, we videotaped each class session. We also gave teachers pre-/post-tests, interviewed them, and kept notebooks of all work produced in the course.

As the research team watched videos of teacher-students solving cognitively challenging (aka high-level) tasks, they noticed a certain pattern in the way I, as the instructor, facilitated work around and discussions of the tasks. I had solved the problems in multiple ways prior to the class, often seeking input from graduate students on alternative approaches. The researchers saw how I interacted with students as they worked and how I made notes of what specific students were doing. They saw how I identified students to present their solutions, how I ordered the solutions in particular ways, and how I helped my students make connections between different strategies, ensuring the mathematical ideas were central. While I was aware of what I was doing, I did not give much thought to why I was doing it, and I did not codify my actions.

The research team noticed the regularity of my teaching pattern and the impact it appeared to have on the quality of the discussions around high-level tasks. They recognized the parallel between a teacher educator teaching teachers and K–12 teachers teaching children. They were excited by the potential this model had to support the work of K–12 classroom teachers. We all knew we were on to something powerful. We gave labels to each of the identified actions so that others could learn them and voila!—the five practices—anticipating, monitoring, selecting, sequencing, and connecting—were born!

From that moment forward—in collaboration with others—I have written about the five practices in journal articles, and my co-author Mary Kay Stein and I published the book that anchors this new series, which you may know as *5 Practices for Orchestrating Productive Mathematics Discussions* (2011). The book sold more than 100,000 copies before we published the second edition in 2018.

What accounts for the surprising success of the five practices? Over the last three decades, there has been a growing consensus that traditional forms of mathematics teaching were not sufficiently preparing students for success in school and beyond. The release of the *Common Core State Standards* (National Governors Association Center for Best Practices & Council of Chief State School Officers, 2010) brought new demands for more ambitious teaching and an increased focus on the importance of engaging students in mathematical discussion. Such discussion gives students the opportunity to share ideas and clarify understandings, develop convincing arguments regarding why and how things work, develop a language for expressing mathematical ideas, and learn to see things from other people's perspectives.

So one answer to the question is that the five practices provides a five-step model of what teachers can do before and during instruction that gives them some control in facilitating discussions—an aspect of instruction that has proven to be especially challenging. The five practices are *doable* and something teachers could continue to get better at doing over time.

Despite the uptake of the five practices by teachers and teacher educators, teachers continue to find aspects of the practices challenging. Questions such as "Where do I find good tasks?," "How do I find time to adequately plan?," "What do I do if students all think about a problem the same way?," and "How do I wrap up the conversation at the end of a lesson without taking over?" abound.

In addition, teachers and teacher educators repeatedly ask me, "Do you have any video of teachers doing the five practices?" The need for authentic examples of what these practices look like in real classrooms was clear.

The Five Practices in Practice: Successfully Orchestrating Mathematics Discussions in Your Elementary Classroom (Smith, Bill, & Sherin, 2019) is the second book in a series that addresses many of the questions that teachers have raised with me over the years, and it provides what teachers and teacher educators have been clamoring for—classroom video of teachers engaged in orchestrating productive discussions. (The middle school book was published in Spring 2019 and the high school book will follow in 2020.)

This book goes beyond the first and second editions of the original *5 Practices* by providing a detailed unpacking of the practices and by identifying specific challenges teachers face related to each practice. The book includes numerous examples drawn from elementary school classrooms to illustrate aspects of the five practices and the associated challenges. A central component of these examples is video excerpts from elementary school classrooms that provide vivid images of real teachers using the five practices in their efforts to orchestrate productive discussions.

We hope this book will be a valuable resource for teachers!

—Peg Smith

Acknowledgments

Since the publication of *5 Practices for Orchestrating Productive Mathematics Discussions* (Smith & Stein, 2011), we have worked with and heard from hundreds of teachers who have reported on their successes and struggles in implementing the five practices in their classrooms. We have taken their feedback to heart. This book is our attempt to provide additional guidance on enacting the five practices in elementary school classrooms.

While the writing herein is the product of our collaboration, this book would not have been possible without the work, support, and commitment of a number of individuals. Specifically, we acknowledge the contributions of the following:

- Erin Null, Executive Editor for Corwin Mathematics, who encouraged us to write this book and provided thoughtful suggestions and insightful feedback at every step of the process.

- The producer at SAGE, Julie Slattery, and the video crew (Mike Labella, Davis Lester, and John Billings), whose expertise is evident in the compelling video clips, which are at the heart of this book.

- Metro Nashville Public Schools, who embraced this project from its inception and provided enthusiastic support throughout the planning, filming, and writing process. In particular,

  - The teachers in Metro Nashville Public Schools—Olivia Stastny (Una Elementary School), Andrew Strong (West End Middle School), and Tara Tyus (Una Elementary School)—who agreed to make their teaching public so that others could learn from their struggles and triumphs.

  - The principals in Metro Nashville Public Schools—Amella Dukes (Una Elementary School) and Russell Young (West End Middle School)—who enthusiastically welcomed us into their schools and accommodated our filming schedule.

- District Leaders—Shawn Joseph (former Superintendent of Schools), David Williams (Executive Officer for the Department of Curriculum and Instruction), and Jessica Slayton (Director of Mathematics)—who were instrumental in making the filming for this book possible.

Publisher's Acknowledgments

Corwin gratefully acknowledges the contributions of the following reviewers:

Cathy Battles
Educational Consultant
University of Missouri–Kansas City Regional Professional
    Development Center
Kansas City, MO

Natalie Crist
Supervisor of Elementary Mathematics
Baltimore County Public Schools
Baltimore, MD

Kevin Dykema
Eighth-Grade Math Teacher
Mattawan Middle School
Mattawan, MI

Cathy Martin
Executive Director, Curriculum and Instruction
Denver Public Schools
Denver, CO

Jennifer Novak
Education Associate, Mathematics
Delaware Department of Education
Elkridge, MD

Lois A. Williams
Adjunct Professor, Mathematics Education Consultant, Author
Mary Baldwin University
Scottsville, VA

Cathy Yenca
Middle School Mathematics Teacher
Eanes Independent School District
Austin, TX

About the Authors

Margaret (Peg) Smith is a Professor Emerita at the University of Pittsburgh. Over the past two decades, she has been developing research-based materials for use in the professional development of mathematics teachers. She has authored or coauthored more than 90 books, edited books or monographs, book chapters, and peer-reviewed articles, including the best seller *5 Practices for Orchestrating Productive Mathematics Discussions* (coauthored with Mary Kay Stein). She was a member of the writing team for *Principles to Actions: Ensuring Mathematical Success for All* and is a co-author of two recent books (*Taking Action: Implementing Effective Mathematics Teaching Practices in Grades 6–8* and *9–12*) that provide further explication of the teaching practices first described in *Principles to Actions*. She was a member of the Board of Directors of the Association of Mathematics Teacher Educators (2001–2003 and 2003–2005), of the National Council of Teachers of Mathematics (2006–2009), and of Teachers Development Group (2009–2017).

Victoria Bill is a former elementary and middle school mathematics teacher. She is currently a fellow and mathematics team lead with the Institute for Learning at the University of Pittsburgh Learning Research and Development Center. She has been designing and facilitating professional development with administrators, coaches, and teachers in urban districts for more than 20 years. She also develops curriculum, intervention materials, and performance-based assessments. Bill was the co-principal investigator on a collaborative research project between researchers from the Learning Research and Development Center, the Institute for Learning, and the Tennessee Department of Education, in which an instructional mathematics coaching model was developed. Bill regularly speaks at the NCTM, the National Council of Supervisors of Mathematics, and NCTM Research Conferences. She is co-author of the NCTM best seller *Taking Action: Implementing Effective Mathematics Teaching Practices, Grades K–5*.

Miriam Gamoran Sherin is Associate Provost for Undergraduate Education and the Alice Gabrielle Twight Professor of Learning Sciences at Northwestern University. Her research interests include mathematics teaching and learning, teacher cognition, and the role of video in supporting teacher learning. Sherin investigates the nature and dynamics of teacher noticing, and in particular, the ways in which teachers identify and interpret student thinking during instruction. *Mathematics Teacher Noticing: Seeing Through Teachers' Eyes*, edited by Sherin, V. Jacobs, and R. Philipp, received the American Educational Research Association Division K 2013 Excellence in Research in Teaching and Teacher Education award. In 2016, Sherin and her colleagues were awarded the NCTM Linking Research and Practice Outstanding Publication Award.

" Our district was introduced to the five practices about three years ago and they were so powerful we decided to infuse them into our professional learning for teachers. We were already working with NCTM's *Principles to Actions* and the idea of facilitating mathematical discourse, and we felt like the five practices really extended that—providing great supports for teachers when they were trying to plan, and determining how they could support students through productive struggle as they were engaging in high-level tasks. "

—JESSICA SLAYTON, DIRECTOR OF MATHEMATICS, METRO
NASHVILLE PUBLIC SCHOOLS

CHAPTER 1

Introduction

At the heart of efforts to help students in Grades K–5 learn mathematics is the idea of *ambitious teaching*. It's referred to as *ambitious* because of the substantial student learning goals that it encompasses—that all students have opportunities "to understand and use knowledge . . . [to] solve authentic problems" (Lampert & Graziani, 2009, p. 492). The Common Core State Standards for Mathematics (National Governors Association Center for Best Practices & Council of Chief State School Officers, 2010) provide a powerful vision of these goals through their description of grade-level, domain-specific content standards and the cross-cutting Standards for Mathematical Practice.

We believe that the phrase *ambitious teaching* is also appropriate because teaching in ways that align with these goals is a formidable task! To help you and other teachers understand what this looks like, *Principles to Actions: Ensuring Mathematical Success for All* (National Council of Teachers of Mathematics, 2014) describes a set of eight teaching practices that serve as a foundation for ambitious teaching (Figure 1.1 on the next page). These practices are based on what we know from research about how to effectively support students' learning of mathematics.

Figure 1.1 • Eight effective mathematics teaching practices

Establish mathematics goals to focus learning. Effective teaching of mathematics establishes clear goals for the mathematics that students are learning, situates goals within learning progressions, and uses the goals to guide instructional decisions.

Implement tasks that promote reasoning and problem solving. Effective teaching of mathematics engages students in solving and discussing tasks that promote mathematical reasoning and problem solving and allow multiple entry points and varied solution strategies.

Use and connect mathematical representations. Effective teaching of mathematics engages students in making connections among mathematical representations to deepen understanding of mathematics concepts and procedures and as tools for problem solving.

Facilitate meaningful mathematical discourse. Effective teaching of mathematics facilitates discourse among students to build shared understanding of mathematical ideas by analyzing and comparing student approaches and arguments.

Pose purposeful questions. Effective teaching of mathematics uses purposeful questions to assess and advance students' reasoning and sense-making about important mathematical ideas and relationships.

Build procedural fluency from conceptual understanding. Effective teaching of mathematics builds fluency with procedures on a foundation of conceptual understanding so that students, over time, become skillful in using procedures flexibly as they solve contextual and mathematical problems.

Support productive struggle in learning mathematics. Effective teaching of mathematics consistently provides students, individually and collectively, with opportunities and supports to engage in productive struggle as they grapple with mathematical ideas and relationships.

Elicit and use evidence of student thinking. Effective teaching of mathematics uses evidence of student thinking to assess progress toward mathematical understanding and to adjust instruction continually in ways that support and extend learning.

Source: Reprinted with permission from *Principles to Actions: Ensuring Mathematical Success for All*, copyright 2014, by the National Council of Teachers of Mathematics. All rights reserved.

Ambitious teaching also requires attention to equity. Mathematics has long been considered a gatekeeper, limiting opportunities for some students while promoting opportunities for others (Martin, Gholson, & Leonard, 2010). These differences are apparent as early as kindergarten, with African American and Latinx students more likely to be in classrooms that focus on procedural aspects of mathematics and/or that underestimate these students' capacities to engage in high-level problem solving (Aguirre et al., 2017; Turner & Celedón-Pattichis, 2011). Ambitious teaching requires you to challenge these long-standing practices and provide access and opportunity for every student so that they can develop strong positive identities as learners of mathematics (Aguirre, Mayfield-Ingram, & Martin, 2013).

At the center of ambitious teaching is a focus on classroom discourse. As you facilitate meaningful discussions with students, you will typically engage in several of the effective mathematics teaching practices, including asking purposeful questions, eliciting and using evidence of student thinking, connecting to various mathematical representations, and supporting productive struggle among students as they learn mathematics (Figure 1.1). In addition, allowing students to share their thinking with the class can help to position all students as valuable resources for learning and promote an equitable learning environment. In these ways, organizing discussions around students' ideas becomes critical for successfully enacting ambitious instruction.

What does it take, then, to organize and implement effective discussions? In this book, we present guidelines for using the five practices described by Smith and Stein (2018) in their book 5 *Practices for Orchestrating Productive Mathematics Discussions.*

The Five Practices in Practice: An Overview

The five practices are a set of related instructional routines that can help you design and implement lessons that address important mathematical content in ways that build on students' thinking (Figure 1.2). Warning: There is actually a Practice 0, which serves as a foundation for the remaining practices—yup, this means there are six practices in total, but for historical reasons, we will still call the set "the five practices." (In case you are wondering how this could have happened, here is the scoop: After some early articles about the five practices were published, a mathematics coach with whom Peg was working suggested to her that a practice was missing—that before teachers could engage with the five practices, they

Figure 1.2 • The five practices in practice

Practices that take place while planning for instruction		**Practice 0: Setting goals and selecting tasks (Chapter 2)** Specifying learning goals and choosing a high-level task that aligns with those goals
		Practice 1: Anticipating student responses (Chapter 3) Exploring how you expect students to solve the task and preparing questions to ask them about their thinking
Practices that take place during instruction but are considered while planning	Students work individually or in small groups	**Practice 2: Monitoring student work (Chapter 4)** Looking closely as students work on the task and asking questions to assess their understanding and move their thinking forward
	As you move from small group work to whole class discussion	**Practice 3: Selecting student solutions (Chapter 5)** Choosing solutions for students to share that highlight key mathematical ideas that will help you achieve lesson goals
		Practice 4: Sequencing student solutions (Chapter 5) Determining the order in which to share solutions to create a coherent storyline for the lesson
	Whole class discussion	**Practice 5: Connecting student solutions (Chapter 6)** Identifying connections among student solutions and to the goals of the lesson that you want to bring out during discussion

needed to set goals and select a task. Though this idea was already implied in the five practices, the coach persuaded Peg to make it explicit, and hence Practice 0 was born!)

Teachers often think that ambitious teaching requires you to make all your instructional decisions during instruction based on what students say and do in class. The five practices, however, help you think through all aspects of the lesson *in advance* of teaching, thus limiting the number of in-the-moment decisions you have to make during a lesson. Careful planning prior to a lesson reduces what you need to think about during instruction, allowing you time to listen more actively, question more thoughtfully, and respond more acutely.

Practice zero, *setting goals and selecting tasks*, lays the groundwork for the remaining five practices. It is essential to be clear on what you want students to learn and to choose a cognitively demanding task that aligns with those goals. Once you have the task in mind, you can move to *anticipating student responses*. Here, the purpose is to think about how students might solve the problem, what challenges they might face, and how you will respond to their thinking. One benefit to doing so is that you can develop—before class—targeted questions you might want to ask students about these different approaches.

Although the next four practices take place during instruction, you will also want to think them through carefully during planning. *Monitoring student work* involves giving students time—usually in groups—to work on the task, while you circulate among them. As you look closely at how students are progressing, you can use the questions you developed earlier to assess what students understand and to try to move their thinking forward. As you prepare to transition students into a whole class discussion, you will engage in *selecting student solutions*—deciding which solutions you want to have shared in the discussion and who should present those solutions—as well as *sequencing student solutions*—deciding how you want to order the presentation of the solutions. Selecting and sequencing require close attention to the mathematical ideas that are highlighted in different solutions and to helping all students have access to the ideas shared in the discussion. As you plan the lesson you will consider what you want to be on the lookout for as you monitor students' work, what solutions will help you surface the mathematical ideas you are targeting, and what order of solutions will provide access to all students.

The final practice, *connecting student solutions*, takes place as the discussion unfolds in your classroom. The purpose is to make explicit the connections between students' solutions and the mathematical goals of the lesson. Drawing out these connections for students is essential to ensure that students take away from the discussion what you intended. This too is something you can consider as you plan the lesson!

Together, the five practices can help you prepare for and carry out meaningful discussions with your students, discussions that revolve around the thinking of your students. And that is the essence of ambitious instruction!

Purpose and Content

The purpose of this book is to deepen your understanding of the five practices as described by Smith and Stein (2018). Toward that end, Chapters 2 to 6 comprise two parts: unpacking the practice (Part One) and challenges teachers face in enacting the practice (Part Two). In Part One, we describe in some detail what is involved in engaging in the practice, provide questions that you should ask yourself as you undertake the practice, and use an example from an elementary classroom to illustrate the components of the practice. In Part Two, we highlight aspects of the practice that have proven to be challenging for teachers, suggest ways you can address the challenge, and provide examples of how teachers are overcoming the challenge.

Throughout these chapters, we encourage you to actively engage with the content. Toward this end, we have created three types of opportunities for engagement: *Pause and Consider* questions (reflection), *Analyzing the Work of Teaching* activities (analysis), and *Linking the Five Practices to Your Own Instruction* assignments (implementation). The Pause and Consider questions give you the opportunity to think about an issue, in some cases drawing on your own classroom experience, prior to reading more about it. The Analyzing the Work of Teaching activities engage you in analyzing aspects of teachers' planning for and enacting of grade-level lessons. The Linking the Five Practices to Your Own Instruction assignments provide you with the opportunity to put the ideas discussed in the chapter to work in your own classroom.

Throughout the book we have included a range of different types of examples drawn from elementary classrooms to illustrate aspects of the five practices and the associated challenges. The video excerpts and related classroom artifacts—featuring the three teachers who are introduced later in the chapter—provide vivid images of real teachers using the five practices in their efforts to orchestrate productive discussions. The narrative examples that appear in the book are based on our experiences working with elementary school teachers through professional development initiatives and teacher education courses. These examples are intended to provide insights into specific challenges teachers face when engaging in the five practices and are not exact representations of a specific teacher's practice. Each of these teachers has been given a pseudonym (e.g., Jada Turner, Carmen Ortiz, Michael McCarthy, and Jesse Samson featured in Chapter 2). The video and narrative examples are not intended as exemplars to be copied but rather as opportunities for analysis, discussion, and new learning.

If you are coming to the five practices for the first time, you might find it helpful to start with *5 Practices for Orchestrating Productive Mathematics Discussions* by Peg Smith and Mary Kay Stein (2018). Smith and Stein's book offers a wonderful, easy-to-read introduction to and overview of the five practices. The book you are reading now takes a much deeper dive into the five practices, asking you to stop and think, watch videos of the practices in action, and consider what is challenging about each practice. While you can certainly start here, the overview of the five practices provided by Smith and Stein (2018) may help you get the big picture before taking a deeper dive!

This book will be a valuable resource for looking closely at what it takes to be successful with the five practices. For each practice, we offer key questions, which identify the essential components of the practice. We suspect these questions will enhance your understanding of the practices and perhaps provide new information about the goals and expectations for each practice. This book also describes challenges associated with each practice that teachers we have worked with have encountered, as well as specific suggestions for successfully addressing these challenges. If you have already been using the five practices, we suspect that some of these challenges may be familiar to you and that these discussions will be particularly useful.

Classroom Video Context

In identifying teachers to feature on video, we felt that it was important to select a school district that would feel authentic to readers—one that faced challenges of diversity, poverty, and student performance but was working hard to improve mathematics teaching and learning. We selected Metro Nashville Public Schools (MNPS) for several reasons—the district met our authenticity criteria. Victoria Bill, the second author, had been working in the district for several years, and the district was willing to be featured in this book.

MNPS is an urban district located in Nashville, Tennessee. MNPS has a diverse student population K–12 (as shown in Figure 1.3) with 50.6 percent of students qualifying for free or reduced lunch and 15.68 percent of students classified as English Language Learners. The nearly 85,000 students attend 76 elementary schools, 31 middle and K–8 schools, and 17 high schools. In addition, there are also 31 charter schools and 17 nontraditional and Special Education schools.

Figure 1.3 • Race/ethnicity of Metro Nashville Public Schools students

American Indian/Alaska Native	0.4%
Black	43%
Hispanic	23%
Asian/Pacific Islander	4%
White	29%

Source: Tennessee Department of Education, 2018.

As stated on its website (https://www.mnps.org/about-mnps/), MNPS is committed to becoming "the fastest-improving urban school system in America, ensuring that every student becomes a life-long learner prepared for success in college, career and life." The mathematical mission for the district is for students to have the opportunity to reason mathematically, communicate their ideas with others, and learn to value mathematics through rigorous instruction on a daily basis.

Jessica Slayton, director of mathematics for MNPS, explains what it will take to make this vision a reality in classrooms:

> *Students need opportunities to communicate their ideas and this means teachers have to be able to facilitate classroom discourse. So we're providing structures and supports for our teachers so that they can effectively facilitate these conversations in their classrooms. The five practices are so essential because discourse is at the heart of our mission.*

A District Engages in the Five Practices

Video Clip 1.1
In Video Clip 1.1, Jessica Slayton, director of mathematics, explains the district's efforts to support teachers in facilitating classroom discourse through their use of the five practices.

To read a QR code, you must have a smartphone or tablet with a camera. We recommend that you download a QR code reader app that is made specifically for your phone or tablet brand.

 Videos may also be accessed at
resources.corwin.com/5practices-elementary

As a result of the professional development in which teachers have engaged, Mrs. Slayton has seen many changes in teachers' practice. She explains:

> The first thing that comes to mind is their belief in the students. We had a lot of timid teachers at first, and they didn't know if the students were actually capable of the mathematics for their grade levels. We said, "Give this a try. Try the five practices, see if you can anticipate, and determine how to support the students." Now that they've done that, they see it: "Oh yes, my students are capable." It doesn't matter if it's a student with limited English; we know how to support them because we've anticipated what some of the struggles might be.
>
> Another change that we've seen is really the self-awareness in planning. If I want to get this out of my students, if this is my mathematical goal, I need to be able to press students towards that goal, which means I need to plan how to do that. It's not going to happen by accident. Planning on your own is challenging. One person might not be able to anticipate five different solution strategies, but working with peers in a grade-level team there are different perspectives and they're able to collaborate, and they can build lessons together that are more meaningful for their students.

Meet the Teachers

The video recordings and related classroom artifacts featured in this book are drawn from the work of three Grade K–5 teachers in MNPS—Olivia Stastny, Andrew Strong, and Tara Tyus. The lesson taught by Tara Tyus will be used in Part One of Chapters 2 to 6 to unpack the focal practice. By focusing on the same teacher across chapters, you will have a coherent picture of instruction in her classroom and a better understanding of how the practices provide synergy. The lessons taught by Olivia Stastny and Andrew Strong will be used in Part Two of Chapters 2 to 6 to provide illustrations of how specific challenges can be addressed.

Olivia Stastny has been teaching at Una Elementary School since she began her career four years ago. She has a bachelor's degree in elementary education and a master's of education in curriculum and instruction. She wanted to become a teacher so she could help all students grow to their fullest potential—academically, socially, and emotionally.

Olivia believes that her third grade students should have daily real-life, rigorous opportunities in the mathematics classroom, allowing them to achieve their greatest abilities. Toward this end, she feels it is important to pick a task for which there is a low floor so that students can enter the task and a high ceiling so that there's the potential to really accomplish something that is mathematically important. Embedded in this is the notion that students could solve the task in multiple ways, because students come to class with different knowledge and experiences, while making it possible for them to also advance their learning.

Olivia sees the five practices as playing a vital role in preparing for instruction. She explains:

> *I can choose the best task for my students and plan, plan, plan, which is one of the biggest parts of doing the five practices. Planning is everything! The teacher needs to know the goals of the lesson, anticipate the solutions, think about possible sequencing, and how it is all going to connect, all before the lesson even starts.*

 **Andrew Strong** has been working in Metro Nashville since he started teaching 16 years ago. He has a bachelor's degree in film production and a master's degree in elementary education. He is currently teaching fifth grade mathematics at West End Middle School (Grades 5–9), where he has been for the past two years. He became a teacher because he believes there is nothing more important to which one can dedicate their life, and he "enjoys the heck out of it."

Andrew feels it is his mission to love his students, instill in them a confidence and joy for the learning process, and provide them with tools they will need to find success wherever they seek it. He wants his students to learn to think and to take responsibility for their own learning so that they will become responsible adults who can think for themselves. This, he feels, is desperately needed in the world, and it gives him a deep sense of purpose.

Andrew sees the five practices as a guideline for organizing his thinking about a lesson. He explains: "This is a solid way to get kids to grapple with their thoughts and then to actually come away with the understanding that they need."

 **Tara Tyus** teaches at Una Elementary School, a position she has held since she started teaching six years ago. She has an undergraduate degree in early childhood education and a master's degree in curriculum and instruction, with a focus on elementary education. Tara believes her mission is to help students become their best selves by engaging them in lessons that make them think.

Tara wants her first-grade students to develop an understanding of the concepts underlying the procedures they are learning so that they are not mindlessly following a series of steps. She explains: "It is necessary to use mathematical tasks so students can learn how to think critically when problem solving. In doing so, they learn multiple solution paths and are able to determine efficient strategies to help them solve problems successfully later. Thus, knowledge learned is retained and not simply regurgitated."

The five practices help Tara plan and facilitate discussions around high-level mathematical tasks. She explains:

> *Students love high-level tasks—to explore and have fun with mathematics. As a teacher, the five practices are so important because they help me get prepared for instruction and make sure I accomplish what I set out to do. Without the five practices, lessons could get very chaotic.*

These three teachers are making their teaching practice public so that others can learn from their efforts. Hiebert, Gallimore, and Stigler (2003) argue that we must respect teachers for being "brave enough to open their classroom doors" (p. 56). To honor their courage, as you read about and view excerpts from their classrooms, we encourage you to avoid critiquing what you see or discussing what the teacher "should have done." Instead, our goal is to use the access we have been given as an opportunity for learning—for serious reflection and analysis—in an effort to improve our own teaching in ways that open up new opportunities for our students to learn.

Using This Book

You will likely get the most out of this book if you are committed to ambitious teaching that provides students with increased opportunities to engage in productive discussions in mathematics classrooms. Through engaging with the ideas in the book, you will learn much about how to increase students' engagement in and learning from classroom discussions.

This book can be used in several different ways. You might read through the book on your own, stopping to engage with the questions, activities, and assignments as suggested. Alternatively, and perhaps more powerfully, you can work through the book with colleagues in professional learning communities, department meetings, or when time permits. The book would also be a good choice for a book study with a group of peers interested in improving the quality of their classroom discussions. You might also encounter this book in college or university education courses for practicing or preservice teachers or in professional development workshops during the summer or school year. We will explore more ideas about ways to make the five practices central to your instruction in Chapter 7.

Norms for Video Viewing

The video excerpts that accompany this book are intended to provide authentic examples from elementary classrooms on which to base discussions of the five practices. To take full advantage of these examples, we encourage you to consider the following three norms for video viewing. These norms are based on recent research that documents how video can support teacher learning and reflection (Sherin & Dyer, 2017; Sherin & van Es, 2009).

Focus on student sense-making. The majority of the video clips that you will watch in this book focus on students. That is intentional. While the five practices describe actions that you as the teacher will take, this work involves looking closely at what students do and say. The videos thus provide an opportunity for you to do just that outside of the immediate demands of teaching.

As you explore students' actions in the videos, we encourage you to look beyond simply whether a student's idea is correct or incorrect. Instead, examine what it is that the student understands. What is the student's idea? Where does it come from? Why is it sensible, given what the student understands? Focus on what it is that makes sense about the students' thinking.

Be specific about what you notice. Much of the value of video viewing is the sense that you can slow down classroom interactions and have the time to notice what is taking place in a detailed way. In addition, with video you can often focus on just a subset of events and look closely, for example, at what a particular student is saying and to whom, what gestures or drawings the student is making, and more.

As you view the video excerpts, we encourage you to be specific about what you notice. Provide detailed evidence to support your claims about what is happening. Explain what it is you see in the video that leads you to a particular interpretation.

Consider alternative interpretations. As you watch the video, you may find yourself quickly making assumptions about what is taking place and why. As teachers, we must often respond quickly, diagnosing student confusions, responding to student questions, and making changes in the direction of a lesson. Video, however, provides the luxury of time. Use this to your advantage!

Once you have an idea of what you think is taking place in the video, look for alternatives. How else might you understand what is happening? This is particularly important when examining students' ideas. Rather than assume you know the reason behind a student's strategy or statement, look for alternatives. Considering alternate interpretations is important because when we assume we understand what a student means, we often limit ourselves to what we have heard from students previously.

Getting Started!

You are now ready to begin a deep dive into the five practices. In the next five chapters, you will learn more about the practices. We encourage you to keep a journal or notebook in which you can respond to questions that are posed and make note of questions you have. Such a journal can be helpful in conversations with other teachers or in reflecting from time to time about how your thinking is evolving and changing.

" Once you set a goal for instruction, you need to find a task that aligns with it. That is, a task that actually has the potential to accomplish what you've said you want to do during the lesson. So in the ideal, when you're having a discussion, you want a learning goal that explicitly talks about what students are going to learn, and a task that is high level, that has the potential to get you there. "

—OLIVIA STASTNY, THIRD-GRADE TEACHER

CHAPTER 2

Setting Goals and Selecting Tasks

Before you can begin to work on the five practices, you must first set a goal for student learning and select a task that aligns with your goal. Smith and Stein (2018) have described this as *Practice 0*—a necessary step in which teachers must engage as they begin to plan a lesson that will feature a whole class discussion. As they explain:

> To have a productive mathematical discussion, teachers must first establish a clear and specific goal with respect to the mathematics to be learned and then select a high-level mathematical task. This is not to say that all tasks that are selected and used in the classroom must be high level, but rather that productive discussions that highlight key mathematical ideas are unlikely to occur if the task on which students are working requires limited thinking and reasoning. (Smith & Stein, 2018, p. 27)

In this chapter, we first unpack what is involved in setting goals and selecting tasks and illustrate what this practice looks like in an authentic elementary school classroom. We then explore challenges that teachers face in engaging in this practice and provide an opportunity for you to explore setting a goal and selecting a task in your own teaching practice.

Part One: Unpacking the Practice: Setting Goals and Selecting Tasks

What does it take to engage in this practice? This practice requires first specifying the learning goal for the lesson and then identifying a high-level task that aligns with the learning goal. Figure 2.1 highlights the components of this practice along with key questions to guide the process of setting goals and selecting a task.

Figure 2.1 • Key questions that support the practice of setting a goal and selecting a task

WHAT IT TAKES	KEY QUESTIONS
Specifying the learning goal	Does the goal focus on what students will learn about mathematics (as opposed to what they will do)?
Identifying a high-level task that aligns with the goal	Does your task provide students with the opportunity to think, reason, and problem solve?
	What resources will you provide students to ensure that all students can access the task?
	What will you take as evidence that students have met the goal through their work on this task?

In the sections that follow, we provide an illustration of this practice drawing on a lesson taught by Tara Tyus in her first-grade classroom. As you read the description of what Ms. Tyus thinks about and articulates while planning her lesson, consider how her attention to the key questions influences her planning.

Specifying the Learning Goal

Your first step in planning a lesson is specifying the goal(s). Consider Goals A and B for each of the mathematical ideas targeted in Figure 2.2. How are the goals the same and how are they different? Do you think the differences matter?

For each of the mathematical ideas targeted in Figure 2.2, the goal listed in Column A is considered a performance goal. Performance goals indicate what students will be able to do as a result of engaging in a lesson. By contrast, each of the goals listed in Column B is a learning goal. The learning goals explicitly state what students will understand about mathematics as a result of engaging in a particular lesson. The learning goal needs to be stated with sufficient specificity such that it can guide your decision-making during the lesson (e.g., what task to select for students to work on, what questions to ask

Figure 2.2 • Different goals for learning specific mathematical ideas

TARGETED IDEA	GOAL A	GOAL B
Counting *Kindergarten*	Students will be able to count numbers of objects up to 20.	Students will understand that when counting a set of objects, the last number said indicates the number of objects counted.
Place Value *Grade 2*	Students will correctly read and write three-digit numbers.	Students will understand that each digit in a three-digit number represents a different magnitude and that each digit to the left is ten times greater than the previous digit.
Equivalent Fractions *Grade 4*	Students will be able to recognize and generate equivalent fractions.	Students will be able to explain why two fractions are or are not equivalent using visual models.

Source: The goals are based on the Common Core State Standards for Mathematics, http://www.corestandards.org/Math/ (National Governors Association Center for Best Practices & Council of Chief State School Officers, 2010).

students as they work on the task, which solutions to have presented during the whole class discussion). According to Hiebert and his colleagues (2007):

> Without explicit learning goals, it is difficult to know what counts as evidence of students' learning, how students' learning can be linked to particular instructional activities, and how to revise instruction to facilitate students' learning more effectively. Formulating clear, explicit learning goals sets the stage for everything else. (p. 51)

In general, "the better the goals, the better our instructional decisions can be, and the greater the opportunity for improved student learning" (Mills, 2014, p. 2).

According to Hunt and Stein (in press), "too often, we define what mathematics we wish students to come to 'know' as performance, or what students will 'do,' absent the understandings that underlay their behaviors." If we want students to learn mathematics with understanding, we need to specify what exactly it is we expect them to understand about mathematics as a result of engaging in a lesson. Hence, goals you set for a lesson should focus on what is to be learned, not solely on performance.

Ms. Tyus's first-grade students were working on subtracting two-digit numbers. They had already established that a two-digit number is made up of a number of tens and a number of ones and had started subtracting two-digit numbers that were both multiples of ten. They had just started to subtract two-digit numbers where the larger number (i.e., minuend) was not a multiple of ten but the number being subtracted (i.e., subtrahend) was a multiple of ten.

As a result of the lesson, Ms. Tyus wanted her students to understand that

1. When subtracting two-digit numbers, tens are subtracted from tens and ones are subtracted from ones. If you are subtracting a multiple of ten, then only the number in the tens place changes because there are no ones to subtract.

2. Decomposing and recomposing numbers in systematic ways can help you solve problems and make relationships among quantities of tens and ones more visible.

3. Numbers can be rounded up or down to make a multiple of ten before subtracting. The amount rounded up or down must then be subtracted from or added to the difference to compensate for the amount added to or taken away initially.

4. Multiple representations (e.g., models, drawings, numbers, equations) can be used to solve problems, and the different representations can be connected to each other.

....
**TEACHING
TAKEAWAY**
Specificity is one of the keys to setting learning goals and finding appropriately aligned tasks.

The level of specificity at which Ms. Tyus articulated the learning goals for the lessons will help her in identifying an appropriate task for her students, and subsequently, it will help her in asking questions that will move students toward the goal and in determining the extent to which students have learned what was intended.

Identifying a High-Level Task That Aligns With the Goal

Your next step in planning a lesson is to select a high-level task that aligns with the learning goal. High-level or cognitively challenging mathematical tasks engage students in reasoning and problem solving and are essential in supporting students' learning mathematics with understanding. By contrast, low-level tasks—tasks that can be solved by applying rules and procedures—require limited thinking or understanding of the underlying mathematical concepts. According to Boston and Wilhelm (2015), "if opportunities for high-level thinking and reasoning are not embedded in instructional tasks, these opportunities rarely materialize during mathematics lessons" (p. 24). In addition, research provides evidence that students who have the opportunity to engage in high-level tasks on a regular basis show greater learning gains than students who engage primarily in low-level tasks during instruction (e.g., Boaler & Staples, 2008; Hiebert & Wearne, 1993; Stein & Lane, 1996; Stigler & Hiebert, 2004).

Tasks that provide the richest basis for productive discussions have been referred to as *doing-mathematics* tasks. Such tasks are nonalgorithmic—no solution path is suggested or implied by the task and students cannot solve them by the simple application of a known rule. Hence students must explore the task to determine what it is asking them to do and develop and implement a plan drawing on prior knowledge and experience in order to solve the task (Smith & Stein, 1998). These tasks provide students with the opportunity to engage in the problem-solving process—understand the problem, devise a plan, carry out the plan, and look back (Polya, 2014). Central to this process is the opportunity for students to wrestle with mathematical ideas and relationships that are inherently part of the task.

While the level of cognitive demand is a critical consideration in selecting a task worthy of discussion, there are other characteristics that you should also consider when selecting a task. Specifically, you need to consider the following: the number of ways that the task can be accessed and solved, the extent to which justification or explanation is required, the different ways the mathematics can be represented and connected, and opportunities to look for patterns, make conjectures, and form generalizations. These characteristics are a hallmark of rich mathematical tasks and help ensure that students will have the opportunity to engage in the mathematics practices/processes (e.g., make sense of problems and persevere in solving them, reason abstractly and quantitatively, construct viable arguments, use repeated reasoning) that are viewed as essential to developing mathematical proficiency. When sizing up the potential of a task, keep in mind the questions shown in Figure 2.3. These questions will help you in selecting rich tasks that will make engagement in key mathematical practices and processes possible.

Figure 2.3 • Questions to help you *size up* the richness of a task

- Are there multiple ways to enter the task and to show competence?
- Does the task require students to provide a justification or explanation?
- Does the task provide the opportunity to use and make connections between different representations of a mathematical idea?
- Does the task provide the opportunity to look for patterns, make conjectures, and/or form generalizations?

Answering "yes" to each of these questions does not guarantee that students will engage in the mathematical practices. However, the use of the five practices, together with doing-mathematics tasks that have the characteristics described, will help ensure that this will occur. So rather than thinking about separate process goals, such as the Standards for Mathematical Practice advocated for in the Common Core State Standards for Mathematics (National Governors Association Center for Best Practices & Council of Chief State School Officers, 2010), we encourage you to consider characteristics of tasks that will provide your students with the opportunities to engage in such processes.

TEACHING TAKEAWAY

Doing-mathematics tasks, rather than procedural exercises, lend themselves to rich and productive mathematical discussion.

For her lesson, Ms. Tyus created the Ms. Tyus's Markers task, shown in Figure 2.4. In creating this task, she paid very close attention to the context and to the numbers she selected. First, the context was one that students would be able to make sense of. Ms. Tyus could actually show students a bucket of markers and act out giving some away. Second, she wanted to have a relatively large number of markers for problems (e.g., 69 and 79) so that students would not be inclined to count out a set of markers. This would encourage them to use other strategies. She also chose a number of markers that was one (or in one case, two) away from a ten so that rounding and compensating would be a viable strategy to consider. She chose a multiple of ten to be subtracted that was sufficiently large so that it would be tedious to count back by ones. Her careful consideration of the context and the numbers was key in ensuring that students would be able to make sense of the task and that they would have the opportunity to engage with the mathematical ideas she was targeting in the lesson.

Figure 2.4 • Ms. Tyus's Markers task

Ms. Tyus's Markers

1. Ms. Tyus has 69 scented markers. She gives 40 scented markers to her friend. How many markers does she have left? Make a diagram and write an equation that shows how Anna can solve this problem.

2. Ms. Tyus has 79 neon markers. She gives 30 neon markers to her friend. How many markers does she have left? Make a diagram and write an equation that shows how Anna can solve this problem.

Solve each of these problems.

$59 - 20 =$ _____ $88 - 30 =$ _____

Source: Task by Tara Tyus. Image from Pixabay.

Download the Task from

resources.corwin.com/5practices-elementary

To ensure that students would have access to the task, Ms. Tyus planned to provide students with a hundreds chart (shown in Figure 2.5a) and base ten blocks (shown in Figure 2.5b) on which they could draw in solving the task along with their usual toolkits, but she would leave it up to the students to decide which, if any of them, would be useful. In addition to these material resources, Ms. Tyus also decided that she would provide "human" resources by having students work on the task in pairs or trios so that they would have others with whom to confer. [NOTE: What Ms. Tyus refers to as the hundreds chart actually goes up to 120. This stems from the fact that first-grade students are expected to be able to count up to 120 and read and write numerals and represent a number of objects with written numerals in this range.]

Figure 2.5 • Material resources provided to Ms. Tyus's students

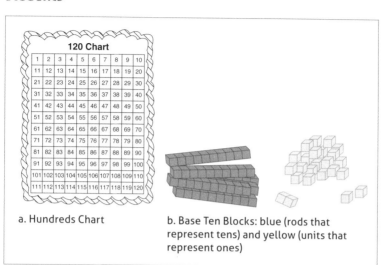

a. Hundreds Chart

b. Base Ten Blocks: blue (rods that represent tens) and yellow (units that represent ones)

When asked what students would say, do, or produce that would provide evidence of their understanding of the goals in the lesson through their work on this task, Ms. Tyus indicated that students would do the following:

- Describe their strategy for subtracting 40 from 69 and explain how different solution strategies are connected;

- Explain that rounding up means getting more markers than they initially had, so they would have to subtract to compensate for the additional markers they added initially; and

- Decompose a two-digit number into tens and ones, then subtract the tens from the tens, and explain that since there are no ones to be subtracted (e.g., $9 - 0 = 9$), you still have the same number of ones, which you then combine with the tens.

Tara Tyus's Attention to Key Questions: Setting Goals and Selecting Tasks

During her initial stage of lesson planning, Ms. Tyus paid careful attention to the key questions. First, in setting her goals for the lesson, she clearly articulated what it was she wanted students to learn about mathematics as a result of engaging in the task. The specificity with which she stated her goals made it possible to determine what students understood about these ideas and to formulate questions that would help move her students forward. While she wanted her students to find the difference between two two-digit numbers, she also wanted to make sure they understood that subtraction requires removing or taking away an amount and that they must attend to the place value of the digits when subtracting.

Second, she created a high-level *doing-mathematics* task that aligned with her goals. Students could not solve the Ms. Tyus's Markers task by applying a known rule or procedure because they had not yet learned one; it would require students' perseverance and sense-making. Ms. Tyus *sized up* the task (see Figure 2.3) to ensure that it had several other important characteristics. Specifically, there were a number of approaches that students could use to enter the task (e.g., making a base ten model of 69 markers with blocks or drawings and removing 4 tens, starting at 69 on the hundreds chart and counting back by 4 tens to 29, rounding 69 to 79, subtracting 40, and then subtracting one more from the difference of 30), and the material and human resources that the teacher planned to provide would support their work. Students had the opportunity to use (e.g., context, base ten blocks, hundreds chart, contents of their toolboxes) and produce (e.g., equations, diagrams) several different representations. Hence through their work on the task, students could learn important mathematics and engage in key practices.

The Ms. Tyus's Markers task, along with the resources the teacher made available to students, allowed all students to enter the task at some level. Rather than differentiating instruction by providing different students with different tasks, she selected one task and met the needs of different learners by providing a range of resources for students to consider and questions that would challenge learners at different levels. In addition, while the teacher's primary intent was to focus on the first two questions in the Ms. Tyus's Markers task, the inclusion of the additional questions (i.e., 59 – 20 and 88 – 30) provided opportunities for students who solved the Ms. Tyus's Markers tasks quickly to engage in repeated reasoning and try out a strategy previously used or a different strategy.

Finally, Ms. Tyus indicated some things that she expected students to say and do that would provide evidence students were making progress on the ideas she wanted them to learn. By considering this evidence in advance of the lesson, she was ready to pay close attention to students' work for indications that they were making progress in their understanding.

Through her careful attention to setting goals and selecting a task, Ms. Tyus's planning was off to a productive start and she was ready to engage in the five practices. In the next chapter we will continue to investigate her planning process as she anticipates what she thinks her students will do when presented with the task and how she will respond. We now turn our attention to the challenges that teachers face in setting goals and selecting tasks.

Part Two: Challenges Teachers Face: Setting Goals and Selecting Tasks

As we described in the chapter opening, setting goals and selecting tasks is foundational to orchestrating productive discussions. Setting goals and selecting tasks, however, is not without its challenges. In this section, we focus on four specific challenges associated with this practice, shown in Figure 2.6, that we have identified from our work with teachers.

Figure 2.6 • Challenges associated with the practice of setting goals and selecting tasks

CHALLENGE	DESCRIPTION
Identifying learning goals	Goal needs to focus on what students will learn as a result of engaging in the task, not on what students will do. Clarity on goals sets the stage for everything else!
Identifying a doing-mathematics task	While *doing-mathematics* tasks provide the greatest opportunities for student learning, they are not readily available in some textbooks. Teachers may need to adapt an existing task, find a task in another resource, or create a task.
Ensuring alignment between task and goals	Even with learning goals specified, teachers may select a task that does not allow students to make progress on those particular goals.
Launching a task to ensure student access	Teachers need to provide access to the context and the mathematics in the launch but not so much that the mathematical demands are reduced and key ideas are *given away*.

Identifying Learning Goals

Identifying learning goals is a challenging but critical first step in planning any lesson. It is challenging because we often focus on what students are going to be able to do as a result of engaging in a lesson, not on what they are going to learn about mathematics.

Consider, for example, a lesson that Jada Turner was planning for her third-grade students. Ms. Turner was beginning a unit on fractions and decided that she would use the Pizza Comparison task (see Figure 2.7) as the basis for the lesson. She selected this task because she thought the pizza context would be engaging for her students who loved pizza. In addition, since students could use drawings, words, and numbers to consider José's claim, there would be different ways to solve it.

Figure 2.7 • The Pizza Comparison task

> ### Pizza Comparison
>
> Think carefully about the following question. Write a complete answer. You may use drawings, words, and numbers to explain your answer. Be sure to show all of your work.
>
> José ate $\frac{1}{2}$ of a pizza.
>
> Ella ate $\frac{1}{2}$ of another pizza.
>
> José said that he ate more pizza than Ella, but Ella said they both ate the same amount. Use words and pictures to show that José could be right.

Source: The Pizza Comparison Task appeared on the National Assessment of Educational Progress in 1992. U.S. Department of Education, Institute of Education Sciences, National Center for Education Statistics, National Assessment of Educational Progress (NAEP), 1992 Mathematics Assessment.

  Download the Task from **resources.corwin.com/5practices-elementary**

Ms. Turner initially indicated that her goal for the lesson was for students to understand fractions. When Ms. Turner was pressed by her mathematics coach to be more specific about what she wanted students to learn about mathematics, she acknowledged, "That is the hard part for me."

In a subsequent team meeting, Ms. Turner, along with her coach and grade-level colleagues, worked together to clarify in detail what understanding of mathematics students would need to solve the Pizza Comparison task and thus determined the following learning goals for the lesson. Specifically, as a result of engaging in the lesson, Ms. Turner wanted her students to understand that

- A fraction $\frac{1}{b}$ is the quantity formed by one part when a whole is partitioned into b equal parts: $\frac{1}{2}$ of a pizza is one part of a pizza that is cut into two equal pieces;

- A fraction must be interpreted in relation to the size of the object (in this case, a whole pizza); and

- Comparisons are only valid when two fractions refer to the same size whole: $\frac{1}{2}$ of one pizza is only equal to $\frac{1}{2}$ of another pizza if the two pizzas are the same size.

With new clarity regarding what she wanted students to understand, Ms. Turner was now ready to anticipate what students would do with the task and prepare questions that would help her illuminate what her students understood about these ideas.

Why does this level of specificity matter? It matters because with this level of specificity, the teacher will be able to determine whether her students understand the meaning of the fraction $\frac{1}{2}$, that all $\frac{1}{2}$s do not represent the same amount, and that the $\frac{1}{2}$s will not be the same size if you have two different-sized wholes. So when Ms. Turner actually interacts with her students as they work on the task, with these targets in mind, she can press them to explain what it would mean for José to be correct and under what conditions that would be possible. In addition, this level of specificity will help Ms. Turner consider the solutions she would want students to share during the whole class discussion and the questions she wants to ask about them later in the lesson. Hence, the specificity of the goal is going to provide guidance to her during the lesson and help her determine what her students do and do not understand. This information will then help her in planning subsequent lessons. (See Hunt and Stein [in press] for a description of three interconnected phases—defining a goal, unpacking the mathematics and refining the goal, and relating goals to pedagogy—that teachers can use individually or collaboratively to create and refine goals for student learning.)

Identifying a Doing-Mathematics Task

While doing-mathematics tasks provide the optimal vehicle for whole class discussions, not all curricular materials are replete with such tasks. Traditional textbooks tend to feature more procedural tasks that provide limited opportunities for reasoning and problem solving. While such resources do include *word problems*, they are often solved using procedures that have been previously introduced and modeled and require limited thinking. While standards-based texts (Senk & Thompson, 2003) contain some procedural tasks, they also include high-level tasks that promote reasoning and problem solving. If you are using a resource that does not include high-level tasks, what should you do? In this section we will explore three possible options—adapt an existing task, find a task in another resource, or create your own task.

Adapting an Existing Task

Most textbooks include low-level tasks that can be solved using the procedure that was introduced in the current chapter. If you can recall the rule, you can simply apply it in order to solve the new problem. If you don't remember the rule, you can usually refer back to an example problem in the chapter that will walk you through the steps involved. While such problems do provide students with the opportunity to practice a learned rule, they provide limited opportunities to think and reason about mathematical relationships and connections. So one thing to consider is how you can provide more thinking opportunities while still providing time for practice.

Take the Baking Cookies task, for example. In the original task (left side of Figure 2.8), students need to recognize the problem as a multiplication situation (most likely implied by the placement of the problem in the textbook chapter) and then apply the standard algorithm to arrive at the answer of 65 minutes.

> **TEACHING TAKEAWAY**
>
> If your textbook does not provide worthwhile enough tasks for discussion, you have options: adapt, find, or create your own!

Figure 2.8 • The original and modified Baking Cookies task

Baking Cookies—Original	Baking Cookies—Modified
Shawna plans to bake five batches of cookies for the class party. Each batch of cookies will take 12 minutes to bake in the oven.	Shawna plans to bake cookies for the class party. Each batch of cookies will take 12 minutes to bake in the oven.
How long will it take to bake all five batches of cookies? 	1. How long will it take to bake five batches of cookies? 2. How long will it take to bake six batches of cookies? Seven? Eight? Nine? Twenty? Write number sentences that describe how long it will take to bake the different batches of cookies. 3. Use drawings, tables, numbers, and/or words to explain any patterns you notice in the set of problems. 4. Describe how to use your pattern to determine how long it will take to bake any number of batches of cookies.

Source: Image from Pixabay.

 Download the Task from **resources.corwin.com/5practices-elementary**

When Carmen Ortiz saw the Baking Cookies task in her textbook, she decided to modify the task so that her students would have to do more thinking and reasoning (see the Modified Task on the right side of Figure 2.8). In comparing the original task to the modified task, you will see that Ms. Ortiz made the following changes:

- She asked students to find the length of time it would take to bake different numbers of batches of cookies and to write number sentences to describe each.

- She asked students to use a range of different representations to explain any patterns they notice.

- She asked students to describe the length of time it would take to bake any number of batches of cookies.

By making these changes, Ms. Ortiz transformed a low-level task into a doing-mathematics task. In addition, her modified task has some of the additional characteristics we previously discussed (see Figure 2.3)—it requires students to use and make connections between different representations, and it asks students to find patterns and to generalize beyond a specific situation. (See Arbaugh, Smith, Boyle, Stylianides, & Steele, 2018; Boyle & Kaiser, 2017; and Smith & Stein, 2018, for more insight on how to modify tasks.)

While the original task focused on numbers and operations (i.e., multiplying a whole number by a one-digit number), the modified task focuses on numbers and operations as well as on algebraic thinking (i.e., analyzing). By adding a sequence of problems to the initial task, students are encouraged to look for a pattern and, ultimately, to generalize. Blanton and Kaput (2003) describe the process Ms. Ortiz used to modify this problem as "algebrafying." They explain:

> *Existing arithmetic activities and word problems are transformed from problems with a single numerical answer to opportunities for pattern building, conjecturing, generalizing, and justifying mathematical facts and relationships.* (Blanton & Kaput, p. 71)

The technique of algebrafying can be applied to a wide range of arithmetic tasks across grade levels and provide students with "large amounts of computational practice in a context that intrigues students and avoids the mindlessness of numerical worksheets" (Blanton & Kaput, 2003, p. 73). Algebrafied tasks provide students with the opportunity to look for and express regularity in repeated reasoning, one of the Standards for Mathematical Practice (National Governors Association Center for Best Practices & Council of Chief State School Officers, 2010).

Finding a Task in Another Resource

You can find high-level doing-mathematics tasks in many print and electronic resources. The challenge is to find a task that meets your mathematical goals, is accessible to your students, has the potential to advance their learning beyond their current level, and fits with the content and flow of your curriculum.

Michael McCarthy's fifth-grade students had some experience in generating and analyzing patterns. He wanted his students to gain experience in analyzing a growth pattern in order to determine the underlying structure of the pattern and use the identified structure to describe any pattern in the sequence. The ability to analyze, describe, and generalize a pattern is a critical component of algebraic thinking (Driscoll, 1999), and Mr. McCarthy wanted to make sure that his students had lots of opportunities to generalize beyond specific numbers and situations.

Although the textbook Mr. McCarthy was using contained some visual pattern tasks, he felt that the problems provided too much scaffolding and left little for students to actually grapple with. As a result, he decided to use the Tables and Chairs Investigation (shown in Figure 2.9) he found online at Mathwire (http://mathwire.com). The task featured a real-world context in which students could explore the relationship between the number of customers who could be seated and the number of square tables needed and ultimately generalize the number of people who could be seated at any number of tables.

....
TEACHING TAKEAWAY
Algebrafying existing tasks can provide students with opportunities to look for patterns and make generalizations while getting computational practice at the same time.

Figure 2.9 • The Table and Chairs Investigation task

Table and Chairs Investigation

Restaurants often use small square tables to seat customers. One chair is placed on each side of the table. Four chairs fit around one square table. Restaurants handle larger groups of customers by pushing together tables. Two tables pushed together will seat six customers.

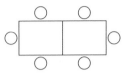

Figure 1   Figure 2

- Draw a diagram showing how many customers would be seated at three square tables pushed together.

- Complete the table for reference:

Number of Tables	Number of Customers
1	4
2	6
3	
4	
5	
6	

- Find a pattern you can use to predict the number of customers that may be seated at any size table. Describe the pattern in words.

CHALLENGE:

- Use your pattern to complete this table without drawing a picture or using manipulatives.

Number of Tables	Number of Customers
10	
25	
100	

Source: This task can be found at Mathwire, http://mathwire.com/algebra/tableschairs.pdf.

By replacing a task in the textbook unit with a doing-mathematics task, Mr. McCarthy provided his students with a rich task that *sized up* nicely (see Figure 2.3). Specifically, the task allowed entry to all students (e.g., students could build or draw subsequent tables, complete the table by building and counting), required making use of different representations (i.e., context, visual diagram, table, verbal description), and pressed students to look for patterns and to generalize beyond specific cases. In addition, there were many different ways to determine the total number of customers that can be seated, each of which could be described algebraically (e.g., $c = 2n + 2$, $c = 2(n+1)$, $c = 4 + 2(n-1)$), or descriptively (e.g., you multiply the number of tables by the seats on the top and bottom and then add two for the sides).

Mr. McCarthy found a website that had a storehouse of good tasks. But not all websites are of equal value. In Appendix A, we have included a list of web resources that may be helpful to you in finding doing-mathematics tasks. This list is not exhaustive but should be helpful in getting started.

Creating a Task

If you cannot find a task you want to use, you may decide to create one yourself. This was the case for Jesse Samson. Mr. Samson's kindergarten students were working on counting and cardinality. He decided to create a mathematical task based on the book *Caps for Sale: A Tale of a Peddler, Some Monkeys and Their Monkey Business* (Slobodkina, 1940). The story is about a peddler who is selling caps. What is unusual about this peddler is that he carries the caps—four gray caps, four brown caps, four blue caps, and four red caps—on his head on top of his checkered cap (see Figure 2.10). One afternoon the weary peddler rests against the trunk of a large tree and falls asleep. When he awakes he finds all his caps are gone.

Figure 2.10 • Image of the peddler and his caps from the book *Caps for Sale*

Source: *Caps for Sale: A Tale of a Peddler, Some Monkeys and Their Monkey Business* by Esphyr Slobodkina, 1940. Harper Collins New York, New York.

He looks up to see monkeys in the tree, each wearing one of his caps. (If you are not familiar with this story, you can find a reading of the book at https://www.youtube.com/watch?v=WTRs9D3H3Lk&feature=youtu.be or search YouTube for "Caps for Sale.")

This book was popular with young children, and Mr. Samson thought it provided a fun context for counting and comparing numbers of objects. Although he did find a number of activities related to the story on the Internet, none of them seemed exactly right, so he created the Caps task (see Figure 2.11). He planned to provide each pair of students with a set of 17 circles—colored to represent the caps—as well as crayons, paper, and a glue stick. In addition, he decided to reproduce and post a large version of the monkeys wearing the caps for students to reference.

Figure 2.11 • The Caps task

> ## Caps Task
>
> Using the illustration, answer the questions below.
>
> 1. How many caps does the peddler have? How do you know? Find a way to keep track of the number of caps so you can tell the peddler how many caps he should collect from the monkeys.
>
> 2. Write numbers and draw a picture to show his total number of caps.
>
> 3. Is the number of blue caps greater than, less than, or equal to the number of red caps? Draw a picture or use your circles to show what you think.
>
> 4. Is the number of checkered caps greater than, less than, or equal to the number of brown caps? Draw a picture or use your circles to show what you think.

 Download the Task from
resources.corwin.com/5practices-elementary

Mr. Samson's idea to connect children's literature with mathematics is a good one. Marilyn Burns, a well-respected mathematics educator and founder of Math Solutions, explains:

> *I've found that children's books are extremely effective tools for teaching mathematics. They can spark students' math imaginations in ways that textbooks or workbooks don't. Connecting math to literature can boost confidence for children who love books but are wary of math. And students who already love math can learn to appreciate stories in an entirely new way.* (Burns, 2015)

While creating tasks is certainly an option, it is a challenging endeavor! If you decide to create a task yourself, we encourage you to ask others to review and solve the task so that you can identify any possible pitfalls before you give it to students. This is exactly what Mr. Samson did with the Caps task! (See Monroe, Young, Fuentes, and Dial [2018] for an extensive annotated bibliography of children's books that can be used for mathematics instruction in the elementary grades. Also see Proud to Be Primary, https://proudtobeprimary.com/childrens-books-teaching-math/, for a list of books that can be used to teach specific mathematical topics or ideas.)

Ensuring Alignment Between Task and Goals

Another challenge teachers often face is making sure that there is alignment between the task and goals—that is, ensuring that the task they have selected as the basis for instruction provides students with the opportunity to explore the mathematical ideas that are targeted during the lesson.

As we described in Part One of this chapter, Ms. Tyus was clear about what she wanted her students to learn about mathematics (not just what they would do) and she selected a high-level doing-mathematics task that was consistent with her learning goals. This combination of a high-level task and a clear learning goal is optimal for providing students with the opportunity to learn mathematics with understanding.

But what would it look like to have a mismatch, and what implications does this have for instruction and learning? Suppose, for example, you are teaching a fourth-grade lesson on multiplication of whole numbers. You decide that you want students to use place value understanding and the properties of operations to perform multidigit multiplication. Specifically, you want students to understand the following:

- The multiplication of two numbers is equivalent to adding as many iterations of one of them, the *multiplicand*, as the value of the other one, the *multiplier* (e.g., $42+42+42+42+42$ is the same as 5×42—where the factor of five tells you how many of the other factor, 42, you are adding).

- A number greater than nine can be decomposed based on place value (e.g., $42=40+2$) and the multiplication statement can be rewritten using the decomposed number(s) (e.g., 5×42 can be rewritten as $5(40+2)$).

- The distributive property of multiplication over addition specifies that you multiply a sum by multiplying each addend separately and then add the products (e.g., $5(40+2)=(5\times40)+(5\times2)$).

- Multiplication can be shown using numbers, rectangular arrays, and area models.

You select a task that asks students only to find a series of products (such as 5×35, 4×64, 9×26, 7×42, and 3×89). This basic *naked numbers* task does not provide students the opportunity to develop an understanding of the meaning of the factors, the relationship between multiplication and repeated addition, or the relationship between place value and the distributive property. In fact, by providing no resources and asking students only for the product, you are implying that students have a procedure for solving such tasks. As a result, students may end up with correct or incorrect solutions but have limited understanding of the targeted mathematical ideas. In this situation, you have established a *learning* goal but have paired it with a low-level task that requires only application of a known procedure. If your goal had been for students to only find the product of a one-digit number and a two-digit number, then the low-level task would be a good match for this goal.

If you want students to understand the distributive property of multiplication over addition, a better choice would be a task such as the one shown in Figure 2.12. The Box of Crayons task provides a context for making sense of the problem and invites students to select from a range of tools for explaining their answers. By including a description of the range of ways students can express their answers and their thinking and making materials such as base ten blocks, base ten paper, and grid paper available, it is likely that the task will generate a range of different approaches that you can use to highlight the underlying meaning of the mathematics and the relationships you have targeted.

Figure 2.12 • The Box of Crayons task

Box of Crayons

Mrs. Phelps bought 4 boxes of crayons at the store to share with her students. Each box contained a total of 64 crayons. What is the total number of crayons Mrs. Phelps bought at the store? Explain your answer using diagrams, pictures, mathematical expressions, and/or words.

Source: Adapted from Smarter Balanced Assessment Consortium, MAT.05.ER.2.00NBT.A.245 Claim 2.

Ensuring alignment between your goals and task is essential and the foundation on which to begin to engage in the five practices. If you find that your task does not fit your goals, consider the ways in which you can modify the task in order to provide more opportunities for students to think and reason as we described previously.

Launching a Task to Ensure Student Access

Launching or setting up a task refers to what the teacher does prior to having students begin work on a task. While it is not uncommon to see teachers hand out a task, ask a student volunteer to read the task aloud, and then tell students what they are expected to produce as a result of the work on the task, research suggests that attention to the way in which the task is launched can lead to a more successful discussion at the end of the lesson. Jackson and her colleagues (Jackson, Shahan, Gibbons, & Cobb, 2012) describe the benefits of an effective launch:

> Students are much more likely to be able to get started solving a complex task, thereby enabling the teacher to attend to students' thinking and plan for a concluding whole-class discussion. This, in turn, increases the chances that all students will be supported to learn significant mathematics as they solve and discuss the task. (p. 28)

So what constitutes an effective launch? In Analyzing the Work of Teaching 2.1, you will explore Ms. Tyus's launch of the Ms. Tyus's Markers task. We invite you to engage in the analysis of a video clip and consider the questions posed before you read our analysis. [NOTE: While the launch of a task occurs during instruction, it is planned for prior to instruction. Rather than describing what Ms. Tyus intended to do, we decided to take you into her classroom so that you could see for yourself!]

Analyzing the Work of Teaching 2.1
Launching a Task

Video Clip 2.1
In this activity, you will watch Video Clip 2.1 from Tara Tyus's first-grade class.

As you watch the clip, consider the following questions:

- What did the teacher do to help her students *get ready* to work on the Ms. Tyus's Markers task?

- What did the teacher learn about her students that indicated they were ready to engage in the task?

- Do you think the time spent in launching the task was time well spent?

online resources
Videos may also be accessed at
resources.corwin.com/5practices-elementary

Launching a Task—Analysis

Ms. Tyus began the lesson by engaging students with the context of the problem. She showed students a basket of the 69 scented markers and had one of her colleagues (Ms. Gibson) come in to borrow 40 markers. (Although Ms. Gibson initially took all the markers, she subsequently returned the basket having removed the 40 markers she needed.) This role-play between Ms. Tyus and Ms. Gibson made clear that markers were being removed or taken away from the total number, thus setting the stage for the subtraction problem the students were to solve. Prior to the lesson, Ms. Tyus explained:

> I want to make it very real life and relevant to the students. I'll have actual markers so they can see. Then someone will say, "Can I borrow some markers?" I'm like, "Okay." Just acting it out, making it very engaging and energetic so they can enter into the task.

Students appeared to be engaged in the launch. They were eager to answer the teacher's questions. When Ms. Tyus asked about how many markers Ms. Gibson had taken and how many markers she had to start with, students were able to respond with 40 and 69, respectively. At this point, Ms. Tyus explained, "Now I want [you] to know how many we would have left" and "that is what you are going to go to your desks to help figure out."

Before Ms. Tyus sent students to their desks to begin work on the task, she first made it clear to students what they were supposed to do: "I want you to make a diagram and write an equation that shows how Anna can solve this problem. Think of if you were Anna. What would you do?" Ms. Tyus then had three students recap the main action in the problem—there are 69 scented markers (Laila), Ms. Gibson took 40 scented markers (Leah), and the mathematical question is how many scented markers does Ms. Tyus have left (Audrey).

As a result of the launch, Ms. Tyus learned that students could relate to the context of the problem and that they were able to make sense of the situation that was presented. They left the launch with a clear sense of what was expected of them. Following the lesson, Ms. Tyus indicated, "The children seemed excited about [the lesson], especially after my launch, and everyone could enter into it." She was glad that students recognized that they were not adding, as this had been the concept they were working on prior to this lesson.

Was the time spent launching the task time well spent? We could argue that it was essential to ensuring that students understood enough about what they were being asked to do to begin their work on the task. Too often, students are given a task and do not understand some aspect of it. When this occurs, the teacher then ends up moving from one group to

the next answering questions that could have been clarified with a more comprehensive launch.

Jackson and her colleagues (2012) list "four crucial aspects to keep in mind when setting up complex tasks to support all students' learning" (p. 26):

1. Key Contextual Features of the Task

2. Key Mathematical Ideas of the Task

3. Development of Common Language

4. Maintaining the Cognitive Demand

Ms. Tyus's launch embodied most of the features described by Jackson and colleagues. She made sure that students understood the context of the Ms. Tyus's Markers task (1), that they were able to explain what the problem was asking them to find (2), and that the cognitive demand of the task was maintained by not suggesting a pathway to follow or giving away too much information (4). Developing a common language (3) is often needed when there is vocabulary used in the task that might not be familiar to some or all of the students. For example, in the Caps task (see Figure 2.11), you would want to make sure that all students understood what a *peddler* was and could describe it in their own words. In the Ms. Tyus's Markers task, however, this did not appear to be necessary.

Perhaps the most challenging part of launching a task is making sure that you do enough to ensure that students understand the context and what they are being asked to do but not so much that there is nothing left for students to figure out. For example, in the Pizza Comparison task (Figure 2.7), you would not want to tell students to start by drawing one small and one large pizza. This would lower the demand of the task by providing a strategy for students to use and limit their opportunity to figure out what to do and how. In the modified version of the Baking Cookies task (Figure 2.8), you would not want to tell students to make a table to show the amount of time it takes to bake a specific number of batches and to find the difference between successive values in the table because this is something you want them to determine.

Conclusion

In this chapter, we have discussed the importance of setting clear goals for student learning and selecting a task that is aligned with the goal, and we have described what is involved in this practice and the challenges associated with it. Our experience tells us that if you do not take the time to seriously consider Practice 0 as a first step in carefully planning your lesson, the remainder of the practices will be built on a shaky foundation.

Ms. Tyus's work in setting a goal and selecting a task provided a concrete example of a teacher who thoughtfully and thoroughly engaged in this practice. Engaging in this practice in a deep and meaningful way does not happen overnight. It takes time and practice. As she said, "Pre-planning is very important and the more you do it, the better you will get at it . . . and your students will love and enjoy mathematics."

Ms. Turner's efforts to determine what students would learn during their lesson and to ensure that the goals and task align made salient the challenges that teachers can face and overcome when engaging in this practice. Working with colleagues helped her make progress on Practice 0.

Setting Goals and Selecting Tasks—Summary

Video Clip 2.2
To hear and see more about setting goals and selecting tasks, watch Video Clip 2.2.

online resources 🔍   Videos may also be accessed at
resources.corwin.com/5practices-elementary

In the next chapter, we explore the first of the five practices: *anticipating*. Here, we will return to Ms. Tyus's lesson and consider what it takes to engage in this practice and the challenges it presents.

Linking the Five Practices to Your Own Instruction

SETTING GOALS AND SELECTING TASKS

Identify a mathematical idea that you will be teaching sometime in the next few weeks. Working alone or with your colleagues:

1. Determine what it is you want students to learn about mathematics as a result of engaging in the lesson. Be as specific as possible. It is okay to indicate what students will do during the lesson, but do not stop there!

2. Select a high-level cognitively demanding *doing-mathematics* task that is aligned with your goals. Make sure that there are different ways to enter and engage with the task. Identify resources that are likely to help students as they work on the task.

3. Identify what students will say and do that indicates that they are meeting the goals you have established.

4. Plan a launch that takes into account the four crucial aspects identified by Jackson and her colleagues.

Reflect on your planning so far. How does it differ from how you have previously thought about goals and tasks? In what ways do you think the differences will matter instructionally?

“ There's a lot of ways of solving this problem. With the anticipating, I have an idea of what students are going to do before it happens. Now, they might do something new, but at least I've already thought about it. ”

—OLIVIA STASTNY, THIRD-GRADE TEACHER

CHAPTER 3

Anticipating Student Responses

Now that you have identified a learning goal and have settled on a task that aligns with that goal, it is time to explore the next practice, anticipating students' responses. Anticipating students' responses takes place before instruction, during the planning stage of your lesson. This practice involves taking a close look at the task to identify the different strategies you expect students to use and to think about how you want to respond to those strategies during instruction. Anticipating helps prepare you to recognize and make sense of students' strategies during the lesson and to be able to respond effectively. In other words, by carefully anticipating students' responses *prior* to a lesson, you will be better prepared to respond to students *during* instruction.

Smith and Stein (2018) explain anticipating in the following way:

> [Anticipating involves making] an effort to actively envision how students might mathematically approach the instructional task or tasks that they will work on and consider[ing] questions that could be asked of the students who used specific strategies. This involves much more than simply evaluating whether a task is at the right level of difficulty or of sufficient interest to students, and it goes beyond considering whether or not they are getting the "right" answer.

> *Anticipating students' responses involves developing considered expectations about how students might mathematically interpret a problem, the array of strategies—both correct and incorrect—that they might use to tackle it, and how those strategies and interpretations might relate to the mathematical concepts, representations, procedures, and practices that the teacher would like his or her students to learn.* (p. 10)

In this chapter, we first unpack anticipating into its key components and illustrate what this practice looks like in an authentic elementary school classroom. We then explore what we have learned is challenging for teachers about this practice and provide an opportunity for you to explore anticipating in your own teaching practice.

Part One: Unpacking the Practice: Anticipating Student Responses

What is involved in anticipating students' responses? This practice involves getting inside the problem (thinking about different ways students might solve the task), planning to respond to students using assessing and advancing questions, and preparing to notice key aspects of students' thinking in the midst of instruction. Figure 3.1 highlights the components of this practice along with key questions to guide the process of anticipating.

Figure 3.1 • Key questions that support the practice of anticipating students' responses

WHAT IT TAKES	KEY QUESTIONS
Getting inside the problem	How do you solve the task?
	How might students approach the task?
	What challenges might students face as they solve the task?
Planning to respond to student thinking	What assessing questions will you ask to draw out student thinking?
	What advancing questions will help you move student thinking forward?
Planning to notice student thinking	What strategies do you want to be on the lookout for as students work on the task?

Getting Inside the Problem

The first step is to get inside the problem! Many teachers find it useful to start by thinking about their own approach. How do you solve the task? You will want to think generally about the approach you use and at a detailed level about steps in your process (which may be different from someone else's). Next, consider how students might approach the task. You might investigate the problem using a different representation or think about how manipulatives might shape the way students explore the task. Do some approaches move students more easily toward the learning goals you established? You could also think about whether the task has different entry points. Often when students begin a task by working on different parts of the problem, their solutions look different (Lambert & Stylianou, 2013). Finally, as you explore these various approaches, keep in mind any challenges you think students will face as they solve the task. Are certain parts of the task likely to be difficult for students? Do you expect that students who use certain approaches will face particular kinds of challenges? Where do you think students might get stuck?

In Analyzing the Work of Teaching 3.1, we return to the Ms. Tyus's Markers task (Figure 2.4) that Ms. Tyus selected for her first-grade students. In this activity, you will engage in solving and thinking deeply about the task. We will then look at the strategies that Ms. Tyus anticipated her students would use in solving the task.

Analyzing the Work of Teaching 3.1

Getting Inside a Problem

Solve the Ms. Tyus's Markers task in at least two different ways. Then consider the following questions:

- What did you need to know to solve the task?

- What do you think might be challenging for students about this task?

Getting Inside a Problem—Analysis

While there are several ways *you* might approach this problem, we will explore two possible methods for solving the first problem. One strategy involves *decomposing and recomposing*. When decomposing, you break a number (the minuend) up into its place value components. In this case, you would decompose 69 into 6 tens (60) and 9 ones (9). You could then subtract tens from tens, $60 - 40 = 20$. Since there are no ones to be subtracted, you would *recompose* the tens and ones, adding the 20 to the 9, which is part of the original 69.

Alternatively, you might choose to use a *rounding and compensating* strategy. First, you would *round* 69 to 70 and then proceed to subtract 40 from 70, $70 - 40 = 30$. Because you *added* 1 to 69 when rounding to 70, you need to *subtract* 1 from your answer of 30 to complete the task, $30 - 1 = 29$. We refer to this process of subtracting at the end to offset the initial adding that you did as *compensating*.

In order to use the first strategy (decomposing and recomposing), you would need to know that numbers can be represented by their place value component parts. You would also need to know that you could operate on those parts independently and then add the subparts back together. In order to use the second strategy (rounding and compensating), you would need to understand that addition and subtraction are inverse operations—if you add an amount to the minuend, then you must subtract the same amount from the difference in order to compensate for what was added initially.

TEACHING TAKEAWAY

Exploring the ways *you* would solve the task is just the first step in anticipating! Leverage colleagues and prior student work to anticipate the various entry points and strategies your students might use.

Elementary students may be challenged by this task if they do not yet have a solid foundation in number sense or may not have access to the same methods that we would tend to apply. Students who have not fully grasped place value and rely on counting strategies may find it difficult to count back 40 ones from 69. Students may not understand the meaning of subtraction and may have difficulty modeling a subtraction problem with concrete objects. Students may not realize that after you decompose the values in a subtraction problem, you need to subtract tens from tens and ones from ones. They may also not realize that if you subtract a multiple of ten, you do not need to subtract any ones from the minuend. Students might also have difficulty relating their solution strategy to an equation.

Ms. Tyus did the task herself in a few ways and also talked with a colleague to come up with other approaches (see Figure 3.2). In anticipating these different methods, Ms. Tyus considered in detail the different ways her students might solve the Ms. Tyus's Markers task and also the reasoning that might underlie their strategies.

Figure 3.2 • Anticipated solutions to the Ms. Tyus's Markers task generated by Ms. Tyus and her colleagues

A. Decompose and Recompose With Base Ten Blocks

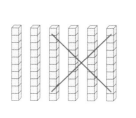

Student decomposes 69 using base ten blocks and then removes 4 tens. Student recomposes the 2 tens and 9 ones.

Student writes

$69 - 40 =$

$60 - 40 = 20$

$20 + 9 = 29$

B. Count Back by Tens on a Hundreds Chart

Student starts at 69 on a hundreds chart, then jumps to 59, 49, 39, 29.

Student writes

$69 - 40 =$

$69 - 10 = 59$

$59 - 10 = 49$

$49 - 10 = 39$

$39 - 10 = 29$

why did you choose this method?

C. Count Back by Tens on an Open Number Line

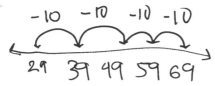

Student draws a number line and labels the point 69. The student then makes 4 jumps back and marks 10 above each, stopping at 29. *why count back by 10's?*

Student writes

$69 - 40 = 29$

D. Round and Compensate

Student adds 1 to 69 to get 70. Student models 70 with base ten blocks or a base ten drawing and then removes 4 tens and has 3 tens left. Student then subtracts 1 from 30 to compensate for the 1 added initially.

Student writes

$69 - 40 =$

$69 + 1 = 70$

$70 - 40 = 30$

$30 - 1 = 29$

E. Subtract Tens, Then Subtract Ones Instead of Add Ones

Student decomposes 69 and then subtracts 40. Student incorrectly subtracts 9 from the remaining 20 rather than recomposing 20 + 9.

Student writes

$69 - 40 =$

$60 - 40 = 20$

$20 - 9 = 11$

F. Round Up, Subtract, and Then Add One Instead of Subtract One

Student adds 1 to 69 to get 70. Student models 70 with base ten blocks or a base ten drawing then removes 4 tens and has 3 tens left. Student then incorrectly adds 1 to 30.

Student writes

$69 - 40 =$

$69 + 1 = 70$

$70 - 40 = 30$

$30 + 1 = 31$

don't correct immediately, have them explain their reasoning

Based on how students were currently solving subtraction problems involving multiples of ten (e.g., $80 - 20$), Ms. Tyus expected that students might use manipulatives to model the situation with the markers. Specifically, she expected a number of students to use base ten blocks because that had been popular with her students recently. Using base ten blocks, a student would first "build" 69 and then remove 4 of the tens blocks (Solution A, Figure 3.2). Ms. Tyus explained that the base ten blocks help students "see the tens and the ones, that decomposition of numbers" and that a student might explain the situation as "Okay, I did 60 minus 40. That gave me 20, plus 9" and represent it with the equations $60 - 40 = 20$ and $20 + 9 = 29$.

Since her class had recently "been looking at patterns on the hundreds chart," Ms. Tyus thought that might be another tool students would use. With this method, a student would first locate the number 69 on the hundreds chart and then subtract 10 four times by moving vertically to 59, 49, 39, and finally to 29. Using the hundreds chart requires the student to understand the organization of the chart—and why moving horizontally reflects adding and subtracting ones, while moving up or down vertically reflects adding and subtracting tens. Ms. Tyus thought students might represent this strategy using a series of equations in which 10 is subtracted four times (Solution B, Figure 3.2).

A third representation Ms. Tyus anticipated students using is an open number line. Because an open number line does not have any markings, the student would select a spot on the line and label it as 69. The student would then take four "hops" to the left to model subtracting 10 four times, ending up at 29. Ms. Tyus thought that a student using this approach might write the corresponding equation as $69 - 40 = 29$ (Solution C, Figure 3.2).

Ms. Tyus also suggested that students might use a rounding and compensating strategy. While she was not confident that students would come up with this approach on their own because they had recently been working on problems involving subtracting multiples of ten from each other, Ms. Tyus thought they might consider "going up 1 to reach a benchmark, a 10." After subtracting 40 from 70, the students "would have to remember that they have to subtract one out to get the correct answer." Students could use base ten blocks, the hundreds chart, or the number line to represent this rounding and compensating strategy (Solution D, Figure 3.2).

As Ms. Tyus anticipated how students might solve the Ms. Tyus's Markers task, she also thought about what might be challenging for students about the task. For example, Ms. Tyus thought that after decomposing 69 and subtracting 40, some students might subtract 9 from 20, rather than recompose $20+9$ (Solution E, Figure 3.2). This might be particularly challenging for students who are still developing their understanding of subtraction. As Ms. Tyus explained, "They might not think about 'What does that 9 represent?'" Also, students who use a rounding and compensating strategy might not fully understand the compensating process and might add 1 rather than subtract 1 in the final step (Solution F, Figure 3.2). Again, if students are just beginning to work with rounding and compensating, the connection between the two processes may not always be apparent.

Planning to Respond to Student Thinking

With your ideas about potential student solutions in mind, the next step is to think about how you will respond to students. We have found two kinds of questions to be particularly useful in supporting students' work (Figure 3.3). Assessing questions help to draw out students' thinking about a problem and are a valuable way for you to investigate what a student understands or why a student decided to take a particular approach. Rather than infer what students are doing or thinking from glancing at their work, assessing questions prompt students to explain their reasoning to you. Franke and colleagues (2009) explain that such questions are important because they help teachers "to more fully understand student thinking and, therefore, to make more informed instructional decisions" (p. 390). Asking students, "Can you tell me what you did?" can often be a good initial assessing question. You can then move to more specific questions that ask students to explain particular parts of their solution strategy and will help you to confirm, for example, whether or not students understand the reasoning behind their approach.

Figure 3.3 • Key characteristics of assessing and advancing questions

ASSESSING QUESTIONS	ADVANCING QUESTIONS
• Are based closely on the work students have produced • Clarify what students have done and what students understand about what they have done • Give the teacher information about what students understand	• Use what students have produced as a basis for making progress toward the target goal of the lesson • Move students beyond their current thinking by pressing students to extend what they know to a new situation • Press students to think about something they are not currently thinking about

Source: Adapted and reprinted with permission from *Five Practices for Orchestrating Productive Mathematical Discussion—Second Edition*, copyright 2018, by the National Council of Teachers of Mathematics. All rights reserved.

TEACHING TAKEAWAY

Assessing questions illuminate what a student knows; advancing questions help students extend their thinking forward toward the lesson goal.

Advancing questions have a different purpose. They are intended to help move students' thinking forward toward the lesson goals. But rather than telling students what to do next, advancing questions are designed to build on what students currently understand and encourage them to "think about something they are not currently thinking about" (Smith & Stein, 2018, p. 44). Advancing questions are not designed as hints. Instead, they ask students to consider particular aspects of their solution or strategy in a new way or to consider how their strategy applies more broadly.

During the anticipating stage, you will want to prepare both assessing and advancing questions that you will be able to use during instruction. One useful strategy is to prepare assessing and advancing questions for each of the student solutions that you anticipate. The assessing questions will help you establish what students know. Sometimes these questions will help confirm what you think a student is doing; other times these questions will help to clarify when the student's intentions are not clear to you. The advancing questions will help students move beyond where they currently are. This could include asking students to examine the limitations in their current approach or generalize their approach to other situations.

 # PAUSE AND CONSIDER

Select two solution strategies from Figure 3.2 for the Ms. Tyus's Markers task and write a few assessing questions for each approach. In addition to general questions that ask students to "Tell me what you did?" identify one or two more specific questions. Next, come up with a few advancing questions for each of the two strategies.

	Assessing Questions	Advancing Questions
Solution Strategy		
Solution Strategy		

Ms. Tyus created a monitoring chart (see Figure 3.4) where she listed the strategies she had anticipated and then developed assessing and advancing questions for each of the strategies identified in Figure 3.2 as well as for the case of students who are not able to get started with the task. (Other features of a monitoring chart, shown in Figure 3.4, will be discussed in the next section of this chapter.) For example, for Solution A in which students use the base ten blocks, her assessing questions aim to uncover what students understand about the relationship between the context and the physical model they created. The question "How do the blocks show what happened with the markers?" may help Ms. Tyus gain information about how students understand the decomposition of 69 as it relates to the initial set of markers. "Why did you add 9 to 20?" will help her assess whether students understand that the 9 is part of the initial set of markers and should be recomposed with the remaining 20 markers. If students seem to understand the relationship between the markers and the blocks but have not yet written an equation, then Ms. Tyus will be in a good position to ask the advancing question, "What equation could you use to represent your model of the task?" This question builds directly on the approach students have used, while encouraging them to extend beyond a physical model of the situation.

Consider also the assessing and advancing questions for Solution B. Here students use the hundred charts to illustrate removing 40 markers from the set of 69 markers. Ms. Tyus's assessing questions first ask for general information about how the students used this approach: "Show me how you used the hundreds chart to explore the task." She wants to understand both what students did and what students understand about the relationship between the strategy and the task. "How did you know how many jumps to make?" and "What does each jump represent?" will help her assess whether students understand both what is represented on the hundreds chart by a vertical jump to an amount directly above a given number and also what it means in the context of the task. Ms. Tyus also has advancing questions prepared that she can use if appropriate—"How could you use the hundreds chart to check your answer? How could you use the hundreds chart to show that the difference between 69 and 29 is 40?" These questions are designed specifically to build on students' understanding of the jumps as representing movement by 10, while also prompting them to consider the reciprocal relationship between vertical jumps up and down as well as horizontal jumps of magnitude 1. The questions will also help students consider the relationship between addition and subtraction in the problem.

Figure 3.4 • Assessing and advancing questions developed by Ms. Tyus as shown in her monitoring chart

SOLUTION STRATEGY	ASSESSING QUESTIONS	ADVANCING QUESTIONS	WHO AND WHAT	ORDER
Solution A. Decompose and Recompose With Base Ten Blocks Student decomposes 69 using base ten blocks and then removes 4 tens. Student recomposes the 2 tens and 9 ones. Student writes $69 - 40 =$ $60 - 40 = 20$ $20 + 9 = 29$	• Tell me about your thinking. • How do the blocks show what happened with the markers? • What does the 69 represent? The 40? • Why did you add 9 to 20?	• (If no equation) What equation could you use to represent your model of the task? • (If there is an equation) Can you show how the parts of your model connect to your equation?		
Solution B. Count Back by Tens on a Hundreds Chart Student starts at 69 on a hundreds chart, then jumps to 59, 49, 39, 29. Student writes $69 - 40 =$ $69 - 10 = 59$ $59 - 10 = 49$ $49 - 10 = 39$ $39 - 10 = 29$	• Show me how you used the hundreds chart to explore the task. • How did you know how many jumps to make? • What does each jump represent? • What does the 69 represent? What does 59 represent? • How did you know which way to move on the hundreds chart?	• How could you use the hundreds chart to check your answer? • How could you use the hundreds chart to show that the difference between 69 and 29 is 40?		

SOLUTION STRATEGY	ASSESSING QUESTIONS	ADVANCING QUESTIONS	WHO AND WHAT	ORDER
Solution C. Count Back by Tens on an Open Number Line Student draws a number line and labels the point 69. The student then makes 4 jumps back and marks 10 above each, stopping at 29. Student writes $69 - 40 = 29$	• Show me how you used the number line to explore the task. • Can you show me how you counted? • How did you know how many jumps to make? • Why did you go backward on the number line? • What does the "10" you wrote represent? • When you subtracted 40 from 69, why did only the tens place change?	• (If no equation) What equation could you use to represent your model for solving the task? • (If there is an equation) How is each part of your equation represented in your model?		
Solution D. Round and Compensate Student adds 1 to 69 to get 70. Student models 70 with base ten blocks or a base ten drawing and then removes 4 tens and has 3 tens left. Student then subtracts 1 from 30 to compensate for the 1 added initially. Student writes $69 - 40 =$ $69 + 1 = 70$ $70 - 40 = 30$ $30 - 1 = 29$	• Tell me about your thinking. • Why did you add 1 to 69? What does 70 represent? • I thought we had 69 markers. What does 70 mean? • Why did you subtract 1 from 30? What does this say about the number of markers Ms. Tyus gave away?	• What would be different about your strategy if Ms. Tyus started with 68 markers? • Would this strategy work on another problem? Try the next problem and see if you can use this strategy. • (If no model) Can you create a physical model or drawing that explains why this strategy works?		

(Continued)

Figure 3.4 (*Continued*)

SOLUTION STRATEGY	ASSESSING QUESTIONS	ADVANCING QUESTIONS	WHO AND WHAT	ORDER
Solution E. Subtract Tens, Then Subtract Ones Instead of Add Ones Student decomposes 69 and then subtracts 40. Student incorrectly subtracts 9 from the remaining 20 rather than recomposing 20 + 9. Student writes 69 − 40 = 60 − 40 = 20 20 − 9 = 11	• Tell me about your thinking. • What does the 69 represent? The 40? • What does the 9 represent? • Why did you take 9 away from 20?	• Can you show how your equations and model connect? • Where does 60 − 40 connect to the situation? Where does 20 − 9 connect to the situation?		
Solution F. Round Up, Subtract, and Then Add One Instead of Subtract One Student adds 1 to 69 to get 70. Student models 70 with base ten blocks or a base ten drawing and then removes 4 tens and has 3 tens left. Student then incorrectly adds 1 to 30. Student writes 69 − 40 = 69 + 1 = 70 70 − 40 = 30 30 + 1 = 31	• Tell me about your thinking. • Why did you add 1 to 69? What does 70 represent? • Why did you add 1 to 30? What does it mean about the number of markers Ms. Tyus gave away?	• Can you use your base ten model or drawing to show how many markers Ms. Tyus has at each step? • When we look at 70 − 40, is that going to be more or less than 69 − 40 and why?		
Students cannot get started.	• What is the problem asking you to find? • How many markers did you start with? • How many markers did Ms. Tyus give away to her friend?	• Can you draw a picture or use your base ten blocks to show what happened in the problem?		
Other				

Planning to Notice Student Thinking

So far, we have focused on identifying the strategies you expect students to use in class as well as how you can respond when students use these strategies during class. The practice of anticipating also involves preparing yourself to notice what students are doing in the midst of instruction. Classrooms are often a whirlwind of activity! As the teacher, there is much for you to attend to—Are students on task? Do they have the materials they need? Are students collaborating productively? How much time is left in the period? Sherin and van Es (2009) explain that the ability to notice students' mathematical thinking in the midst of all that is taking place is a key component of teaching expertise today. In particular, teachers need to be able to sift through all the *noise* of the activity to identify what is important in what students are doing and saying.

Planning to notice involves preparing yourself to attend to those aspects of the lesson that you expect to be significant, while also being open to new ideas that might arise. Preparing a monitoring chart prior to instruction is a valuable approach for doing this (see Figure 3.4). The monitoring chart is a place where you can organize the strategies you anticipate that students will use along with the corresponding assessing and advancing questions for each strategy. Teachers often find it useful to list *Other* as a final strategy to remind them to be on the lookout for additional approaches that students might use. The monitoring chart also includes a *Who and What* column as a reminder to prepare to notice not just which strategies are being used but also who is using them. (We will discuss how to use the *Who and What* and *Order* columns in Chapters 4 and 5, respectively.) (A blank copy of the monitoring chart can be found in Appendix B.)

In addition to preparing yourself to be aware of how students will approach the task, you may want to also identify key ideas that you think are particularly important to keep track of as the lesson unfolds. For example, as Ms. Tyus prepared for instruction, she had in mind a few key aspects of students' thinking that she planned to be on the lookout for. First, as stated earlier, she was concerned that if students decomposed the 69 into 6 tens and 9 ones and then subtracted 4 tens, they might not know what they to do with the remaining 9 (in particular, what the 9 means in the context of the task). Because she thought this could get in the way of students' progress on the task, she planned to be on the lookout for this issue. Second, she was curious to see if any students used the rounding and compensating strategy, and if so, if they understood why it was necessary to subtract 1 from 30 as the final step; thus this was something she was also planning to attend to during the lesson.

> **TEACHING TAKEAWAY**
>
> A monitoring chart helps keep track of the work you anticipated and the questions you prepared *in advance* of the lesson but also helps you stay focused, intentional, and actively listening *during the lesson*!

Tara Tyus's Attention to Key Questions: Anticipating

As Ms. Tyus anticipated what her students would do, how she would respond to them, and what she would be on the lookout for, she kept her focus on the key questions. She approached this work by first *getting inside the problem* and identifying different solution strategies that she thought her students might use. Ms. Tyus then created assessing and advancing questions for each of these strategies. Her assessing questions were designed to draw out students' thinking, while the advancing questions were intended as prompts to move students' thinking forward. Finally, Ms. Tyus prepared herself to notice students' responses during instruction by developing a monitoring chart (shown in Figure 3.4). Her monitoring chart included the key strategies she anticipated students would use, assessing and advancing questions for each, as well as a column labeled *Who and What* where she planned to record what students did in class. Let's now look at some of the key challenges teachers face as they anticipate students' responses.

Part Two: Challenges Teachers Face: Anticipating Student Responses

As we described at the beginning of the chapter, anticipating what students are likely to do in a lesson, how you will respond, and what you will keep track of during the lesson is foundational to orchestrating productive discussions. Anticipating, however, is not without its challenges. In this section, we focus on three specific challenges associated with this practice, shown in Figure 3.5, that we have identified from our work with teachers.

Figure 3.5 • Challenges associated with the practice of anticipating students' responses

CHALLENGE	DESCRIPTION
Moving beyond the way *you* solve a problem	Teachers often feel limited by their own experience. They know how to solve a task but may not have access to the array of strategies that students are likely to use.
Being prepared to help students who cannot get started on a task	Teachers need to be prepared to provide support to students who do not know how to begin work on the task so that they can make progress without being told exactly what to do and how.
Creating questions that move students toward the mathematical goals	The questions teachers ask need to be driven by the mathematical goals of the lesson. The focus needs to be on ensuring that students *understand* the key mathematical ideas, not just on producing a solution to the task.

Moving Beyond the Way YOU Solved the Problem

You may, at times, feel limited by your own experiences—you know one way to solve a task and cannot imagine other ways to do it. Why do you need more than one solution method? When students are presented with a high-level task, one for which "a predictable, well-rehearsed approach or pathway is not explicitly suggested by the task, task instructions, or a worked-out example" (Smith & Stein, 1998, p. 348), students must determine a course of action based on their prior knowledge and experiences. Since their prior knowledge and experiences are different from yours, they are likely to think about the situation in very different ways. By anticipating what students are likely to do *prior* to a lesson, you will be better positioned to support students *during* the lesson.

In exploring this challenge, we begin by examining the third-grade lesson planned by Olivia Stastny. Ms. Stastny's students had been working on understanding what it means for fractions to be equivalent. As a result of engaging in the lesson, she wanted her students to understand that

1. A fraction describes the division of a whole or unit (area/region, set, linear/measurement) into equal parts. The size of the fraction is relative to the size of the whole or unit.

2. A fraction in which the number of parts you have (numerator) is the same as the size of the parts into which the whole is divided (denominator) is called one whole. So $\frac{4}{4}$ means there are four parts, each of which represents $\frac{1}{4}$ of the whole.

3. Two fractions are equivalent if they represent the same area of the same size whole even though the number of parts and the size of the parts are different.

Ms. Stastny selected the Lasagna task, shown in Figure 3.6, as the basis for her lesson. Unlike previous equivalent fraction tasks where students were given a fraction and asked to find another fraction equivalent to it, this task requires students to create two fractions equivalent to each other when given the number of parts eaten by each of two students— one student ate 2 parts and the other student had 4 parts. She selected this task because it was consistent with her lesson goals and would challenge students to draw on prior experiences with creating and subdividing whole units. In addition, the context was one that students could relate to since lasagna was a food with which they were familiar and they knew that it was their teacher's favorite food.

Figure 3.6 • The Lasagna task

Lasagna

There were two pans of lasagna at the school picnic. The parents cut each pan of lasagna into equal portions.

Tanesha has 2 portions from one pan, while David has 4 portions from the other pan. They both received the same amount of lasagna. How is this possible?

1. Show how the lasagna was divided into portions so Tanesha's 2 portions are equal to David's 4 portions.

2. Shade in the portion of lasagna eaten by each child.

3. Write fractions that describe each student's portion of the pan of lasagna.

4. Explain how you know that Tanesha and David each received the same amount of lasagna. Explain your thinking by referring to the pictures, symbols, and words.

Source: Adapted from Hamilton County Department of Education Grade 4 Task 11.

 Download the Task from **resources.corwin.com/5practices-elementary**

Ms. Stastny began the practice of anticipating by solving the task herself. She then conferred with colleagues in order to gain additional insight regarding how students could solve the task. Working together, Ms. Stastny and her colleagues first identified what students would need to do in order to correctly solve the task and then generated specific examples of what the actual work might look like (see Solutions A, B, and C in Figure 3.7). They agreed that students would need to

- Draw a model that shows two wholes the same size, subdivide them so one whole had twice as many pieces as the other, and accurately shade two pieces of one and four pieces of the other.

- Label each drawing with the correct fraction.

- Provide an explanation regarding why the two amounts are equal, drawing on equivalent fractions and/or area.

Figure 3.7 • Anticipated solutions to the Lasagna task generated by Ms. Stastny and her colleagues

A. Comparing Different Size Pieces	B. Comparing Two Wholes	C. Comparing Areas Covered
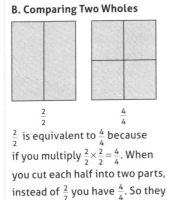		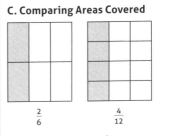

A. Comparing Different Size Pieces

$\frac{2}{4}$ $\frac{4}{8}$

David and Tanesha get the same amount. It looks like David got more but he really got the same amount as Tanesha. He just got more pieces that are smaller.

B. Comparing Two Wholes

$\frac{2}{2}$ $\frac{4}{4}$

$\frac{2}{2}$ is equivalent to $\frac{4}{4}$ because if you multiply $\frac{2}{2} \times \frac{2}{2} = \frac{4}{4}$. When you cut each half into two parts, instead of $\frac{2}{2}$ you have $\frac{4}{4}$. So they both ate a whole lasagna.

C. Comparing Areas Covered

$\frac{2}{6}$ $\frac{4}{12}$

Both students have the same amount of lasagna. If you put their shares on top of each other they will be the same amount of lasagna.

In addition to considering what complete and correct solutions would look like, Ms. Stastny and her colleagues also thought about solutions that were incomplete or incorrect. They determined that students might

- Draw a correct diagram (such as those shown in Figure 3.7) but not label it with the fraction it represents and/or not provide an explanation regarding why the amount of lasagna eaten by each student was the same.

- Draw a diagram that shows two different size wholes (Solution D in Figure 3.8).

- Interpret the 2 pieces that Tanesha was to eat and 4 pieces that David was to eat as the number of pieces in each lasagna rather than the number of pieces eaten from a whole (Solution E in Figure 3.8).

- Draw two wholes the same size but subdivide them into unequal parts (Solution F in Figure 3.8).

Figure 3.8 • Possible misconceptions about the Lasagna task generated by Ms. Stastny and her colleagues

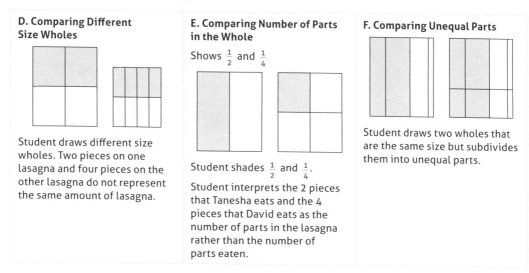

D. Comparing Different Size Wholes

Student draws different size wholes. Two pieces on one lasagna and four pieces on the other lasagna do not represent the same amount of lasagna.

E. Comparing Number of Parts in the Whole

Shows $\frac{1}{2}$ and $\frac{1}{4}$

Student shades $\frac{1}{2}$ and $\frac{1}{4}$.

Student interprets the 2 pieces that Tanesha eats and the 4 pieces that David eats as the number of parts in the lasagna rather than the number of parts eaten.

F. Comparing Unequal Parts

Student draws two wholes that are the same size but subdivides them into unequal parts.

The key factor in Ms. Stastny's anticipating is that she did not have to *go it alone.* By working in collaboration with colleagues, she was able to expand on the set of ideas she was able to come up with on her own. As Ms. Stastny explained:

A big part of doing the five practices is the anticipating and figuring out what the students might do so that I'm not stumped in class. Sometimes you have to collaborate with other people to see all of those different strategies. Because sometimes you miss them but somebody that you might work with will see it.

Fifth-grade teacher Mr. Andrew Strong echoed the importance of collaboration when anticipating student solutions and also recognized the value in saving student responses to a task from previous years as a resource for anticipating. For his lesson, students would be continuing their work on division with fractional divisors. As a result of the lesson, he wanted his students to understand that

1. To divide a whole number by a fraction (e.g., $4 \div \frac{1}{3}$) means to determine how many iterations of the fraction ($\frac{1}{3}$) fit inside the whole number (4).

2. The quotient of a whole number divided by a fraction can be found by multiplying (e.g., $4 \div \frac{1}{3} = 4 \times 3$) because you are determining how many iterations of the fraction there are in 1 unit of the dividend then multiplying the number of iterations in 1 unit by the total number of units in the dividend (e.g., there are three $\frac{1}{3}$s in 1 mile so the number of $\frac{1}{3}$s in 4 miles is 4×3).

3. When dividing by a number less than 1, the quotient will be greater than the dividend because you are making groups of an amount less than 1.

For this lesson, Mr. Strong decided to use Mr. Strong's Hike task (see Figure 3.9). He used a version of this task (Bobby's Hike) the previous year but decided to make the task about a hike he was planning to take. He planned to launch the task by talking about his own hiking experiences and how he makes sure to drink water at regular intervals throughout the hike in order to stay hydrated using his hydration pack, which he planned to wear and use during the lesson.

Figure 3.9 • Mr. Strong's Hike task

Mr. Strong's Hike

This weekend I'm going for a 4-mile hike!

I'm going to stop and take a drink every $\frac{1}{3}$ mile. How many times will I stop for a drink? Be sure to show how you found your answer with both diagrams and an explanation in words. What fraction equations match your diagram?

Source: Adapted from the University of Pittsburgh, 2015.

 Download the Task from **resources.corwin.com/5practices-elementary**

Mr. Strong began his planning by reviewing student responses to the Bobby's Hike task from the previous year. Most students, he noted, solved the problem by creating number lines—they drew a line, broke it into four sections to represent the miles, and then subdivided each mile into three pieces to represent thirds. He noted, however, that all students did not do this the same way. Some students took each mile as a whole and labeled the number line as $0, \frac{1}{3}, \frac{2}{3}, 1, \frac{1}{3}, \frac{2}{3}, 2, \frac{1}{3}, \frac{2}{3}, 3, \frac{1}{3}, \frac{2}{3}, 4$ (see Solution A in Figure 3.10), while other students seemed to consider the entire 4 miles as the whole and labeled all points on the graph in terms of a number of thirds (i.e., $\frac{1}{3}, \frac{2}{3}, \frac{3}{3}, \frac{4}{3}, \frac{5}{3}$, etc.) as shown in Solution B in Figure 3.10. Still other students created a number line that did not show equal subdivisions (see Solution C in Figure 3.10).

Figure 3.10 • Solutions to the task produced by Mr. Strong's students the previous year

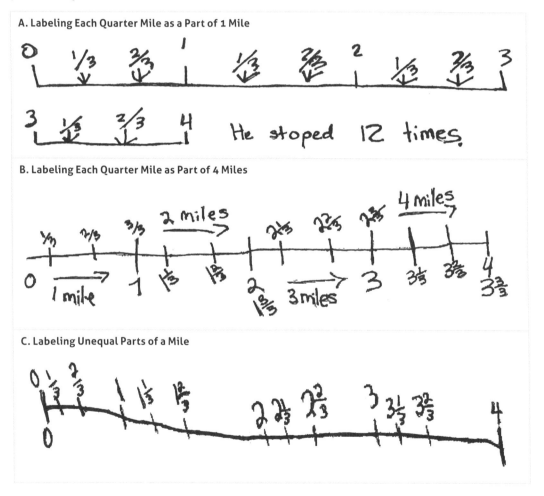

Mr. Strong shared the solutions his students produced the previous year with his grade-level colleagues. They agreed that the number line solutions (shown in Figure 3.10) were ones that current students would likely produce. In addition, in reviewing the student work from the

Bobby's Hike task and reflecting on their own experiences in teaching this content, the teachers felt that they could also expect to see students doing some or all of the following:

- Create an accurate number line and determine that Mr. Strong would stop for a drink 12 times, but not be able to explain why or write an equation.

- Create an equation (3×4) that contains no fractions and not be able to explain what happened to the $\frac{1}{3}$ in the problem.

- Create the equation $\frac{1}{3} \div 4$ instead of $4 \div \frac{1}{3}$ and have trouble explaining how it fits the situation.

- Struggle to make sense of why $4 \div \frac{1}{3}$ is the same as 4×3.

With these anticipated solution strategies in hand, Mr. Strong was now ready to create his monitoring tool and to prepare questions to assess and advance his students' learning. We will explore this component of anticipating in the next section.

So what can you do to anticipate multiple possible solution paths? A first step is to consider different ways to represent the situation. The diagram shown in Figure 3.11 describes five different ways to represent a mathematical idea—visual, symbolic, verbal, contextual, or physical.

Figure 3.11 • Different ways to represent a mathematical idea

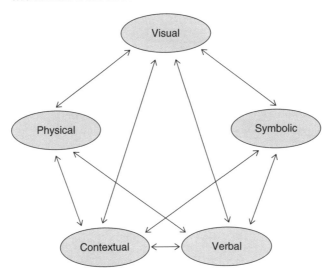

In order to illustrate how this diagram might be helpful in anticipating solution strategies, let us consider the Treat Bags task shown in Figure 3.12.

Figure 3.12 • Treat Bags task

Treat Bags

Julia's mother made 153 cookies for her birthday party. Julia's job is to put them into treat bags for each of her 12 friends who are coming to her party. How many cookies will be in each bag if all her friends get the same number of cookies? How many cookies will be left over?

 Download the Task from **resources.corwin.com/5practices-elementary**

⏸ PAUSE AND CONSIDER

How could you solve the Treat Bags task shown in Figure 3.12 using each of the representations shown in Figure 3.11?

Physical: *Verbal:*

Visual: *Symbolic:*

Contextual:

Your first instinct in solving this problem may have been to use the division algorithm. However, students who have not been formally taught this procedure will use one of several other ways to solve the problem as shown in Figure 3.13. The point is to think through what students might do so that you are prepared to deal with a range of different strategies that are likely to appear during the lesson. This level of anticipating will also help you think about the resources that you need to make available to students so they can pursue various pathways. For example, if you want students to be able to create physical models of the situation, you need to provide materials they could use for this purpose. If you want students to feel free to use an area model, you should have grid paper available for them to use. If you want students to draw a picture, you should provide paper and colored pencils, markers, or crayons. (A caution here—providing colored pencils, markers, or crayons can encourage students to turn their work into an art project. Be sure to make clear that this is not an art activity and the colors are available to help them keep track of the amounts.)

Figure 3.13 • Different ways of representing the relationships in the Treat Bags task

Visual—Area Model

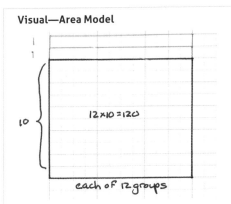

I know $12 \times 10 = 120$ so I start by putting 10 in each column/group. Then I add 1 to each of the 12 groups, which means I used 132. Then I add another 1 to each of the 12 groups, which means I used 144. I have 153 cookies so I can't add any more to each of the 12 groups. So each treat bag has 12 cookies and there are 9 cookies left.

Visual—Base Ten Model

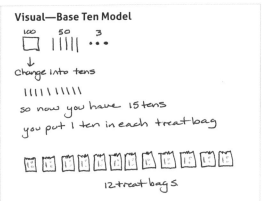

You have 3 tens left and 3 ones after you put 1 ten in each of the treat bags. So you change the 3 tens into 30 ones, which gives you 33 ones. You put 1 more cookie in each bag so that uses up 12. Now you have 21 cookies left. So you put 1 more cookie in each bag and that uses up 12 more. So now you have only 9 cookies left. So each treat bag has 12 cookies and there are 9 left over.

Symbolic—Repeated Multiplication

$12 \times 12 = 144$, so if you do one more 12 you get 156 and you don't have that many cookies.

$156 - 144 = 9$, so there are 9 cookies left over.

Each treat bag has 12 cookies.

$12 \times 1 = 12$
$12 \times 2 = 24$
$12 \times 3 = 36$
$12 \times 4 = 48$
$12 \times 5 = 60$
$12 \times 6 = 72$
$12 \times 7 = 84$
$12 \times 8 = 96$
$12 \times 9 = 108$
$12 \times 10 = 120$
$12 \times 11 = 132$
$\boxed{12 \times 12 = 144}$
$12 \times 13 = 156 \rightarrow$

Symbolic—Repeated Subtraction

I took 12 away 12 times and had 9 left over.

So each treat bag has 12 cookies in it.

$$
\begin{array}{r}
153 \\
-12 \\
\hline
141 \\
-12 \\
\hline
129 \\
-12 \\
\hline
117 \\
-12 \\
\hline
105 \\
-12 \\
\hline
93 \\
-12 \\
\hline
81 \\
-12 \\
\hline
69 \\
-12 \\
\hline
57 \\
-12 \\
\hline
45 \\
-12 \\
\hline
33 \\
-12 \\
\hline
21 \\
-12 \\
\hline
9
\end{array}
$$

(Continued)

Verbal—Language

I know that 12 × 12 is 144. If I add 12 more, I get 156. This is too many, since there are only 153 cookies. So each of the 12 treat bags will have 12 cookies in it. There will be 9 cookies left over because 153−144 is 9. So Julia gets to eat the 9 cookies.

Physical—Manipulatives

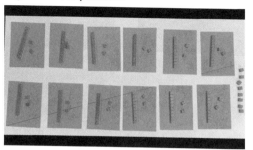

While you may not be able to generate an array of strategies yourself, consider ways to collaborate with others. You may be able to work with a colleague who teaches the same grade level or a different grade level, in or outside of your building. If you do not have math-teacher colleagues to help generate and discuss an expanded set of solutions to a particular task, consider one of the following options:

- Ask your friends (either face-to-face or virtually) to solve the task. Adults who are not mathematics teachers often produce solutions that approximate what students will do!

- Post a question on Twitter, My NCTM (https://my.nctm.org/home), or other social media outlets. This will give you access to a community of educators, many of whom will be eager to respond!

- Take photos of solutions students produce to a particular task the first time you teach it, and add to it every time you use the same task. Over time, you will have a robust collection of approaches to consider as you prepare for subsequent lessons. (This will also be a great resource to share with colleagues who are using the task for the first time.)

Being Prepared to Help Students Who Cannot Get Started

Regardless of how carefully you set up or launch the lesson, there is often a student who is unsure how to begin the task. Smith, Steele, and Raith (2017) argue,

> when a student can't get started on a problem, it generally is not because he or she has no relevant knowledge to bring to bear on the situation. More often, the student, for some reason, is unable to connect what he or she does know with the task at hand. (p. 187)

This could be due to a reading comprehension issue, lack of familiarity with the context of the problem, or a lack of confidence in their ability to engage with a task for which a strategy is not provided.

TEACHING TAKEAWAY

Be prepared to help students who do not know how to get started on a problem by eliciting what they understand about the task rather than by suggesting specific steps to try or by having another student show them what to do.

Common approaches to this challenge include suggesting a strategy for the student to use or pairing the student with a student who knows how to begin. While these approaches give the student something to do, they provide you with no insight regarding what the student understands about the task, do nothing to build the student's capacity to persevere in the face of struggle, and probably add to the student's self-perception as someone who cannot do mathematics. When students move forward based on someone else's thinking, it is unlikely that they will be able to retain and appropriately use a strategy they do not understand. Therefore, it is critical to have a plan in place regarding how to support students who struggle to get started.

⏸ PAUSE AND CONSIDER

What questions could you ask a student who could not begin the Lasagna task (Figure 3.6)?

Ms. Stastny anticipated that some students in her class might have trouble getting started on the task, so she planned questions that would provide her with insight regarding what students understood about the problem context. As she explained:

> If my students can't get started I'm going to start with a very basic question, "What do we know about the story?" They might go back and say that we know that she has two pieces and he has four pieces. So I might say, "Draw me a picture. Can you draw that for me?" Or I'll go back to our launch. I have a picture with a rectangular pan of lasagna. So I might say, can you draw that lasagna for me and show me the two pieces? They will also have fraction strips at their desks if they choose to use them. I have a couple that may need manipulatives.

The goal is to be able to support students' productive struggle—finding ways to support students so that they can move forward on their own steam. Warshauer (2015) argues that while telling students what to do or providing them with directed guidance helps them to move forward, it tends to lower the cognitive demand of the task and limit students' opportunities to learn.

Creating Questions That Move Students Toward the Mathematical Goal

The questions that teachers ask students during a lesson need to be driven by the mathematical goals. You need to first determine what students know in comparison to what you ultimately want them to learn and then ask questions that move them toward the goal. You will not ask all students the same set of questions because they are not all thinking about the problem in the same way, and your questions will be driven by the different solutions they have produced.

In preparation for her lesson, Ms. Stastny created a series of assessing and advancing questions that she planned to ask her students, based on the strategies she anticipated they would use (see Figures 3.7 and 3.8).

 PAUSE AND CONSIDER

Review the models shown in Figure 3.7 Solution C and in Figure 3.8 Solution A. What questions could you plan to ask students who produced these models, given the lesson goals (shown below)?

1. A fraction describes the division of a whole or unit (area/region, set, linear/measurement) into equal parts. The size of the fraction is relative to the size of the whole or unit.

2. A fraction in which the total number of pieces in the whole is the same as the total number of the pieces is called one whole because all of the pieces of the whole are accounted for (e.g., $\frac{4}{4}, \frac{5}{5}, \frac{6}{6}$).

3. Two fractions are equivalent if they show the same area of the same size whole even though the number of parts and the size of the parts are different.

Two of the solutions that Ms. Stastny anticipated students would use, and the questions she planned to ask about those solutions, are shown in Figure 3.14. The first assessing question she plans to ask each student is, "What did you do?" By asking this question (or some variant), the teacher is honoring the student's thinking by giving the student the opportunity to explain what he or she has done, not assuming that she knows what

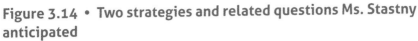

Figure 3.14 • Two strategies and related questions Ms. Stastny anticipated

STRATEGY	ASSESSING QUESTIONS	ADVANCING QUESTIONS
$\frac{2}{6}$ $\frac{4}{12}$ Both students have the same amount of lasagna. If you put their shares on top of each other, they will be the same amount of lasagna.	• What did you do? • What do your diagrams show about how much lasagna Tanesha and David ate? • Who got the most lasagna and how do you know?	• You explained how you know the portions are equivalent. What equation can you write to show why this is true? • What equation can you write to show that $\frac{2}{6}$ is equivalent to $\frac{4}{12}$?
	• What did you do? • What do your diagrams show about how much lasagna Tanesha and David got?	• Can you show David and Tanesha's shares and write a fraction, if the students have the same size pans?

the student is thinking, and laying the foundation on which to build subsequent questions. The remaining assessing questions are intended to elicit more details on what the student understands about the solution the student has produced should they be needed.

Even if a student produces an accurate and correctly labeled diagram and a clear explanation (as shown in the first row of Figure 3.14 and Solution C in Figure 3.7), Ms. Stastny will be interested in what this student *understands* and would not equate answering the questions posed in the task with understanding. Toward this end, she plans to ask the student two additional assessing questions, each of which corresponds to the goals she had targeted in the lesson.

- *What do your diagrams show about how much lasagna Tanesha and David ate?* By asking this question, the teacher is trying to get the student to explain how her diagram shows that David and Tanesha had different numbers of pieces of lasagna (4 and 2, respectively) but had the same amount of lasagna. By phrasing the question in this way, the student has to articulate what the problem is asking her to find and how her diagram helped in answering the question. Ms. Stastny might expect the student to say something similar to "Tanesha's lasagna is cut into 6 pieces and she ate 2 of them like the problem said. David's lasagna is the same size, but if he was going to eat 4 pieces instead of 2 but have the same amount, the pieces need to be smaller. So I cut each sixth into 2 pieces and that gave me 12 pieces. David's pieces are smaller but he is getting 4 pieces—twice as many as Tanesha." A response such as this would make clear that the student understood that a fraction describes the division of a whole into equal parts (Goal 1) and that 2 parts of a whole divided into sixths is equivalent to 4 parts of the same size whole divided into 12ths (Goal 3).

- *Who got the most lasagna and how do you know?* The phrasing of the question is important because the teacher did not ask how the student knows David and Tanesha had the same amount, which is what the problem asked her to show. The teacher is looking for the student to articulate that David and Tanesha got the same amount of lasagna *and* to explain why. Although the student stated in writing that the amounts would be the same if you put one on top of the other, she might also expect the student to say that $\frac{2}{6}$ and $\frac{4}{12}$ were equivalent because they show the same area. This directly relates to Goal 3 (two fractions are equivalent if they show the same area of the same size whole even though the number of parts and the size of the parts are different).

Armed with answers to these questions, Ms. Stastny is then positioned to advance the student's thinking by asking how the diagram shows $\frac{2}{6}$ is equivalent to $\frac{4}{12}$ and what equation can be written to show the change. Although these questions go beyond the goals the teacher had stated for the lesson, given the progress the student had made on the task, challenging the student to making connections between a symbolic and pictorial representation is a logical next step in advancing this student's understanding of equivalent fractions.

The solution with two different size wholes (shown in the second row of Figure 3.14 and Solution D in Figure 3.8) is not correct. While the student has shown $\frac{2}{4}$ and $\frac{4}{8}$, giving Tanesha and David the desired number of pieces, the size of the wholes is not the same and therefore the fractions do not represent that same amount. Here the teacher wants to help the student recognize that there is a problem with the diagram.

- *What do your diagrams show about how much lasagna Tanesha and David got?* This question provides an opportunity for the student to articulate what she understands about the size of the pan of lasagna and for the teacher to clarify that the pans are the same size. (While this is implied in the problem, it is not stated.)

Once it is established that the two pans of lasagna must be the same size, Ms. Stastny can ask the student to revise her solution in light of the fact that the pans of lasagna are the same size and to write a fraction that shows each student's shares. This provides the student with the opportunity to rethink her diagram and to write fractions that reflect the diagrams. Hence this advancing question addresses Goals 1 and 3.

The bottom line is that the lesson goals need to drive the questions you ask. If your goal is for students to understand a mathematical relationship, then the questions you ask need to focus on getting students to recognize and articulate the relationship. Being satisfied with an answer such as

"$\frac{2}{4} = \frac{4}{8}$" in the Lasagna task or "Mr. Strong took 12 sips of water" in Mr. Strong's Hike without further probing tells you nothing about what the student understands. Some students are good at finding answers but do not know why they are doing it or what it means.

TEACHING TAKEAWAY

Posing questions carefully crafted around your lesson's mathematical goals *and* students' work will tell you what students understand, not just how well they perform.

It is important to note that while the teacher establishes specific learning goals for the lesson, students will be at different places in their learning based on their prior knowledge and experiences. Therefore, students are asked questions that help them make progress *toward* the goals based on their current understanding. All students may not enter the whole class discussion having made the same amount of progress on the task. This is not imperative. What is important is that the conversation provides the opportunity for students to extend and solidify their own understandings. The discussion should provide an opportunity for learning, not just a chance for students to report out what they have done.

Conclusion

In this chapter, we explored the components of the practice of *anticipating* and focused on a set of challenges that teachers often face when engaging in this practice. Anticipating is critical to planning a lesson because it provides the teacher with the opportunity to think deeply about what students are likely to do and how they will respond. This in-advance-of-the-lesson thinking eliminates much of the on-the-fly decision-making that often is required in teaching. While you will not be able to anticipate everything that students will do, our experience tells us that you may be able to anticipate much of what will happen, especially if you do not plan alone.

Ms. Tyus's work on anticipating provides insight into what a teacher needs to consider as he or she engages in the process. In planning her lesson, Ms. Tyus thought deeply about what students were likely to do when presented with the task, including identifying aspects of the task she thought would be challenging for students, and the questions that she would ask students to assess their thinking and to move them toward the goals of the lesson. In addition, she identified specific aspects of student thinking that she planned to be on the lookout for during the lesson. This level of preparation before the lesson is likely to have a positive impact on the quality of the lesson itself because she has thought deeply about the mathematics she wants students to learn, the task, and what her students are bringing to the task.

By examining the work of Ms. Stastny around the Lasagna task, we saw that while there are challenges associated with anticipating, collaborating with colleagues can go a long way in addressing the challenges. Ms. Stastny's work also makes clear how important it is to never lose sight of the lesson goals—they should serve as a resource throughout the lesson and a way of evaluating students' learning.

Anticipating Student Responses—Summary

Video Clip 3.1
To hear and see more about anticipating student thinking and using the monitoring tool to plan your responses, watch Video Clip 3.1.

 Videos may also be accessed at
resources.corwin.com/5practices-elementary

We now invite you to apply what you have learned from your work in this chapter to your own teaching practice by engaging in the Linking the Five Practices to Your Own Instruction activity. We encourage you to find one or more colleagues with whom to collaborate on this activity. As one teacher commented, "A best practice for anticipating strategies for a specific task is to sit with a team of teachers to identify all of the possible inroads, rather than completing this as a teacher in isolation" (Smith & Stein, 2018, p. 49).

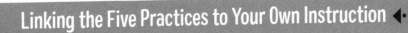

Linking the Five Practices to Your Own Instruction

ANTICIPATING

Identify a mathematical idea that you plan to teach sometime in the next two weeks.

1. Specify a clear goal for student learning and select a high-level task that is aligned with your learning goal.

2. Anticipate—get inside the problem, plan to respond, and plan to notice. If possible, get input from colleagues either virtually or face-to-face in order to gain additional insights into the task, its solutions, and its challenges.

3. Create assessing and advancing questions that are driven by your goals for the lesson but build on where students are in their thinking.

4. Produce a monitoring chart you can use to record data during the lesson that includes possible solutions, assessing and advancing questions that are driven by your goals, and questions you can ask students who cannot get started.

"The assessing and advancing questions asked during the monitoring and exploring phase help me see where students truly are and then push them further."

—TARA TYUS, FIRST-GRADE TEACHER

CHAPTER 4

Monitoring Student Work

The next practice we explore is monitoring students' work. Having carefully selected a goal and corresponding task, and anticipated the different strategies students will use, we now turn to instruction. How do you, as the teacher, keep track of what students are doing and saying, as the lesson unfolds in your classroom? Monitoring involves paying close attention to students' ideas and methods as they relate to your goals for the lesson. With many students working at the same time, this can be quite challenging. Who is using what strategy? How far did they get? Monitoring also involves asking students questions both to clarify their thinking and to move their thinking forward. Interacting with students during instruction in ways that productively move the lesson forward is complex work. The practice of monitoring is designed to help you manage this complexity by having a clear, focused lens for attending to and keeping track of students' thinking.

Smith and Stein (2018) describe monitoring in the following way:

> *Monitoring is the process of paying attention to the thinking of students during the actual lesson as they work individually or collectively on a particular task. This involves not just listening in on what students are saying and observing what they are doing, but also keeping track of the approaches that they are using, identifying*

those that can help advance the mathematical discussion later in the lesson, and asking questions that will help students make progress on the task. This is the time when the assessing and advancing questions that you created prior to the lesson will come in handy. These questions include those that will make students' thinking explicit, get students back on track if they are following an unproductive or inaccurate pathway, and will press students who are on the right course to think more deeply about why things work the way that they do. (p. 54)

In this chapter, we first describe key aspects of monitoring and illustrate what this practice looks like in an authentic elementary school classroom. We then discuss what aspects of monitoring are challenging for teachers and provide an opportunity for you to explore monitoring in your own teaching practice.

Part One: Unpacking the Practice: Monitoring Student Work

What is involved in monitoring students' thinking? This practice involves tracking the thinking of students in your class and asking questions to uncover what students understand (assessing questions) and to move students' thinking forward (advancing questions). Figure 4.1 highlights the components of this practice along with key questions to guide the process of monitoring.

Figure 4.1 • Key questions that support the practice of monitoring

WHAT IT TAKES	KEY QUESTIONS
Tracking student thinking	How will you keep track of students' responses during the lesson?
	How will you ensure that you check in with all students during the lesson?
Assessing student thinking	Are your assessing questions meeting students where they are?
	Are your assessing questions making student thinking visible?
Advancing student thinking	Are your advancing questions driven by your lesson goals?
	Are students able to pursue advancing questions on their own?
	Are your advancing questions helping students to progress?

In the next sections, we illustrate the practice of monitoring by continuing our investigation of Ms. Tyus's implementation of the Ms. Tyus's Markers task. As you view video clips from her class and read the descriptions of what took place, consider how Ms. Tyus's attention to the key questions may have shaped her teaching.

Tracking Student Thinking

Once your students begin working on the task, you will want an efficient and productive way to follow what they are doing. Who is making progress? Who has questions? Who is feeling stuck? Tracking the diversity of students' thinking during instruction is complex work. Kazemi, Gibbons, Lomax, and Franke (2016) emphasize that it is not sufficient to wait for students to complete the task in order to check their progress. Instead, teachers need a way to "gain insight into student thinking that [is] manageable" during "face-to-face conversations with students" during class (p. 184).

The monitoring chart you developed during the anticipating phase can be a valuable resource for tracking student thinking. As you observe and talk with your students, you can quickly note what strategy students are using and record it in the *Who and What* column of your monitoring chart. This is where listing the anticipated strategies on your monitoring chart really comes in handy! You may also want to note anything particularly interesting that a student is doing—a question or variation in a strategy or a connection between two strategies, for example. Indicating when students are using a strategy that was not anticipated is equally important, both for the day's lesson and for the future, particularly if those strategies have the potential to illuminate the mathematical goals of the lesson. There is typically little time to make elaborate comments on the monitoring chart during instruction. Still, making some notes throughout the lesson can help you stay abreast of what is happening. Many teachers choose to print their monitoring chart before the lesson and take notes by hand as the lesson progresses. Others prefer to annotate an electronic version of the monitoring chart during instruction. Either way, the monitoring chart can help you quickly reference how students are thinking about the task.

As you track students' responses, you want to make sure that you are circulating throughout the classroom. Some teachers opt to move in a designated pattern around the room as a way to ensure they check in with each student during the lesson. Having students work in groups can increase collaboration and make it easier to touch base with more than one student at a time (Horn, 2012). Using the monitoring chart can help you keep track of which students you have spoken with as well as how many times you have visited each group. It may be hard, at times, to pull yourself away from a group that is having a particularly interesting discussion. Or you may find yourself spending extra time with students who are having trouble getting started with the task. In either case, making a plan for how you will circulate among and keep track of students as you monitor their thinking is an important consideration. For Ms. Tyus, the monitoring chart is a key part of her instruction: "I carry it as I'm

> **TEACHING TAKEAWAY**
>
> Taking quick notes on your monitoring chart can help you track which students use which strategies.

> **TEACHING TAKEAWAY**
>
> Using the monitoring chart can help you track your interaction with students, in terms of both what students are doing and with whom you have spoken.

conferencing with students. I write down their names and what they did." She explained, "Sometimes it is challenging to remember to take down those notes on the monitoring tool. Learning is happening so fast and you can't catch it all on that tool, but the tool is very important for you to look back later so that drives your instruction. So it is challenging, but very necessary."

PAUSE AND CONSIDER

How do you track students' ideas during instruction?

How do you circulate among your students as they are working?

What techniques might help you more effectively track student thinking in your classroom?

Assessing Student Thinking

As you monitor students' progress, you want to interact with students in ways that take them from where they are now and move them toward the lesson goals. Jacobs and Philipp (2010) highlight the importance of this goal when they explain that teaching that "builds on children's ways of thinking can lead to rich instructional environments and gains in student achievement" (p. 101).

To start, be on the lookout for those strategies that you anticipated that students might use. Once you recognize that a student is using one of the anticipated approaches, you can examine the assessing questions you designed for that approach. The assessing (and advancing) questions in the monitoring chart are not meant to be a script. Rather, they are intended as a reference for you to use to help you consider what questions you want to ask particular students. For example, when Ms. Tyus sees a student using the hundreds chart, she does not automatically ask, "What does each jump represent?" Instead, she looks at what this particular student is doing or saying and decides what question is appropriate to ask.

When selecting an assessing question to use in class, there are two main considerations. First, aim to meet students where they are in their current thinking about the task. Ball, Lubienski, and Mewborn (2001) emphasize that "sizing up students' thinking and responding" depends on the details of what a student is doing (p. 451). Be sure to ask about the students' ideas, about what they have written or drawn. Using students' own terminology can often be helpful. Be aware that what you anticipated students might do is not always what they end up doing. Asking students specific questions about their work is an important way to uncover how they are thinking about the task and their solution. As Ms. Tyus explained, "I have my strategies outlined and I have my assessing questions. But anything can happen in the task. They might do different things." Mr. Strong echoed this point, saying, "You never know what you're going to get sometimes" and that for him, the next step is "just to assess their thinking. Why did you do this? Explain it to me." Assessing questions are important because they can help you uncover what students are doing, whether or not that aligns with what you anticipated.

> **TEACHING TAKEAWAY**
>
> Look and listen *carefully*. Modify your planned assessing questions in real time based specifically on what students are doing and saying, rather than what you thought they would do or say.

Second, assessing questions are most useful when they make students' thinking visible in ways that can then help you move their thinking forward toward the lesson goals. You want to understand not only *what* students did but *why* they did it. Understanding the reasons behind a student's strategy often provides the clues you need to help the student reconsider her position or move deeper into the task.

What does this look like in practice? In Analyzing the Work of Teaching 4.0, you will explore how students in Ms. Tyus's class begin to make sense of the Ms. Tyus's Markers task. We encourage you to look at the student work and consider the questions posed before you read our analysis.

Analyzing the Work of Teaching 4.0

Exploring Student Problem-Solving Approaches

After launching the Ms. Tyus's Markers task, Ms. Tyus asks students to spend a few minutes working on the problem individually. Here you will investigate the initial work of two students, Jacey and Leah, on the first problem: *Ms. Tyus has 69 scented markers. She*

CONTINUED

CONTINUED FROM PREVIOUS PAGE

gives 40 scented markers to her friend. How many markers does she have left? Make a diagram and write an equation that shows how Anna can solve this problem.

Jacey's Work

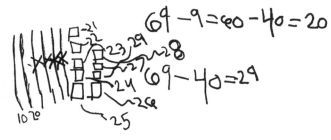

Leah's Work

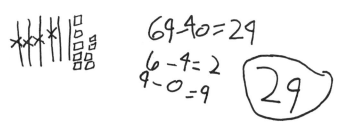

As you examine Jacey and Leah's written work, consider the following questions:

1. What can you infer from their written work about how Jacey and Leah are thinking about the problem?

    •   What does Jacey's drawing reveal about her understanding of the task? What do her equations reveal?

    •   What does Leah's drawing reveal about her understanding of the task? What do her equations reveal?

2. What strategies are Jacey and Leah using? Can you identify each strategy as one listed on Ms. Tyus's monitoring chart? (See Figure 3.4)

3. What assessing questions would you want to ask Jacey and Leah in order to be sure that you understand their reasoning about the problem?

Exploring Student Problem-Solving Approaches—Analysis

Jacey's written work on the Ms. Tyus's Markers task shows a base ten drawing, with lines representing tens and boxes representing ones. She has crossed out 4 of the 6 tens, likely to represent the 40 markers that

Ms. Tyus gave away. Jacey has labeled the remaining 2 tens as "10, 20." It may be that she is counting the tens that are left after taking away 4 tens. Jacey has also labeled each of the ones from 21 to 29. One possible explanation is that she is adding on from the 20 to determine the total number of markers that Ms. Tyus has left. Jacey's equations also seems to indicate that she is decomposing and recomposing using base ten blocks, Solution A in Ms. Tyus's monitoring chart (Figure 3.4). Jacey decomposes 69 into 6 tens and 9 ones and later seems to recompose the 2 tens and 9 ones when working with her model and then writes the difference equation.

While Ms. Tyus had anticipated that students using this strategy would write the equations $60 - 40 = 20$ and $20 + 9 = 29$ to represent their solution, Jacey has written something different. At the top of her work she has written $69 - 9 = 60 - 40 = 20$. Even though Jacey has written a single equation, it is possible that she understands it as two separate operations, $69 - 9$ and $60 - 40$. Or it may be that Jacey's understanding of equality is still developing and that she sees the equal sign as a direction to "do something" rather than an indication that two things are equal (Falkner, Levi, & Carpenter, 1999; Leavy, Hourigan, & McMahon, 2013). What might Ms. Tyus want to ask Jacey to help understand her approach? Here are some possible assessing questions she could ask: "Can you tell me what your equations mean?" "What does the 60 mean in the top equation?" "Can you tell me what these numbers next to the boxes mean?"

Similar to Jacey, Leah has created a base ten drawing showing 6 tens and 9 ones with 4 of the tens crossed out, reflecting Solution A in Ms. Tyus's monitoring chart (Figure 3.4). Leah has written three equations: $69 - 40 = 29$, $6 - 4 = 2$, and $9 - 0 = 9$. We might wonder what the equation $6 - 4 = 2$ means. Does Leah intend the 6 and the 4 to represent tens as in 6 tens $-$ 4 tens $=$ 2 tens? While this equation may raise questions for us about Leah's understanding of place value, Leah is able to model 69 as a decomposition of tens and ones. In addition, Leah does accurately represent place value in the equation $69 - 40 = 29$, and she has circled the answer 29, suggesting that she understands that the 2 represents 2 tens.

There can be a great deal to process in the moments of instruction. Effective assessing questions help students articulate their thinking and give you insight into how they are making sense of the task. What questions might you ask Leah to help her reveal her ideas? Potential assessing questions include "What does the equation $6 - 4 = 2$ mean?" "Can you tell me what the 29 means?" and "How did you determine it?"

In Analyzing the Work of Teaching 4.1, you will investigate what Ms. Tyus does to support her students as they work on the task.

Analyzing the Work of Teaching 4.1

Assessing Student Thinking

Video Clip 4.1

As students continued to work individually on the Ms. Tyus's Markers task, the teacher circulated around the room checking in with her students. In this video clip, she first talks briefly with Jocelyn and then with DuJuan about their progress on the task.

First take a look at Jocelyn and DuJuan's written work. What can you infer about how they might be thinking about the task?

Jocelyn's Work

DuJuan's Work

As you watch Video Clip 4.1, consider the following questions:

1. What assessing questions does Ms. Tyus ask Jocelyn and DuJuan?

2. How do her assessing questions help Ms. Tyus make sense of how Jocelyn and DuJuan are thinking about the problem?

3. How do her assessing questions help Ms. Tyus diagnose challenges these students are facing?

 Videos may also be accessed at
resources.corwin.com/5practices-elementary

Assessing Student Thinking—Analysis

As Ms. Tyus approaches Jocelyn, she uses a series of assessing questions to try to figure out how she is thinking about the task. Ms. Tyus starts with a general question from her monitoring chart: "Tell me about your thinking." Jocelyn responds, "I put 60 tens." Mrs. Tyus seems surprised by this and repeats Jocelyn's words back to her in the form of a question: "You put 60 tens?" Jocelyn clarifies that she meant "6 tens" and continues with her explanation. Ms. Tyus then asks additional questions to unpack what it means to Jocelyn to "x out 4 of the tens." In particular, the teacher asks, "What made you think to 'x' out 4 of the tens?" and "The 'x' means what?" Here, Ms. Tyus's goal is to explore the meaning that Jocelyn attributes to removing 4 of the tens.

Next, we see Ms. Tyus talking with DuJuan, who is working with the hundreds chart and also created a drawing and an equation. Ms. Tyus again uses a general assessing question: "Tell me about your work." DuJuan begins by sharing that he identified the number 69 on the hundreds chart: "I got 69." In an effort to explore what DuJuan understands about the 69 he is pointing to, Ms. Tyus asks, "What does that 69 represent?" When DuJuan responds, "Markers," Ms. Tyus has learned something important—that DuJuan is aware of the connection between the 69 on the hundreds chart and the 69 markers that Ms. Tyus has at the start of the task. DuJuan continues to explain how he used the hundreds chart and states that "I hopped 40 times and got 29." What might he mean by "40 hops?" To investigate this, Ms. Tyus asks DuJuan to show how he counted, and DuJuan responds by counting by tens, moving up vertically on the hundreds chart. Finally, Ms. Tyus turns to his base ten drawing and equation. As the video ends, Ms. Tyus starts to ask DuJuan how the task is represented in his written work.

Throughout these conversations, Ms. Tyus's questions aim to uncover her students' thinking—she is not asking them to think differently; rather her goal is to better understand how they approached the problem. Having assessed their understanding, Ms. Tyus notes in her monitoring chart that "Jocelyn is working on 69−40" and "DuJuan starts at 69 and hops four times to 29."

It is worth noting that in her conversation with students, Ms. Tyus does not always use the assessing questions she had prepared in advance word-for-word, and in addition, she also uses several assessing questions that she had not prepared in advance. This is to be expected! Developing assessing questions prior to instruction helped Ms. Tyus get her head around how she might draw out students' thinking in specific cases. In the moment, however, as she interacts with students, she also develops new questions based on what students are doing and saying.

Advancing Student Thinking

Once you have an idea of how students are thinking about the problem, the next step is to advance their thinking. For some students, this might involve helping them reconsider what the task is asking them to do. For other students, it might mean encouraging them to consider a special case or pressing them to be able to explain why an approach was successful. Once again, your monitoring chart can be a resource as you decide how to help move students' thinking forward, as you select from or adapt the assessing questions you anticipated earlier.

As you choose an advancing question to use, you want to make sure that the question is driven by your goals for the lesson, and not just a way to help students produce an accurate solution. For example, for the Ms. Tyus's Markers task, the teacher's goal is not simply for students to identify that the number of markers remaining is 29; her goal is for them to do so in a way that relates to exploring the decomposition of numbers in strategic ways. Similarly, Ms. Stastny explained that advancing questions should be designed to "move students towards the math goals" so she can know if students "truly, deeply, understand where I'm trying to get them." As you select advancing questions, you will want to keep your goals for the lesson clearly in mind.

Another important feature of advancing questions is that they usually cannot be answered immediately. Instead, an effective advancing question should prompt students to think, explore, or reconsider ideas about the task. As Mr. Strong explained, an advancing question should prompt students to "have real conversations with each other." Similarly, Ms. Tyus explained that after she poses an advancing question to a group of students, she expects to see "students bouncing ideas off of each other, and learning from each other."

This ability for students to pursue an advancing question is key. Thus, as you pose advancing questions, you will want to gauge students' initial

Handwritten margin note: "walk away questions" push student thinking further

TEACHING TAKEAWAY

You can often gauge the effectiveness of an advancing question by noticing whether students immediately begin to explore it!

reaction. Do they begin working? Can you see them thinking, mulling something over? Often that's how you will be able to tell if they were ready for that advancing question.

Of course, what is most essential is that your advancing questions prompt students to move forward in their thinking. After you ask an advancing question, you will want to give students time to work but will also want to check back in with the group to see how they have progressed. Ms. Tyus explained that advancing questions allow her to "take a backseat" and then return later to see how students are thinking. Ms. Stastny explained that in her experience, when you return to a group, "Depending on what their answer is, you can see if that was the right advancing question" and that at times, she may have to "tweak a question" or "think of another off the top of my head." While advancing questions are designed to help students make progress, it is important that you take time during the lesson to check whether or not they have successfully done so.

What does this look like in practice? In Analyzing the Work of Teaching 4.2, you will explore how Ms. Tyus's use of advancing questions helps students make progress on the Ms. Tyus's Markers task. We encourage you to view the video clip and consider the questions posed before you read the analysis.

Analyzing the Work of Teaching 4.2

Advancing Student Thinking—Part One

Video Clip 4.2
Now you will investigate Leah and Elsie's work on the Ms. Tyus's Markers task.

You examined Leah's written work earlier in Analyzing the Work of Teaching 4.0. Take a moment and remind yourself of her approach. Elsie's written work is provided below. What can you infer about how Elsie might be thinking about the task?

CONTINUED

CONTINUED FROM PREVIOUS PAGE

Elsie's Work

Next, watch Video Clip 4.2 in which Ms. Tyus talks with Leah and then Elsie about their approaches to the task.

As you watch the clip, consider the following questions:

1. What advancing questions does Ms. Tyus ask Leah and Elsie? What goals were the advancing questions targeting?

2. Is there evidence that the advancing questions can or cannot be pursued by the students?

online resources 🔎 Videos may also be accessed at
resources.corwin.com/5practices-elementary

Advancing Student Thinking, Part One—Analysis

When Ms. Tyus approaches Leah, she begins by asking assessing questions in order to explore how Leah is thinking about the task. She begins generally with "Tell me what you've got here." As Leah explains her thinking, she discusses two of the equations she has written: $6 - 4 = 2$ and $9 - 0 = 9$. She points to the $6 - 4 = 2$ and states, "That's the tens . . . since $6 - 4$ is first. So I know that 2 is the tens and 9 is the ones." This response clarifies for Ms. Tyus that Leah understands, at least to some extent, that the 2 in $6 - 4 = 2$ represents 2 tens.

Ms. Tyus then asks another assessing question to further explore Leah's understanding of place value. Here she asks Leah whether it is appropriate to combine the 2 and the 9 that resulted from the subtraction problems using addition. Ms. Tyus asks, "But wait a minute. I'm confused. How come it's not $2 + 9$ is 11? Because you have a 2 and 9. A 2 and 9, that can equal an 11." Leah then responds, "We had to subtract $69 - 40$. You can't add these two; these two are the answers." Leah's comment that we cannot add the 2 and 9 to get a sum of 11 may suggest that she understands that these values do not both represent a quantity of ones. Instead, Leah's statement that "these two are the answers" may provide evidence that Leah understands that the correct operation on the two numbers is to add $20 + 9$ and produce the answer of 29, which she has circled on her paper.

With these clarifications in mind, Ms. Tyus is ready to try to advance Leah's thinking. She asks Leah, "Can you write another equation for this [pointing to $6 - 4 = 2$] for somebody like me that didn't understand the $6 - 4$?... Because I heard you say they were tens." As Ms. Tyus walks away, we see Leah begin to consider her question.

While not shown on the video clip, after Ms. Tyus left, Leah added to her written work (see the circled portion of Figure 4.2). Interestingly, rather than write a new equation such as $60 - 40 = 20$, Leah drew a new base ten diagram to illustrate that 29 is composed of 2 tens and 9 ones. In doing so, Leah provides evidence that the 2 in $6 - 4 = 2$ is 2 tens, while the 9 in $9 - 0 = 9$ is 9 ones.

Figure 4.2 • Leah's final written work

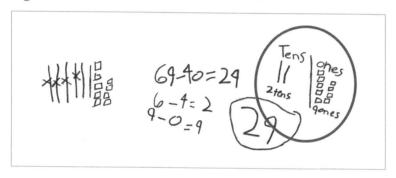

Elsie's written work displays two solution strategies. One is a base ten drawing and corresponding equation $69 - 40 = 29$. In addition, Elsie has written $70 - 40 - 1 = 29$. This equation suggests that Elsie used a rounding and compensating strategy (Solution D in Figure 3.4). There is also what appears to be a hand-drawn hundreds chart but it is crossed out.

In the video clip, Ms. Tyus asks a general assessing question: "What have we got going on?" Elsie explains that she "x'd out" 40 and found the answer to be 29. Ms. Tyus seems familiar with this strategy from an earlier visit to Elsie. Ms. Tyus then proceeds to ask Elsie about the second strategy she has written using a series of assessing questions. "What is this right here?" she asks. Elsie explains that is how Anna "might have solved it and she might have solved it my way too." Ms. Tyus's next questions aim to understand why Elsie decided to round up to 70: "Wait. But you have 70. I thought we had 69. But why would she go to 70?" Elsie's responses focus on the fact that both methods have the same answer of 29. Elsie does not talk, for example, about it being easier to subtract 40 from 70, or that 70 is one away from 69.

Ms. Tyus wants to advance Elsie's thinking around this solution—why it works and why it might be reasonable to use. She sees that Elsie previously tried to use a hundreds chart to illustrate this solution. The teacher thinks this is a worthwhile approach, likely to illuminate why the strategy makes sense. Ms. Tyus's advancing question therefore involves asking Elsie to redraw the solution "so that you can explain that to someone else."

After students work on the Ms. Tyus's Markers task individually, the teacher gives the class time to work with a partner at their table. She instructs students to discuss the task together and for each partner to share their strategy. In Analyzing the Work of Teaching 4.3, you will explore Ms. Tyus's interactions with one pair of students who have just started working together.

Analyzing the Work of Teaching 4.3

Advancing Student Thinking—Part Two

Video Clip 4.3

As students move to partner work, DuJuan and Allison begin to work together. In this video clip, Ms. Tyus is talking with DuJuan and Allison about their approaches to the task.

You examined DuJuan's work earlier in Analyzing the Work of Teaching 4.1. Take a moment and remind yourself of his approach, which involved creating a drawing and using the hundreds chart. Allison's written work is provided below. What can you infer about how Allison might be thinking about the task?

Allison's Work

Next, watch Video Clip 4.3 in which Ms. Tyus talks with
DuJuan and Allison.

As you watch the clip, consider the following questions:

1. What advancing questions does Ms. Tyus ask the students?
   What goals were the advancing questions targeting?

2. Is there evidence that the advancing questions can or
   cannot be pursued by the students?

 Videos may also be accessed at
resources.corwin.com/5practices-elementary

Advancing Student Thinking, Part Two—Analysis

Allison's written work is similar to what we have seen other students
do: create a base ten drawing and write the corresponding equation
$60 - 40 = 29$. When Ms. Tyus approaches DuJuan and Allison, she
comments first on the overall difference in their approaches ("You did the
base ten blocks and you did the hundreds chart") and then asks several
assessing questions to see what DuJuan and Allison understand about the
relationship between their methods. The students indicate that they both
"took away 40" and it is clear from their written work that both students
found that the number of remaining markers is 29.

Ms. Tyus then wants to see if the students understand the connection
between counting by tens on the hundreds chart and using base ten
blocks. She asks, "You both took away 40 . . . What if somebody can't see
it here? . . . How can you explain that the hundreds chart is like base ten
blocks?" Allison's response ("They can count the hops?") suggests that
she is not sure of the answer. Ms. Tyus thus leaves this as an advancing
question for the two students to consider. With both the base ten blocks
and the hundreds chart in mind, she asks, "How can you prove to them
that this is why you counted by tens?"

As Ms. Tyus leaves the group, there is some evidence that DuJuan and
Allison are able to start exploring this question on their own. DuJuan
suggests that "to count by tens to get to 29, you have to 'x' out 69 four
times." Allison recommends, "You maybe could count the hops by 1."
Both of these ideas have merit and could serve as a productive foundation
for looking across the two strategies.

Tara Tyus's Attention to Key Questions: Monitoring

Once students begin working on a task, it is essential that the teacher carefully monitor their progress. To do this, Ms. Tyus tracks her students' thinking by paying close attention to what her students do and say. Because she has already listed the strategies she anticipated students will use on her monitoring chart, she can quickly note who is doing what as she circulates throughout the classroom. Using assessing and advancing questions allows Ms. Tyus to draw out and make sense of students' ideas, as well as to try to move students' thinking forward.

We now take a look at key challenges teachers face as they monitor students' progress during instruction.

Part Two: Challenges Teachers Face: Monitoring Student Work

Although you can prepare for monitoring prior to the lesson by setting goals, selecting a high-level task, and anticipating what students will do and how you will respond, as we discussed in Part One, monitoring occurs *during* instruction. Collecting as much information as you can about what students are doing and thinking—and providing them support to help them make progress—arms you with data that will be vital to making decisions regarding the whole class discussion. Monitoring, however, is not without its challenges. In this section, we focus on three specific challenges associated with this practice, shown in Figure 4.3, that we have identified from our work with teachers.

Figure 4.3 • Challenges associated with the practice of monitoring

CHALLENGE	DESCRIPTION
Trying to understand what students are thinking	Students do not always articulate their thinking clearly. It can be quite demanding for teachers, in the moment, to figure out what a student means or is trying to say. This requires teachers to listen carefully to what students are saying and to ask questions that help them better explain what they are thinking.
Keeping track of group progress—which groups you visited and what you left them to work on	As teachers are running from group to group, providing support, they need to be able to keep track of what each group is doing and what they left students to work on. Also, it is important for a teacher to return to a group in order to determine whether the advancing question given to them helped them make progress.
Involving all members of a group	All individuals in the group need to be challenged to answer assessing and advancing questions. For individuals to benefit from the thinking of their peers, they need to be held accountable for listening to and adding on, repeating and summarizing what others are saying.

Trying to Understand What Students Are Thinking

Students are not always very articulate when they are asked to explain their thinking. They often use nonacademic language to describe things (e.g., "I flipped it over"), make vague references (e.g., "I took *this* away from *that*"), and have difficulty providing a concise description of what they have done. In addition, students may come up with ways of solving problems (both correct and incorrect) that you had not anticipated. And even when you think that you know exactly what a student is thinking because their work resembles what *you* did, you could be dead wrong!

Trying to understand what students are thinking can be challenging work for a teacher, yet it is critical for teachers to make an effort to do so. If students have arrived at a correct solution, you will want to know how they got there so you can determine whether the process they used makes sense, always works, and how (or if) it might connect to more standard approaches. If students have arrived at an incorrect solution, you will want to know what led to the result so that you can provide an opportunity for students to consider some aspect of the task they may have not attended to. It would be easier for the teacher to just tell students that they are wrong and provide them with a new pathway to pursue or ask students to use a more standard or recognizable approach, but such *help* is short term. It may allow students to get a correct answer to the problem at hand using a standard method, but since students are moving forward based on the thinking of the teacher rather than their own thinking, it is not clear whether students will have access to the strategy the next time they are presented with a similar problem. Telling students what to do or how to do it does not help build their capacity to figure things out on their own or develop their identities as capable mathematics doers.

Assessing questions help make student thinking visible. Once student thinking is clear, then the teacher is in the position to help move the thinking forward. According to Smith, Steele, and Raith (2017),

> Questions are the primary tool that teachers have to help them determine what students know and understand about mathematics. Specifically, purposeful questions should reveal students' current understandings; encourage students to explain, elaborate, or clarify their thinking; and make mathematics more visible and accessible for student examination and discussion. (p. 77)

In Analyzing the Work of Teaching 4.4, you will have the opportunity to make sense of the thinking of students in Mr. Strong's class. (Recall that Mr. Strong's fifth-grade students were working on the Mr. Strong's Hike task, shown in Figure 3.9.)

Analyzing the Work of Teaching 4.4

Determining What Students Are Thinking—Part One

Video Clip 4.4

In Video Clip 4.4, you will visit the small group that includes Lucian, Markel, Ester, and Jasper. They had written on their paper as shown below.

As you watch the video clip, consider the following questions:

1. What are the students thinking?

2. What does the teacher do in order to be sure he understands what students are thinking?

3. Why does the teacher press students to explain what happened to $\frac{1}{3}$?

 Videos may also be accessed at
resources.corwin.com/5practices-elementary

Determining What Students Are Thinking, Part One—Analysis

In this clip, Mr. Strong is not making any assumptions about what students are thinking just because they came up with the correct answer to the problem. Although students have written 3×4, he wants to make sure that they are not simply applying a learned rule (i.e., keep-change-flip) and can explain what each of the numbers means in the context of the problem and why the $\frac{1}{3}$ in the original problem does not appear in their equation. Through his questioning, it becomes clear that students understand what the numbers (3, 4, and 12) in their multiplication equation mean. Specifically, when Mr. Strong asks, "What does the 4 mean in this?" Lucian, Jasper, and Markel all respond that it is the number of miles. When he asks, "The three means what to me?" Lucian responds, "How many times you drink per mile," echoing Jasper's initial explanation. When asked what 12 means, Markel and Lucian both indicate that it is the number of times he stopped to drink.

What is less clear in this exchange is what Ester is thinking. When Mr. Strong asks, "The three means what to me?" Ester responds that it means $\frac{1}{3}$ (her only contribution to the discussion). Since Lucian quickly jumps in and indicates that the three is the number of drinks per mile, Mr. Strong does not immediately pursue Ester's response. What is not clear is what the students understand about the relationship between stopping for a drink every $\frac{1}{3}$ mile and stopping three times each mile and why the $\frac{1}{3}$ does not appear in their equation. Rather than pursue this immediately, Mr. Strong's final question, "Where did the fraction go?" raises the issue that while the initial problem included a fraction, their equation did not. Rather than wait for an answer to this question, Mr. Strong walks away and gives the group time to explore this relationship on their own. His parting comment, "I'm going to come back," makes it clear that the students are going to be held accountable for figuring this out.

Throughout his interaction with the group, Mr. Strong asked questions. His initial set of questions was intended to assess what students understood about the work they had produced. His final question, "Where did the fraction go?" was intended to move students beyond where they currently were. This advancing question was tied directly to his second goal. He wanted students to understand that the quotient of a whole number divided by a fraction can be found by multiplying because they are determining how many iterations of the fraction there are in one unit of the dividend and then multiplying the number of iterations in one unit by the total number of units in the dividend. While he had evidence that students were able to solve a division problem by multiplying, he wanted to be sure they understood why it would make sense to do so.

Mr. Strong had anticipated that students might create an equation that contained no fractions and would not be able to explain what happened to the $\frac{1}{3}$ in the problem, so he was prepared for his interactions with Lucian, Markel, Ester, and Jasper. In Analyzing the Work of Teaching 4.5, you will explore Ms. Stastny's interaction with a small group in her class who came up with a solution that she had not anticipated.

Analyzing the Work of Teaching 4.5
Determining What Students Are Thinking—Part Two

Video Clip 4.5
In Video Clip 4.5, you will visit the small group that includes Anasimon, Selvia, Vinny, and Johanna. Students in the group produced three different solutions (shown below) to the Lasagna task (shown in Figure 3.6).

Anasimon's Solution

Tanesha   David

Selvia's Solution

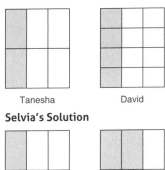

Tanesha   David

Vinny's Solution

Tanesha   David

As you watch the video clip, consider the following questions:

1. What does Selvia appear to be thinking?

2. What is the source of disagreement within the group?

3. What does the teacher do to understand the nature of students' disagreement and to help them move beyond it?

 Videos may also be accessed at resources.corwin.com/5practices-elementary

Determining What Students Are Thinking, Part Two—Analysis

An initial review of Selvia's written work shows that she has created two pans of lasagna, each of which she divided into six pieces. She allocated two pieces from one pan to Tanesha and four pieces from the other pan to David: $\frac{2}{6}$ and $\frac{4}{6}$, respectively. Hence, she seems to be attending to the fact that both pans are the same size (a condition specified by Ms. Stastny, although not stated in the problem) and that Tanesha got two pieces and David got four pieces (a condition clearly stated in the problem). She does not appear to be attending to the fact that the problem also stated that both students got the same amount of lasagna.

Selvia's explanation to her group provides additional insight into why she divided the lasagna into sixths. As she explained, "I added 4 plus 2, which gives me 6. I got that for both on the bottom." This suggests that the denominator of six was chosen because it represented the sum of the total number of pieces eaten by Tanesha and David. She then gave two pieces to Tanesha and four pieces to David as specified. Despite the fact that in her diagrams the shaded areas showing the portion each student got are not the same, she does not appear to notice or be concerned about the fact that she did not address all of the criteria specified in the task.

The source of the disagreement, initially between Selvia and Anasimon, stems from the fact that Anasimon thought David's share of the lasagna would be $\frac{4}{12}$, while Selvia thought David's share should be $\frac{4}{6}$. Although their diagrams for Tanesha are identical, their diagrams for David are not. (The diagrams created by Anasimon and Selvia are shown in Analyzing the Work of Teaching 4.5.) Anasimon subdivided each of the six pieces in Tanesha's pan into two pieces, giving her a total of 12 pieces. Anasimon explains, "I kept on splitting it more" and later "Instead of me doing two-sixths, I split it more. Instead of six, I got 12." Anasimon, however, did not explain why she did this or that David had more pieces than Tanesha but the same amount as Tanesha. Although Selvia acknowledges that Anasimon doubled both the numerator and the denominator while she only doubled the numerator, she does not see that Tanesha and David got the same amount of lasagna in Anasimon's diagram while in her model they did not. When Selvia concludes, "I still think that they are equal," it is not clear what she thinks is equal or why.

In an effort to gain more clarity, Anasimon asks Vinny what he did. Vinny explained that he got $\frac{2}{4}$ for Tanesha and $\frac{4}{8}$ for David. He explained, "I just doubled one-half to get the amount four-eighths and two-fourths." Selvia appears to pick up on the fact that he also doubled something and asks Johanna, "So, did you double them or what did you do?" Johanna explains, "I doubled—So, the six had the same denominator, and the numerator, it has the same." Selvia presses her: "You said that you doubled the bottom number?" Johanna responds, "Yeah." Selvia then goes on to say, "Okay. That gets you to 12. So, for David, what did you get?" Johanna responds that she got two-sixths for David, and when questioned she indicates that she received two-fourths for Tanesha. Hence through this exchange it is unclear what Johanna actually did and how she made sense of the problem.

Ms. Stastny arrives at the group during the exchange between Johanna and Selvia. The first thing she does is listen to the discussion the two girls are having without interrupting, in an effort to determine what they are thinking. Once she sees that the discussion is focused on the number of pieces each student received with no attention to the size of the pieces, she asks the group, "Did they eat the same amount or different amounts?" While Selvia does confirm that Tanesha and David ate the same amount, she states, "Yeah, because what I did was that I just—that I got the same denominator, but it just doubled the numerator."

At this point, Ms. Stastny draws students' attention to the diagram that Selvia has created and asks the question, "If she ate this much [referring to the shaded $\frac{2}{6}$ eaten by Tanesha] and he ate this much [referring to the shaded $\frac{4}{6}$ eaten by David], did they eat the same amount? See if y'all can talk about that." She then lets the group know that she will be back to check in with them. This advancing question was intended to refocus students' attention on the size of the pieces rather than the number of pieces and help them realize that in Selvia's diagrams Tanesha and David did not eat the same amount. This question was critical to students making progress, since one of Ms. Stastny's goals for the lesson was for students to understand that two fractions are equivalent if they show the same area of the same size whole. Since Selvia's diagrams did not show the same area for the same size whole, $\frac{2}{6}$ could not be equivalent to $\frac{4}{6}$. While Ms. Stastny could have pointed this out to students, she knew that giving students time to grapple with this question on their own would lead to greater learning. Letting students know that she would be returning to the group to check on their progress held them accountable for pursuing her inquiry.

You may also have noticed that Ms. Stastny was actively using her monitoring chart during her visit to the group to make note of what students were doing and saying. These notes help her remember whom she needs to return to and what the students were doing. Ms. Stastny's notes would also help her when she is ready to make decisions about what solutions to feature during the discussion, what students to ask to present, and which students to be checking in with during the whole group discussion. For example, given Johanna's lack of clarity in her explanation, Ms. Stastny might want to look for an opportunity to check in with her to see if she can better explain the relationship between Tanesha and David's portions after hearing different student presenters discuss their solutions.

Keeping Track of Group Progress

When you have students working in groups, it is important to keep track of which groups you have visited, what they are doing, and what you have left them to work on. Without a method of tracking this information, it is easy to forget to return to a group or to miss a group completely. To address this challenge, some teachers move around the room in a defined pattern so they know where they have been and where they need to go next. You could start with the group closest to the door and moved counterclockwise on your initial pass around the room. Some teachers put a small colored dot on the table with each visit to a group so that they can easily tell which groups they have visited and how many times they had been there. Alternatively, you could give each group a number tent, list the group numbers on a sticky note, and place a check next to the group number on the sticky note each time you visit the group.

Once you have checked the progress of each group, however, you may find that given time limitations it is more important to revisit some groups than others. For example, if you encountered a group that had trouble getting started or was struggling to move forward, you would want to make sure that they were able to move beyond the impasse they had encountered. Also, if you found that a group had started to use a strategy that you had planned to share but had not yet completed their work, you might want to check in with them again to see what progress they had been able to make.

While the *Who and What* column of the monitoring chart can be used to record what a group is doing, it is also important to keep track of the advancing question you encouraged the group to pursue when you left them. Asking advancing questions is critical in moving students forward, but you need to make sure that the question you asked is having the desired effect. You could track this by highlighting the question on your monitoring chart and indicate the group to whom you asked the question next to it. Alternatively, you could jot the question on the sticky note next to the group number if you used the sticky note approach. Elizabeth Brovey, a former teacher and current coach, indicates that she takes notes but also holds the group responsible for telling her what they were asked to do. As she described it,

> *I have to keep track of what I told them to work on, so I try to take notes. But the other thing I do is when I come back I make them say, "What was it I was asking you to work on? . . . I told you guys, what did I ask you to do before I left?" And they have to tell me. So that's not just about them. That's about me too. 'Cause I also have to honor the frame that I've given them.* (Conversation with Elizabeth Brovey, September 11, 2015)

In Analyzing the Work of Teaching 4.6, you will return to Mr. Strong's class where students continue to work on the Mr. Strong's Hike task. You will observe Mr. Strong as he visits Lucian, Markel, Ester, and Jasper a second time and consider what progress, if any, they have made.

Analyzing the Work of Teaching 4.6
Following Up With Students

Video Clip 4.6

When Mr. Strong first visited Lucian, Markel, Ester, and Jasper (see Analyzing the Work of Teaching 4.4), he noted that they had solved the task by multiplying 3×4. After a brief conversation, he challenged them to explain what happen to the $\frac{1}{3}$ that was in the original problem. In Video Clip 4.6, he returns to the group to see what progress they have made.

The work shown below appeared on Lucian's paper—other group members had a similar set of computations.

As you watch Video Clip 4.6, consider the following questions:

1. Did the advancing question students were left with help them move forward?

2. What does the teacher do to push their thinking further?

 Videos may also be accessed at resources.corwin.com/5practices-elementary

Following Up With Students—Analysis

At the end of his first visit to the group that included Lucian, Markel, Ester, and Jasper, Mr. Strong challenged the students to explain what happened to $\frac{1}{3}$ in the original problem, since it did not appear in their equation. When Mr. Strong returns to group, he notes that students have written several new equations that included the fraction $\frac{1}{3}$ (i.e., $\frac{1}{3} \div 4$, $\frac{1}{3} \times \frac{1}{4}$, and $4 \div \frac{1}{3}$). Students seem to know that when they divide by a fraction, they multiply by the reciprocal, as evidenced by the two sets of related division and multiplication equations they had produced. They appear to have rejected the equation $\frac{1}{3} \div 4$, perhaps because it did not yield the answer of 12 that they had previously determined, as evidenced by the fact they crossed it out. So in Mr. Strong's absence, the group produced an equation that included $\frac{1}{3}$ and that yielded a correct answer.

Since the students had written both multiplication and division equations, Mr. Strong begins his discussion with the group by asking whether this was a multiplication or division problem. Markel responds, "Technically it's kind of both. Kind of sort of, but since we multiply by the reciprocal it will be multiplication even though it starts off as division." The students agree with Markel.

Mr. Strong then asks, "What is actually being divided in this problem?" While it appears from their written work that students had rejected the equation $\frac{1}{3} \div 4$ in favor of $4 \div \frac{1}{3}$, he wants to make sure that they really understood the meaning of these statements. Ester indicates that 4 was being divided, while Lucian states that $\frac{1}{3}$ was being divided because it is $\frac{1}{3}$ of a mile. When Mr. Strong challenges them by saying, "Oh, so I'm dividing $\frac{1}{3}$ up?" students come to the conclusion that they are dividing 4 into one-thirds. Mr. Strong then presses further by asking, "Does it matter if I put the four on this side or the four on that side [referring to whether the four goes before or after the division symbol]?" Lucian responds that it does matter because $\frac{1}{3} \div 4$ doesn't give you the right answer. Mr. Strong wants students to really understand what the equation $4 \div \frac{1}{3}$ means and why it is equivalent to $\frac{4}{1} \times \frac{3}{1}$ or $\frac{12}{1}$. He is not satisfied with students just stating that "it gives you the right answer"—they need to know why. At this point Mr. Strong asks, "Okay, so four is the one being divided and I'm dividing it by one-third. What is this then [referring to the equation $\frac{4}{1} \times \frac{3}{1}$]?" Ester responds, "That's when you go in to work on the problem. You have to multiply by the reciprocal." Mr. Strong then asks, "What does that mean?" Ester responds, "Wait, but since there are three in one mile, then would it . . . so I was trying to think, how would one-third become three over one? 'Cause that's the reciprocal."

At this point, Ester is very close to getting to the meaning—there are three *one-thirds* in 1 mile, so there would be 3×4, or 12 one-thirds in 4 miles. Mr. Strong asks, "Where is the three in here [referring to the diagram they have drawn, shown in Figure 4.4]?" Ester responds, "Yeah, that's what I'm trying to think." At this point, Mr. Strong turns to the other members of the group and asks, "Do you know where? Do you guys want to pitch in on this?" He then leaves the group to continue the discussion.

Students pursued the advancing question Mr. Strong left them to explore after his first visit, and as a result they were able to create a division equation that included the fraction $\frac{1}{3}$. The written work they produced during their exploration provided the grist for a new series of assessing questions that pressed students to make sense of the meaning of division and the relationship between the multiplication and division equations that they had written. Although students still were not able to clearly articulate why dividing by $\frac{1}{3}$ turns into multiplication by 3, they had made considerable progress in making sense of the situation. By drawing students' attention to their diagram, Mr. Strong's final advancing question

Figure 4.4 • The diagram created by Lucian, Markel, Ester, and Jasper

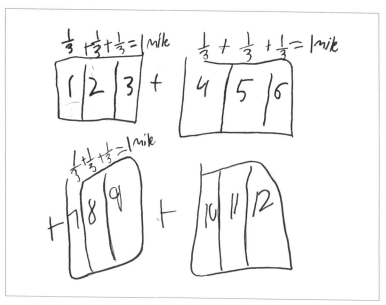

("Where is the three?") provided students with a model that could help them in making this important connection. If they are not able to make this connection before the whole group discussion, this is a point that Mr. Strong can raise and challenge the entire class to consider.

Involving All Members of a Group

The purpose of having students work in groups is so they can serve as resources for each other as they engage in solving challenging problems (Horn, 2012). But getting students to actually work together requires more than just telling them to do so. The teacher needs to set clear expectations regarding group work and to reinforce these expectations through her interactions with small groups. For example, if one student in the group has a question, the teacher might indicate that she will only answer a question if no one in the group can so that students see members of the group as a first source of support. When the teacher begins a discussion with one member of a group, she needs to bring in other group members to make sure they are following the discussion. There is limited value in having student desks pushed together if they are not benefitting from what their peers have to contribute. One of the teachers with whom we have worked describes how she stays with a group in order to ensure that all of the group members are invested in the work of the group:

> I do decide to stay when I recognize that the students aren't in
> that place of being able to work with each other. So I stay if one

or more of the students in a group are working in isolation . . . I consciously pull students in who may not be explicitly letting me know that they're part of the conversation. They may be listening . . . I can't assume. They may be where we're at when we're talking. But until I get evidence from them, I can't be sure of that. So, I stay until I make sure each person has demonstrated to me they have a vested interest in pursuing whatever aspect of the learning goal they happen to be working on at that time. (Conversation with Elizabeth Brovey, September 11, 2015) [See Smith, Steele, and Raith (2017), Chapter 8, for an example of Elizabeth Brovey applying these principles in her interaction with a small group.]

While involving all members of a group in a discussion is important, it is extremely difficult for several reasons. First, it takes time. The more time you spend with one group, the less time there is to visit other groups. Second, it is challenging enough for the teacher to understand some explanations without making sure that everyone else in the group understands them too. Hence, it may not be realistic to make sure that every student speaks every time you interact with a single group. What is important is that you set norms for work that make clear what your expectations are and that you make an effort to ensure that members of the group are at a minimum paying attention to the discussion.

For example, Ms. Tyus consistently tells her students that when they work in groups they need to work together. She stresses that every member of the group needs to be able to explain what the group is doing and thinking. In Analyzing the Work of Teaching 4.7, you will drop in on Ms. Tyus's first-grade class as they work on the second problem in the Ms. Tyus's Markers task and consider how she operationalizes her commitment to holding students accountable to working together.

Analyzing the Work of Teaching 4.7

Holding All Students Accountable

Video Clip 4.7

In this video clip, Ms. Tyus checks in on Markiya, Jacey, and John as they work on a second problem, shown below.

Ms. Tyus has 79 neon markers. She gives 30 neon markers to her friend. How many markers does she have left? Make a diagram and write an equation that shows how Anna can solve this problem.

As you watch Video Clip 4.7, consider the following questions:

1. What aspects of monitoring do you see Ms. Tyus engage in as she interacts with Markiya, Jacey, and John?

2. What does Ms. Tyus do to ensure that all three students understand the solution presented by Jacey?

 Videos may also be accessed at
resources.corwin.com/5practices-elementary

Holding All Students Accountable—Analysis

Ms. Tyus's interactions with Markiya, Jacey, and John highlight many of the aspects of monitoring that we have discussed in this chapter. Throughout her visit to the group, Ms. Tyus makes notes on her monitoring chart. In fact, a review of her monitoring chart shows that next to *Other*, she recorded the initials of the members of the group (JY, MC, and JG) along with the equations students generated ($79 - 9 = 70$, $70 - 30 = 40$). This provided her with a record of what the group was doing and thinking that she could later refer to.

Throughout her interactions with the group, Ms. Tyus asks assessing questions. For example, after Jacey explains that she subtracted 9 from 79, the teacher asks, "What does that 9 represent?" After students produced the equation $70 - 30 = 40$, she asks, "But I heard you guys say something about the answer is 49. So, where did 9 come back in?" These questions allowed her to continue to check for understanding within the group and to ensure that students were able to explain what the numbers represented and why they could decompose and recompose them.

Her final question to the group, which she leaves them to pursue on their own, is to write the equation to represent the fact that they need to add the 9 they initially took away from the 79 to the 40 they now have. This advancing question would provide an opportunity for students to discuss and come to agreement about the equation without the teacher's assistance.

Perhaps what is most striking in Ms. Tyus's interactions with the group is the way in which she holds Markiya and John accountable for making sense of Jacey's solution. Ms. Tyus has stressed the need for students to work together and has made it clear that every member of the group needs to be able to explain what the group is doing and thinking. There are several instances of this in the video clip. After Jacey explains how she arrived at the answer of 49, Ms. Tyus makes sure that Markiya and John understand what Jacey has done. She first asks Markiya if she understands. Markiya responds, "Yeah." Ms. Tyus then turns to John and asks, "What did she [Jacey] say she did?" John indicates that $79 - 9 = 70$, and Ms. Tyus asks, "Then what?" She specifically asks Markiya to continue with the next step. After Markiya indicates that Jacey subtracted 30 from 70, Ms. Tyus asks John what equation would represent this. She leaves the group with the charge, "You guys talk about that last equation."

The key to holding students accountable for working together is setting clear expectations regarding what you expect and then reinforcing these expectations through your actions and interactions. Ms. Stastny's classroom provides a good example of what can happen once these expectations become the norm in the classroom. In Analyzing the Work of Teaching 4.5, we saw Anasimon, Selvia, Vinny, and Johanna discussing their solutions to the Lasagna task prior to the teacher's arrival. During the exchange, we saw students questioning each other. For example, after Anasimon explained that she got $\frac{2}{6}$ for Tanesha and $\frac{4}{12}$ for David, Selvia asked, "Can you at least tell me why you got 4 over 12?" Selvia continued to press Anasimon for more information, ultimately asking, "Can you try— can you be a bit more specific?" In addition, we saw the students asking for input from other members of the group. For example, Anasimon asked Vinny, "What did you do?" and Selvia asked Johanna what she had done. Hence through the teacher's actions and interactions with small groups, students can learn to question and solicit input from their peers.

Conclusion

In this chapter, we explored the practice of monitoring. This is perhaps one of the more challenging practices because the actual practice of monitoring takes place during instruction as the lesson is unfolding in real time. There is a lot to attend to as students work individually and in small groups, and it can be overwhelming. Our experience suggests that careful attention to anticipating prior to the lesson, including the preparation of a monitoring chart, can help make monitoring more manageable.

This was evident in the work of Ms. Tyus. As a result of the care she took in planning the lesson (as described in Chapters 2 and 3), she entered the class with clarity about what she wanted students to learn and how she would support them in reaching the goals she set. She asked assessing questions that made students' thinking clear and public, asked advancing questions to move students forward in thinking about the mathematics of the lesson, and checked on their progress. She made notes as she interacted with groups so that she would be able to make purposeful decisions about who and what to highlight during the whole group discussion that would follow. (You can see Ms. Tyus's annotated monitoring chart in Appendix C.) Ms. Tyus's work during the monitoring phase makes salient that assessing and advancing questions occur in cycles—you assess, then you advance, you return, and you assess again, then you advance again. The intent is that each time you return to a group, you move them further toward the goal. While one visit to some groups may be sufficient, other groups may require multiple visits.

As you will note on Ms. Tyus's monitoring chart, she managed to capture a great deal of what was going on while students worked on the task. Did she record everything that happened when she interacted with students as they worked on the task? No. She was able to capture sufficient detail about what students were doing to give her a good sense of what they understood and what they were struggling with. While we discussed in this chapter what would be ideal to try to capture on the monitoring chart, the reality is that you may not get every single thing. The point is to do the best you can to get an accurate picture of the ideas students have generated that will help you in achieving the goals for the lesson.

In our analysis of Ms. Stastny's and Mr. Strong's interactions with small groups, we saw the importance of asking questions that help clarify what students are thinking. You cannot move students forward if you do not know where they are to start with. It is critical to use questions to make student thinking visible. In Mr. Strong's and Ms. Tyus's classes, we saw the teachers calling on different students in the group to contribute to the discussion. In doing so, the teacher was holding all students accountable for listening to and making sense of what their peers were saying.

Because monitoring generally involves interaction with small groups of students, it is critical to consider how you can help build students' capacity to work together. Ms. Tyus's interactions with Markiya, Jacey, and John provide some insights on how to hold students accountable for working together, but getting students to work together productively will not happen overnight. This will require time, patience, and persistence on your part! You will know you are making progress if groups are able to work collaboratively and independently and you hear conversations like the one that took place in Ms. Stastny's classroom.

Your ability to effectively monitor will improve over time as you continue to do it, reflect on what went well and what did not, make midcourse corrections, and do it again. The key is to keep at it, even if the first few times are not as successful as you would like.

> **TEACHING TAKEAWAY**
>
> Assessing and advancing questions occur in cycles.

▶ Monitoring Student Work—Summary

Video Clip 4.8
To hear and see more about monitoring student work using the monitoring tool, watch Video Clip 4.8.

 Videos may also be accessed at
resources.corwin.com/5practices-elementary

In the next chapter, we explore the next two practices: *selecting* and *sequencing*. There, we will return to Ms. Tyus's lesson and consider what it takes to engage in these practices and the challenges it presents.

Linking the Five Practices to Your Own Instruction ◀

MONITORING

It is now time to teach the lesson you planned in Chapters 2 and 3! (Or if you prefer, select another lesson. Just make sure that you have engaged in Practice 0 and have anticipated student responses and questions before you begin.) We encourage you to video record the lesson so that you can reflect back on what occurred during the lesson.

1. Before teaching the lesson, consider how you are going to make sure you visit every group and remember the questions you leave groups to pursue. Also, consider whether there are any specific instructions you want to give students regarding your expectations for how you expect them to work in their groups.

2. As you teach the lesson, use your monitoring chart to keep track of the strategies students are using. Be sure you are checking in with every group and returning to groups to see if they are making good progress.

3. Following the lesson, use these questions to guide reflection on your monitoring:

- Did you interact with each group in the class? If not, what could you do differently to ensure that you have a chance to check in with all of your students? Did you return to groups when you said you would to check on their progress?

- To what extent did students use the strategies you had anticipated? What was unexpected?

- To what extent were the assessing questions you anticipated in planning useful in your interactions with students? Did they help you make students' thinking clear and public?

- To what extent were the advancing questions you anticipated in planning useful in your interactions with students? Did they help students make progress on the task?

- To what extent were you able to involve all members of a group in the conversation? What might you do differently in the future to hear the voices of more students?

4. What did you learn about students' understanding of mathematics as a result of teaching the lesson?

5. What lessons have you learned about monitoring that will help you in planning and enacting the next lesson you teach?

" While students are working and I'm checking in with them, I'm going to be thinking about how to sequence the math and the kids. I might have ideas, but I have to wait and see what they do. I'll be trying to see who's got something that can help us make sense of the math goals for today. "

—ANDREW STRONG, FIFTH-GRADE TEACHER

CHAPTER 5

Selecting and Sequencing Student Solutions

Once students have had the opportunity to explore the task individually or in small groups, and you as the teacher have monitored their discussions, the next step is to bring the class together for a whole group discussion of the key mathematical ideas of the lesson. To help ensure that the discussion is meaningful for all students, you will want to engage in the next two practices, selecting and sequencing student solutions.

Selecting and sequencing builds on the careful monitoring you did as students worked on the task. These practices involve choosing which solutions will be shared with the class, who will share those solutions, and the order in which the solutions will be shared. Selecting particular solutions to highlight provides you with an opportunity to help students move beyond the specific strategies they used to consider other approaches. In addition, being intentional about the order in which the solutions are presented provides an opportunity to build strategically on what students have done.

Smith and Stein (2018) describe selecting and sequencing in the following way:

> *Selecting is the process of determining which ideas (what) and students (who) the teacher will focus on during the discussion. This is a crucial decision, since it determines what ideas students*

will have the opportunity to grapple with and ultimately to learn. Selecting can be thought of as the act of purposefully determining what mathematics students will have access to—beyond what they were able to consider individually or in small groups—in building their mathematical understanding. (pp. 63–64)

Sequencing is the process of determining the order in which the students will present their solutions. The key is to order the work in such a way as to make the mathematics accessible to all students and to build a mathematically coherent story line. (p. 64)

In this chapter, we first unpack selecting and sequencing into their key components and illustrate what these practices look like in an authentic elementary school classroom. Next, we explore what we have learned is challenging for teachers about selecting and sequencing and provide an opportunity for you to explore these practices in your own teaching.

Part One: Unpacking the Practice: Selecting and Sequencing Student Solutions

Selecting and sequencing involve identifying the student work you wish to highlight, purposefully selecting individual presenters, and establishing a coherent storyline for sequencing students' presentations. Here we explore each of these components by looking inside Ms. Tyus's classroom. Figure 5.1 highlights the components of these practices along with key questions to guide the processes of selecting and sequencing.

Figure 5.1 • Key questions that support the practices of selecting and sequencing

WHAT IT TAKES	KEY QUESTIONS
Identifying student work to highlight	Which student solution strategies would help you accomplish your mathematical goals for the lesson?
	What challenges did students face in solving the task? Were there any common challenges?
Purposefully selecting individual presenters	Which students do you want to involve in presenting their work?
	How might selecting particular students promote equitable access to mathematics learning in your classroom?
Establishing a coherent storyline	How can you order the student work such that there is a coherent storyline related to the mathematical learning goal?

Identifying Student Work to Highlight

The first step in selecting and sequencing is to identify the student work that you want to highlight for the class. As you monitored students' progress, you will likely have noticed a range of solutions that students produced and will have noted them on your monitoring chart. Remember that you intentionally chose a task that invited multiple approaches!

Having access to different solution strategies during the discussion has the potential to help students deepen their understanding of the mathematics involved in the task (Zbiek & Shimizu, 2005). To realize this, you want to identify those solution paths that put the key mathematical ideas in the spotlight and will therefore help you to achieve your lesson goals. As you review students' work on the task, look for similarities and differences among the paths students took to solve the task, while keeping in mind the mathematical features of students' solutions that are important for the class to consider.

You will also want to consider the challenges that students faced as they solved the task. Were there any common challenges that you want to highlight? Often, we shy away from discussing incorrect solutions with students when in fact there can be important benefits to discussing errors and false starts (Santagata & Bray, 2016). As Kazemi and Hintz (2014) explain,

> How we respond to errors and partially developed ideas sends important messages about taking risks. It is not easy for students to express their ideas if there is a high burden to be correct and understand everything the first time around. (p. 5)

As you consider which solution strategies to focus on with the whole class, keep in mind the potential value in discussing some of the difficulties that students may have encountered.

As she reviewed her monitoring chart, Ms. Tyus could see that her students had solved the Ms. Tyus's Markers task in a number of different ways, as shown in Figure 5.2. To determine the number of markers Ms. Tyus had left, two students initially attempted to model the task by drawing 69 circles or lines to represent the markers (Solution I). Most students decomposed 69 into tens and ones using a base ten drawing and wrote one of several different equations to represent the situation (Solution II). The most common equation was $69 - 40 = 29$, in which the 4 tens are "x'd out" in the drawing to reflect subtracting 40 in the equation (Solution IIa). Two students used addition in their equation and wrote $69 + 40 = 29$ (Solution IIb). These students seemed to recognize that, according to their drawing, there were 29 markers left but they did not write an equation that captured what they did.

Two other students wrote equations in which tens were represented as $6 - 4 = 2$ rather than $60 - 40 = 20$. As discussed in Analyzing the Work of

Teaching 4.0, in the case of Leah, her final answer of 29 suggests that she was aware that the difference of 2 actually represented 20 (Solution IIc). One student created a "run-on-equation," $69 - 9 = 60 - 40 = 20$, combining two equations incorrectly into one equation (Solution IId). (While $69 - 9 = 60$ and $60 - 40 = 20$, it is *not* true that $69 - 9 = 20$!) Another approach that Ms. Tyus observed two students using was to count back by tens on the hundreds chart (Solution III). In addition, one student used a rounding and compensating strategy, where 1 was added to 69 to round up to 70 and later subtracted from the difference (Solution IV).

Figure 5.2 • Solutions Ms. Tyus noted on her monitoring chart

Solution I. Direct Modeling of 69

"I'm thinking to draw 69 circles"

Solution II. Create a Base Ten Drawing and an Equation	
Solution IIa. $69 - 40 = 29$ "I x'd out 4 tens and counted 29 left." 	**Solution IIb.** $69 + 40 = 29$ "I took 40 of them and then I had 29."
Solution IIc. $6 - 4 = 2$, $9 - 0 = 9$ "6 minus 4 equals 2 and 9 minus 0 equals 9." 	**Solution IId.** $69 - 9 = 60 - 40 = 20$ "I know that 69 is 60 and 9, and then I took away the 40 markers that you gave away."
Solution III. Count Back by Tens on a Hundreds Chart	**Solution IV. Round and Compensate**
"I found 69 and then I jumped four times." 	"70 minus 40 minus 1 equals 29."

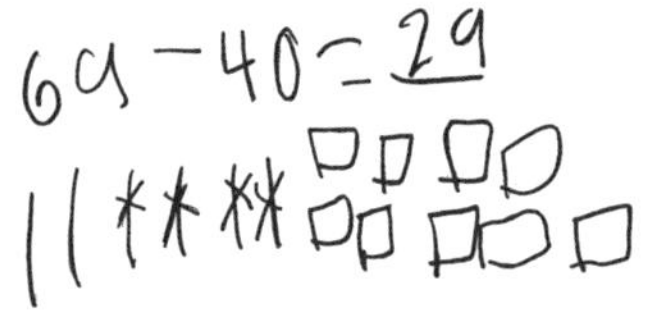

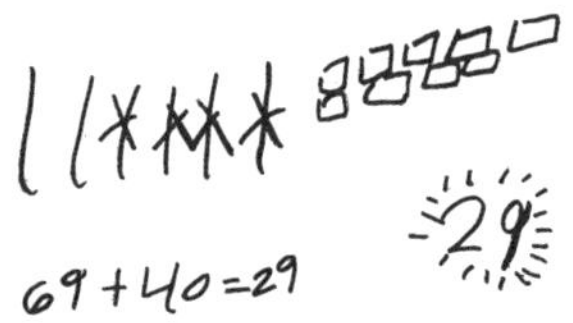

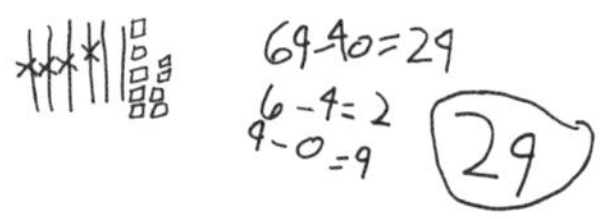

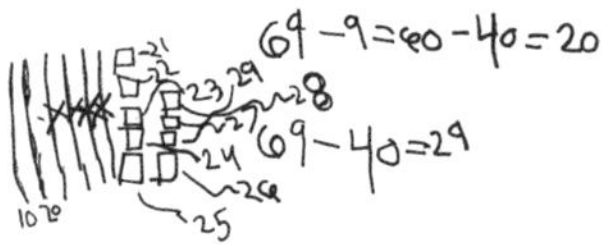

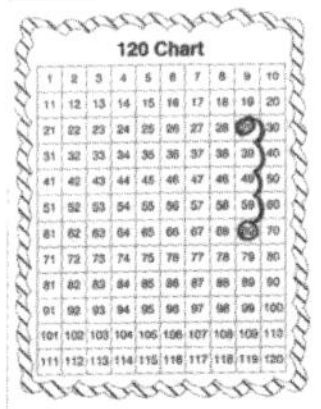

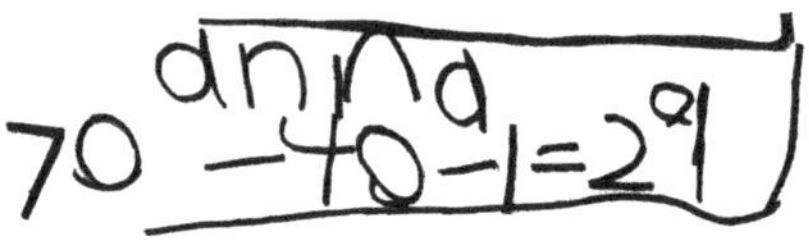

There were also a few strategies that Ms. Tyus anticipated students would use that she did not observe. No students counted back by tens on an open number line, nor did any students subtract 4 tens from 69 and then also subtract 9 ones. Ms. Tyus also expected that some students might use a rounding and compensating strategy incorrectly, by rounding to 70 and then adding 1 to the difference (rather than subtracting 1), but she did not see any students use this approach.

In Analyzing the Work of Teaching 5.1, you will analyze the approaches taken by Ms. Tyus's students in solving the problem and consider which strategies would be most useful in addressing the mathematical goals she had for the lesson.

Analyzing the Work of Teaching 5.1
Selecting Student Solutions

Consider the solutions shown in Figure 5.2 in light of Ms. Tyus's goals for the lesson.

Goal 1: When subtracting two-digit numbers, tens are subtracted from tens and ones are subtracted from ones. If you are subtracting a multiple of ten, then only the number in the tens place changes because there are no ones to subtract.

Goal 2: Decomposing and recomposing numbers in systematic ways can help you solve problems and make relationships among quantities of tens and ones more visible.

Goal 3: Numbers can be rounded up or down to make a multiple of ten before subtracting. The amount rounded up or down must then be subtracted from or added to the difference to compensate for the amount added to or taken away initially.

Goal 4: Multiple representations (e.g., models, drawings, numbers, equations) can be used to solve problems and the different representations can be connected to each other.

- Which solutions do you think Ms. Tyus might want to select in order to address her goals for the lesson?

- Students who used Solutions IIb, IIc, and IId determined that the number of markers left was 29 but wrote equations that did not always capture this clearly. What might be the benefit of sharing one of these solutions?

Selecting Student Solutions—Analysis

The solutions produced by Ms. Tyus's students address the lesson goals in several different ways.

Goal 1: When subtracting two-digit numbers, tens are subtracted from tens and ones are subtracted from ones. If you are subtracting a multiple of ten, then only the number in the tens place changes because there are no ones to subtract.

One of Ms. Tyus's goals for the Ms. Tyus's Markers task is for students to understand that when you subtract a multiple of ten, the number in the ones place does not change because there are no ones to subtract. While this is not explicitly stated in any of the solutions that she observed, it is implicit in Solutions II and III. In Solution II, 69 is decomposed using a base ten drawing, and subtraction of 40 is represented by crossing out 4 tens. No ones are crossed out because none are being subtracted. Similarly, in Solution III, subtracting 40 on the hundreds chart is illustrated by four vertical jumps down, each representing a subtraction of ten. No horizontal movement is required because no ones are being subtracted.

Goal 2: Decomposing and recomposing numbers in systematic ways can help you solve problems and make relationships among quantities of tens and ones more visible.

Central to Ms. Tyus's goals for the lesson is for students to decompose and recompose numbers as they model subtraction. Solution II addresses this goal as students create base ten drawings in which tens are represented with lines and ones are represented with boxes. Once students cross out 4 tens to represent the 40 markers that Ms. Tyus gave away, they can recompose the remaining 2 tens and 9 ones to represent the 29 markers that remain.

Goal 3: Numbers can be rounded up or down to make a multiple of ten before subtracting. The amount rounded up or down must then be subtracted from or added to the difference to compensate for the amount added to or taken away initially.

Solution IV directly illustrates Goal 3. In this case, the student rounds up 69 to 70 by adding 1, and then later compensates by subtracting 1. As Ms. Tyus explained, "I want to have them see that you can round up, and then compensate. So if you have 69, you can take that to 70. Then once you subtract 40, you have to subtract one more in the end to get the correct answer."

Goal 4: Multiple representations (e.g., models, drawings, numbers, equations) can be used to solve problems and the different representations can be connected to each other.

Ms. Tyus's final goal involved having students use multiple representations to solve the task: "I want every child to see that you can solve place-value problems using multiple representations." Solutions I, II, and III illustrate this goal as students model 69 objects directly, create base ten drawings, use a hundreds chart to explore the task, and create various equations to represent the situation. Each of these approaches highlights different ways to indicate the 69 markers that Ms. Tyus started with, the 40 markers that are removed, and the remaining 29 markers.

In Solutions IIb, IIc, and IId, students use equations that do not always clearly reflect their base ten drawings or what is taking place in the problem situation. Still, discussing the challenges students faced in writing an equation to represent their solution has several potential benefits. For example, exploring the relationship between the equations $6 - 4 = 2$ and $60 - 40 = 20$ can be a valuable jumping-off point for a discussion of place value. And looking closely at $69 - 9 = 60 - 40 = 20$ can provide an opportunity to examine the meaning of the equals sign. In general, discussing incorrect thinking can potentially illustrate for students that the classroom is a place where all mathematical ideas are respected and where errors are a time for reflection and discussion.

After reviewing the solution strategies in light of her lesson goals, Ms. Tyus decided that she wanted to highlight Solutions IIa, IIc, III, and IV. She had noted on her monitoring chart that most students "show base 10 with $69 - 40 = \square$," so she thought highlighting a base ten drawing and the corresponding equation $69 - 40 = 29$ would be a good way to connect with what many of her students had done. In addition, Solution IIa would allow her to address Goal 2, decomposing and recomposing numbers, as well as implicitly address Goal 1, subtracting a multiple of ten.

Ms. Tyus also wanted to highlight Solution IIc for the class, in which the student creates a base ten drawing and uses the equation $6 - 4 = 2$ to illustrate subtracting 4 tens from 6 tens. During her planning for the lesson, Ms. Tyus remarked, "Some students may have trouble writing an equation. I want to make sure I focus on some of those students." In particular, this solution would allow Ms. Tyus to address Goals 1 and 2, as students explore the relationship between the base ten drawing and the equation. Solution III would also be a way to explore Goal 4 and the use of a hundreds chart. Finally, Solution IV would allow Ms. Tyus to address Goal 3, rounding and compensating.

Ms. Tyus could have made other choices. For example, she might have decided to use Solution I to motivate for students the need to decompose tens and ones systematically in order to efficiently solve the task. Similarly, she could have chosen Solution IIb as a way to examine the relationship between the base ten drawing and the equation. Because the base ten drawing models the task using subtraction while the equation states the relationship as addition, it could have been a good choice if Ms. Tyus wanted the class to examine the inconsistency between the base ten model and the equation. Ms. Tyus might also have chosen to highlight Solution IId with the class. Doing so could have had the result of illustrating for students the need for more than one equation to represent the solution. The point is, there is not just one *right way* to select the set of solutions that are shared during the whole class discussion. The key is ensuring that the selected solutions will make it possible for you to surface the mathematical ideas that are central to the lesson.

Purposefully Selecting Individual Presenters

Once you identify the solutions that you want to highlight, you will need to purposefully select students to present those solutions to the class. But how should you decide? One factor, of course, is which students produced the solutions that you want to share with the class. Having students present their own solutions can validate the importance of different kinds of mathematical thinking and help the class recognize their peers as valuable intellectual resources for learning mathematics (Aguirre et al., 2013; Jilk, 2016). In addition, because it is students' own work, they can authentically answer questions about the reasoning behind their representations and solution strategies (Imm, Stylianou, & Chae, 2008). Although you may find it more efficient and less messy to share a student's work yourself, doing so robs the student of the opportunity to be seen as an author of mathematical ideas, contributing to both a student's authority and identity. [See Aguirre et al. (2013) for a set of equity-based teaching practices that are intended to strengthen mathematics learning and the development of positive mathematics identities.]

*Sometimes
learning from a
peer is better
than a novice ?*

Being purposeful about the students you select can also promote equitable access to mathematics learning in your classroom. Classroom discourse in the United States is often stratified with certain students contributing more frequently than others (Hung, 2015). In addition, students from diverse racial backgrounds are often considered not as good at mathematics as their White and Asian peers (Louie, 2017; Shah, 2017). Particularly troubling is recent research that shows that as early as elementary school, students are aware of racial stereotypes concerning who is good at mathematics (Nasir, McKinney de Royston, O'Connor, & Wischnia, 2017).

Your choice of which students will present their solutions sends an important message about who and what is valued mathematically in your classroom. You will want to pay attention to who has recently had an opportunity to share their work with the class, and who has not; who might be comfortable sharing an incorrect or unusual solution, and who might benefit from sharing a solution that was used by many students in the class.

To be clear, decisions about what solutions to select and whom to select as presenters are often closely related. Here, we have suggested that you first select the solutions you want students to share in class and then choose who should present those solutions. In practice, these decisions often happen in an integrated way. You may recognize that a particular student is more engaged than usual and decide to have her present her solution. Or you may recognize a solution as novel and interesting but realize the student who created it presented recently and decide to forgo that solution for a different one.

Two teachers with whom we have worked, Jennifer Mossotti and Michelle Saroney, explained their approach to selecting student presenters. Mrs. Mossotti explained that she makes a conscious effort to vary which students present in class. In addition, she often tells students in advance that she plans to have them present: "I'll give them a little tap on the shoulder and say, 'Do you mind saying this in front of the room?'" Mrs. Saroney described a similar process:

> As I walk around and make notes about what students are doing, I'll be trying to figure out who I want to come up. And I tend to let students know so they can be prepared to talk about that particular piece of their work. Also if a student's nervous, it helps that they're not put on the spot all of a sudden.

Mrs. Mossotti also explained that while she often asks students to present individually, she also finds it productive to ask students who have worked together to present together. She has found, particularly at the beginning of the year, that it can build students' confidence if they have "somebody who thought about it the same way up there" with them. In addition, she stated that she routinely looks to highlight "somebody who thinks about it different than everybody else. I like to put a spotlight on that student so that the rest of the kids can get access to different kinds of thinking." Clearly, there is much to keep in mind as you coordinate what ideas you want students to share in class and which students you want to present those ideas! (For more information about Jennifer Mossotti and Michelle Saroney's use of the five practices, see Smith and Sherin, 2019.)

A final consideration is the process through which students share their work. If a document camera is available in your classroom, students can share their own written work for the rest of the class to see. If not, you might ask students to re-create their solution on the board, or if there is time, you might ask them to prepare a poster to present to the class. In cases where students are completing their work electronically, you may be able to project the work directly for the class to view. As technology continues to advance, we may see more technologically based solutions for easy sharing of student work.

PAUSE AND CONSIDER

How do you make decisions about which students should present in class? How do your decisions promote or constrain an equitable learning environment?

For the Ms. Tyus's Markers task, the teacher decided to have Jocelyn present Solution IIa and Leah present Solution IIc. While many students in class produced Solution IIa, Ms. Tyus explained that she chose Jocelyn in part because "I haven't called on her in a while." Ms. Tyus thought that it was important for different students to have a chance to share their thinking. Leah was one of two students who used Solution IIc. Ms. Tyus decided to call on Leah because in talking with her during class, Leah had expressed that the "2 was really 2 tens" and Ms. Tyus planned to discuss that idea with the class.

Ms. Tyus also decided that she would have DuJuan present Solution III. She wanted to make sure that the class had a chance to discuss the use of the hundreds chart, since looking at different representations was essential to her lesson goals. While two students had used the hundreds charts, DuJuan, like Jocelyn, had not presented recently so Ms. Tyus thought that he was a good choice. Ms. Tyus planned to call on Elsie to present Solution IV. As she explained, "I called on Elsie because I wanted to show the class this new idea to help them reach the mathematical goal, and she was the only student at that moment that tried it."

Establishing a Coherent Storyline

The final step in selecting and sequencing is to decide on the order in which students will present their solutions. Being intentional about the order provides you with an important opportunity to build a coherent storyline around the goals of the lesson. Just as the materials in a curriculum unit are carefully sequenced to build on each other in ways that support students' learning, you will want to be strategic in how you sequence students' presentations. One teacher we have worked with, Michelle Musumeci, explained it in the following way: "I'm trying to build almost like a story about this problem that moves us toward the

goal so that we can make connections along the way." (You can explore a lesson from Michelle Musumeci's classroom in detail in Smith and Sherin, 2019.)

 PAUSE AND CONSIDER

What factors do you think may be important to consider when deciding how to sequence students' presentations of solution strategies in class?

There are a number of issues you may want to consider in thinking about how to effectively create a story that brings students together and highlights the lesson goals. To build conceptual coherence, you might find it beneficial to move from the most concrete strategies to more abstract approaches. This could involve starting with solutions that involve specific cases and then presenting ones that offer generalized solutions. Some teachers find it productive to move from less sophisticated representations to more sophisticated representations, for example, from a physical model, to a drawing, to a number sentence.

Attending to the social organization of the classroom can also be an important consideration in thinking about how to sequence the class discussion (Horn, 2012). You may, for instance, choose to first share a solution strategy that many students used so that students will initially see work similar to their own being presented (Aguirre et al., 2017). Once students' own strategies are validated, they may be more interested in hearing about strategies that differ from their own. You will also want to think carefully about when and how to address incorrect strategies (this is explored further in Part Two of this chapter).

Whatever criteria you chose to use, it is important that you vary your approach over time. Students can become accustomed to routines, even when they are not made explicit. If students have a sense, for example, that you typically introduce the simplest strategies first, they may feel disappointed if they are asked to be the first presenter. Mixing up the criteria you use to sequence class discussions may also help to increase opportunities for all students to participate.

In thinking about how to organize the discussion of the Ms. Tyus's Markers task, the teacher decided to start with Jocelyn and have her explain her base ten drawing and corresponding equation (Jocelyn's final work is shown in Figure 5.3, Solution IIa). Many students in the class had used this approach, and Ms. Tyus thought it was a good place to begin the discussion. Next, she planned to have DuJuan explain how he used the hundreds chart to find the number of markers left after giving away 40 (Figure 5.3, Solution III). Ms. Tyus wanted to have this strategy shared next so that the class could explicitly compare using the hundreds chart with the base ten drawing.

Figure 5.3 • Jocelyn and DuJuan's solutions

First Presentation—Jocelyn	Second Presentation—DuJuan
Solution IIa. Create a Base Ten Drawing and Equation $69 - 40 = 29$ 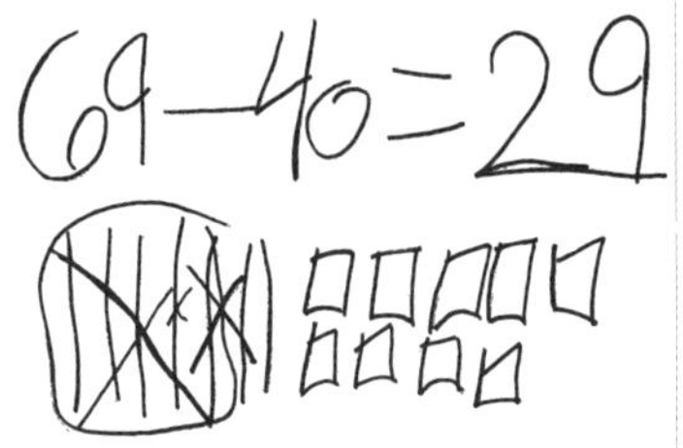	Solution III. Count Back by Tens on a Hundreds Chart 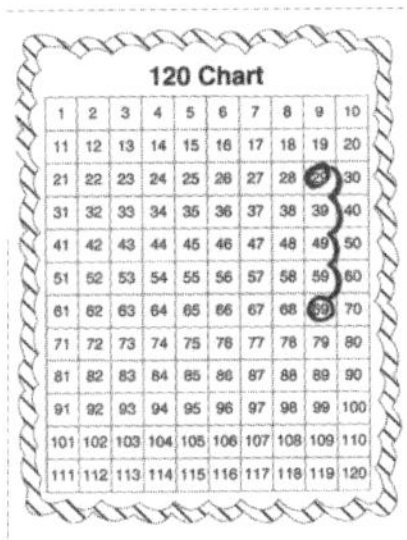

Following DuJuan, Ms. Tyus planned to have Leah share her approach (Figure 5.4, Solution IIc) including her use of the equation $6 - 4 = 2$. Ms. Tyus hoped that Leah would highlight the relationship between her equation and her base ten drawing. In the storyline for the Ms. Tyus's Markers task, Ms. Tyus considered the use of the rounding and compensating strategy as key to moving students forward in their facility with numbers. But because this was a new approach for most students,

Figure 5.4 • Leah and Elsie's solutions

Third Presentation—Leah	Fourth Presentation—Elsie
Solution IId. Create a Base Ten Drawing and Equations $6 - 4 = 2$ and $9 - 0 = 9$ 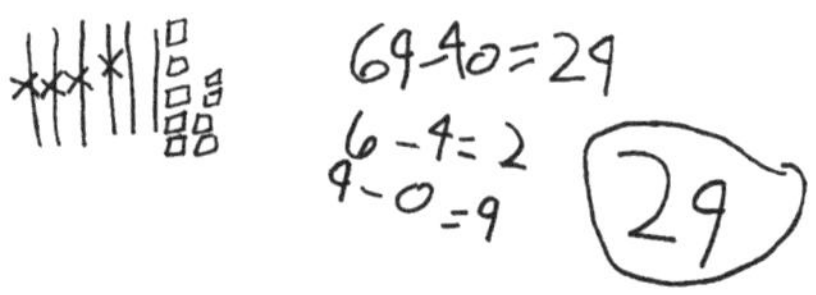	Solution IV. Round and Compensate 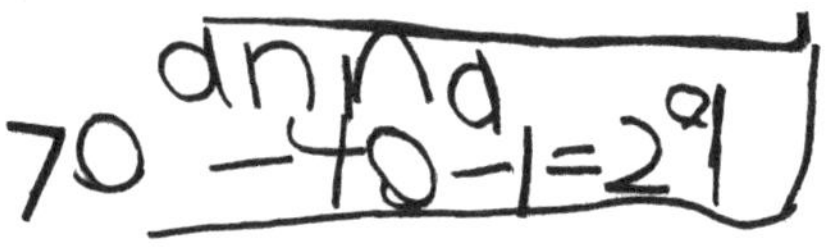

she chose to leave this strategy for the end of the discussion (Figure 5.4, Solution IV). Ms. Tyus hoped that first examining the decomposition of numbers in the base ten drawings as well as moving among tens using the hundreds chart would help students understand this new approach.

Tara Tyus's Attention to Key Questions: Selecting and Sequencing

As Ms. Tyus prepared for her class to discuss the strategies students used to solve the Ms. Tyus's Markers task, she focused on the key questions. Using her monitoring chart, she reviewed students' solutions with the lesson goals in mind. What solutions would highlight the goal for students to understand that they had to subtract tens from tens and ones from ones? What solutions would highlight the connections between different representations? These questions were critical for Ms. Tyus as she thought about which solutions she wanted to call attention to during the class discussion. In addition, she reviewed the challenges students faced as they worked on the task and considered whether it would be valuable to discuss those with the class as well.

Ms. Tyus also gave careful attention to *who* would share these solutions with the class. She considered a number of factors, including who had recently presented, whether to have students present individually or in groups, and the kinds of supports she might want to offer students as they present. She kept in mind that her selection of presenters matters and could play a role in promoting an equitable learning environment for students in her class.

Finally, in deciding how to sequence the presentations, Ms. Tyus attempted to create a coherent structure that would allow the learning goals to become visible for all students, even those who had not used those particular solution strategies. We now take a look at some of the challenges teachers face as they select and sequence students' solutions.

Part Two: Challenges Teachers Face: Selecting and Sequencing Student Solutions

You must purposefully select and sequence the solutions that will be shared in order to ensure that the goals of the lesson are met and that class time is used efficiently and effectively. Selecting and sequencing can be particularly challenging because, although you can give some consideration to what you would ideally like to share as you plan the lesson, the actual decisions about *what* is shared, *who* is going to share it, and *how* the solutions will be ordered are made during the lesson. In this section, we focus on four specific challenges associated with these practices, shown in Figure 5.5, that we have identified from our work with teachers.

Figure 5.5 • Challenges associated with the practices of selecting and sequencing

CHALLENGE	DESCRIPTION
Selecting only solutions that are most relevant to learning goals	Teachers need to select a limited number of solutions that will help achieve the mathematical goals of the lesson. Sharing solutions that are not directly relevant can take a discussion off track, and sharing too many solutions (even if they are relevant) can lead to student disengagement.
Expanding beyond the usual student presenters	Teachers often select students who are articulate and on whom they can count for a coherent explanation. Teachers need to look for opportunities to position each and every student as a presenter and help students develop their ability to explain their thinking.
Deciding what work to share when the majority of students were not able to solve the task and your initial goal no longer seems obtainable	Teachers may on occasion find that the task was too challenging for most students and that they were not able to engage as intended. This situation requires the teacher to modify her initial plan and determine how to focus the discussion so students can make progress.
Moving forward when a key strategy is not produced by students	In planning the lesson, a teacher may determine that a particular strategy is critical to accomplishing the lesson goals. If the success of a lesson hinges on the availability of a particular strategy, then the teacher needs to be prepared to introduce the strategy through some means.
Determining how to sequence errors, misconceptions, and/or incomplete solutions	Teachers often choose not to share work that is not complete and correct for fear that students will remember incorrect methods. Sharing solutions that highlight key misconceptions in a domain can provide all students with an opportunity to analyze why a particular approach does not work. Sharing incomplete or partial solutions can provide all students with the opportunity to consider how such work can be connected to more robust solutions.

Selecting Only Solutions Relevant to Learning Goals

You may be tempted to have every group publicly share their work on a task in order to motivate students to produce a complete product, give all students an opportunity to share their thinking, or acknowledge students' effort. While this strategy is well intended, it often results in long, drawn-out discussions where similar solutions are repeated, mathematical ideas get lost, and students begin to disengage. Limiting the number of solutions that are shared to those that will help you explicitly address the mathematics you are targeting in the lesson will allow you to make the best use of your instructional time and keep the class focused and engaged.

Consider, for example, Mr. Strong's lesson on the Mr. Strong's Hike task (see Figure 3.9). As we discussed in Chapter 3, as a result of engaging in the lesson, Mr. Strong wanted his students to understand that

1. To divide a whole number by a fraction (e.g., $4 \div \frac{1}{3}$) means to determine how many iterations of the fraction ($\frac{1}{3}$) fit inside the whole number (4).

2. The quotient of a whole number divided by a fraction can be found by multiplying (e.g., $4 \div \frac{1}{3} = 4 \times 3$) because you are determining how many iterations of the fraction there are in 1 unit of the dividend and then multiplying the number of iterations in 1 unit by the total number of units in the dividend (e.g., there are three $\frac{1}{3}$s in 1 mile so the number of $\frac{1}{3}$s in 4 miles is 4×3).

3. When dividing by a number less than 1, the quotient will be greater than the dividend because you are making groups of an amount less than 1.

Of the five groups in the class, four groups (1, 3, 4, and 5) produced a number line. Each number line was divided into 4 miles and each mile was subdivided into three equal pieces. Two of the groups (1 and 4) labeled the three equal pieces as fractions of a mile ($\frac{1}{3}, \frac{2}{3}, 1, \frac{1}{3}, \frac{2}{3}, 2$, etc.), while two groups (3 and 5) labeled the thirds as the distance from the origin (i.e., $\frac{1}{3}, \frac{2}{3}, \frac{3}{3}, \frac{4}{3}, \frac{5}{3}$, etc.). Each of the five groups included two equations, one that represented division ($4 \div \frac{1}{3}$) and one that represented multiplication (4×3). While all five groups included some level of explanation, only Group 1 explained that 4 was the number of miles, that each mile was being divided into groups of $\frac{1}{3}$, and that the number of $\frac{1}{3}$ markings in each mile was the number of drinks per mile. In addition, Group 2 included the incorrect equation ($\frac{1}{3} \div 4$) on their poster as well the two correct equations, and Group 4 included a more general rule for finding the number of drinks given any number of miles and the frequency of the stops each mile.

Mr. Strong decided to begin the discussion with the number lines produced by Group 1 (Zane, Henry, Kamaria, and Aidyn) and Group 3 (Connie, Jackson, Zalijah, and Jahnisa) as shown in Figure 5.6. As Mr. Strong explained,

I think we can learn more by looking at a number line, or at least it's a little easier to talk about. We had two different types of number lines that we wanted to address. One just divided the total up into four whole miles. Then each mile was divided up into thirds [see top of Figure 5.6]. The other number line kind of used the total number of miles as the whole, and divided it up into 12 thirds [see bottom of Figure 5.6]. That gave us the opportunity to be able to discuss a number of different viewpoints.

Figure 5.6 • Number lines produced by Group 1 (Zane, Henry, Kamaria, and Aidyn) and Group 3 (Connie, Jackson, Zalijah, and Jahnisa)

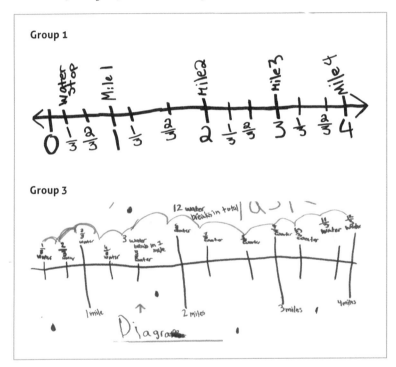

Mr. Strong then decided to have Group 2 (Ester, Lucian, Markel, and Jasper) discuss their equations. They had initially written the equation incorrectly as $\frac{1}{3} \div 4$ but soon realized that it did not make sense. As Mr. Strong described it,

They tried to divide $\frac{1}{3}$ by 4, instead of 4 by $\frac{1}{3}$. They quickly realized that their answer didn't make sense. In that process of explaining why it didn't make sense and how it did make sense to divide 4 by $\frac{1}{3}$, I heard a lot of things that showed me that they did understand that they're dividing a total by a fraction. They were able, also, to *explain to me through that, that the quotient becomes larger than the dividend, which was one of my goals for the day.*

Finally, Mr. Strong selected Group 4 (Rutland, Joaquin, Aniya, Isaac, and Youstina), who went a step beyond what was required in the problem. In addition to providing a number line and an equation, they had generalized their findings: "You can figure out how many times he stops by multiplying the number of miles by how many times he stops each mile." As Mr. Strong noted,

> *They not only were able to put things into a number line and determine the equation. They were able to determine, if I changed how often I took my drink, and if I changed the number of miles, it didn't matter. Based on that denominator, they knew how many iterations there would be within 1 mile, and then however many miles there were. They took it to the ultimate end!*

So why didn't Mr. Strong invite each group to present their poster? We would argue that given the fact that there was considerable duplication in what the groups produced, it made sense for Mr. Strong to strategically target aspects of specific solutions that made salient the three key ideas he had targeted for the lesson. Specifically, the meaning of division of a whole number by a fraction (Goal 1) could be made clear through a discussion of the number lines and the equations. Based on his earlier conversation with Group 2, Mr. Strong was confident that a discussion of their equations would make clear what happens when you divide by a number less than 1 (Goal 3) and the relationship between dividing by $\frac{1}{3}$ and multiplying by 3 (Goal 2). Although Group 4's contribution to the discussion would not explicitly address one of the identified goals, it provided students with the opportunity to generalize beyond a specific case, an important component in algebraic reasoning—a standard at Grade 5. Hence, the targeted solutions provided sufficient fodder for a rich whole class discussion.

Let us now consider how Ms. Stastny selected and sequenced student solutions to the Lasagna task (see Figure 3.6). As we discussed in Chapter 3, as a result of engaging in the lesson, Ms. Stastny wanted her students to understand that

1. A fraction describes the division of a whole or unit (area/region, set, linear/measurement) into equal parts. The size of the fraction is relative to the size of the whole or unit.

2. A fraction in which the number of parts you have (numerator) is the same as the size of the parts into which the whole is divided (denominator) is called one whole. So $\frac{4}{4}$ means there are four parts, each of which represents $\frac{1}{4}$ of the whole.

3. Two fractions are equivalent if they represent the same area of the same size whole even though the number of parts and the size of the parts are different.

While many students in the class ultimately produced accurate models showing that Tanesha and David had either $\frac{2}{2}$ and $\frac{4}{4}$, $\frac{2}{4}$ and $\frac{4}{8}$, or $\frac{2}{6}$ and $\frac{4}{12}$ portions of lasagna, Ms. Stastny noted that many students struggled initially. She commented:

What surprised me was there were quite a few that ended up not being able to start or starting differently than I had anticipated. For example, incorrectly showing shares of one-half and two-fourths, or two-fourths and four-fourths. Those were two that I didn't quite anticipate happening.

As a result of this initial confusion, Ms. Stastny decided to begin the discussion by considering the misconceptions she noted. Ms. Stastny explained:

I chose to start with a misconception because so many of my students had that misconception and I wanted them to see it with their model. I wanted everybody to hear it a couple times in a couple different ways to really understand why those were misconceptions and not addressing what the question was asking.

Just prior to the discussion, Ms. Stastny prepared the poster shown in Figure 5.7. She wanted students to be clear on why $\frac{2}{4}$ and $\frac{4}{4}$ (left side of the figure) were not equivalent and did not meet the condition stated in the problem that Tanesha and David ate the same amount. She also wanted students to see that while $\frac{1}{2}$ and $\frac{2}{4}$ (right side of the figure) were equivalent, they did not meet the conditions that Tanesha ate two pieces while David ate four pieces. She also wanted students to see that while $\frac{2}{4}$ and $\frac{4}{8}$ were equivalent to each other and to $\frac{1}{2}$, they also gave Tanesha and David the correct number of pieces.

Figure 5.7 • Poster produced by Ms. Stastny based on students' work

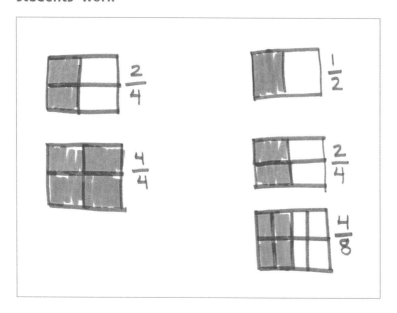

Ms. Stastny decided to not have the students who had the misconceptions actually present their own work for a practical reason. She explained:

> *A lot of them, during the group talk, they had actually changed their answers. They'd either erased it or crossed it out and so it wasn't very legible on their paper, so I wanted people to be able to see clearly what we were talking about.*

Following the discussion of the misconceptions, Ms. Stastny planned to have two different correct solutions presented, $\frac{2}{2}$ and $\frac{4}{4}$ (Ahmed) and $\frac{2}{6}$ and $\frac{4}{12}$ (Anasimon), as shown in Figure 5.8 (at the top of the next page). She explained:

> *I chose the two-halves and four-fourths because at least half of the class had that as their model. Some of them started off with the misconception but after talking with their groups they realized that two-halves and four-fourths could be one of the models. I wanted to also do one that some of them didn't see—two-sixths and four-twelfths—and have them make those connections as the equivalence and also the doubling of the fractions.*

Figure 5.8 • Ahmed (left) and Anasimon's (right) solutions to the Lasagna task

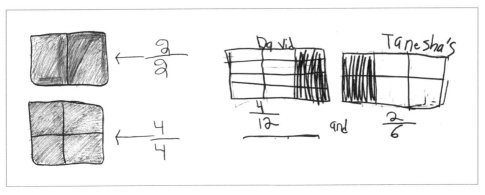

In addition, including Anasimon's solution, even though no other students produced it, provided an opportunity for Ms. Stastny to assess student understanding of the concept of equivalence because students had to think about a solution they had not considered when they initially explored the problem.

By examining both correct and incorrect responses to the Lasagna task, Ms. Stastny's students would have the chance to explain what fractions describe (Goal 1), what constitutes a whole (Goal 2), and when fractions are equivalent (Goal 3). Although only three correct solutions were presented, they represented what most of the students in the class actually did. As a result, many students beyond the presenters would be able to contribute to the discussion.

So what do you do if there are *lots* of different solutions? How do you limit the solutions that are discussed to a manageable number? To answer this question, consider a lesson you might teach to a second-grade class. Suppose you want your students to represent and solve a problem involving addition and equal groups. You select the Sheep and Ducks task, shown in Figure 5.9, because it would allow all students entry to the problem (questions 1 to 4 provided scaffolding), question 5 could be approached and answered in several different ways, and it aligned with your lesson goals. Your students produced the strategies shown in Figure 5.10. In Analyzing the Work of Teaching 5.2, you will consider how you could select and sequence students' solutions in order to accomplish your goals for the lesson.

Figure 5.9 • Sheep and Ducks task

Sheep and Ducks

The farmer raises sheep and ducks.

1. How many legs on 1 duck? _____

2. How many legs on 4 ducks? _____

3. How many legs on 5 sheep? _____

4. Next to the barn is a pen with 2 sheep and 3 ducks.

   How many legs altogether? _____

   Show how you know your answer is correct.

5. One of the farmer's pens has a high fence around it. He can see 32 legs under the fence. Use words, pictures, and numbers to show one way to have sheep and ducks with 32 legs in all.

Source: Adapted from Noyce Foundation (2007). Sheep and duck from biscotto87/iStock.com.

Analyzing the Work of Teaching 5.2

Selecting Solutions That Highlight Key Ideas

Review the student solutions to question 5 of the Sheep and Ducks task shown in Figure 5.10. Keeping your goals for the lesson in mind (elaborated below), determine

1. Which solutions you should select for the whole class discussion;

2. What each solution will contribute to the discussion; and

3. How you would sequence them in order to ensure that all students have access to the discussion.

Specifically, you wanted students to

- Understand situations that involve equal groups of objects (as a foundation for multiplication);

- Use addition and subtraction to solve word problems;

- Communicate their reasoning using words, numbers, equations, and/or pictures; and

- Make connections between different representations.

Figure 5.10 • Solutions to the Sheep and Ducks task

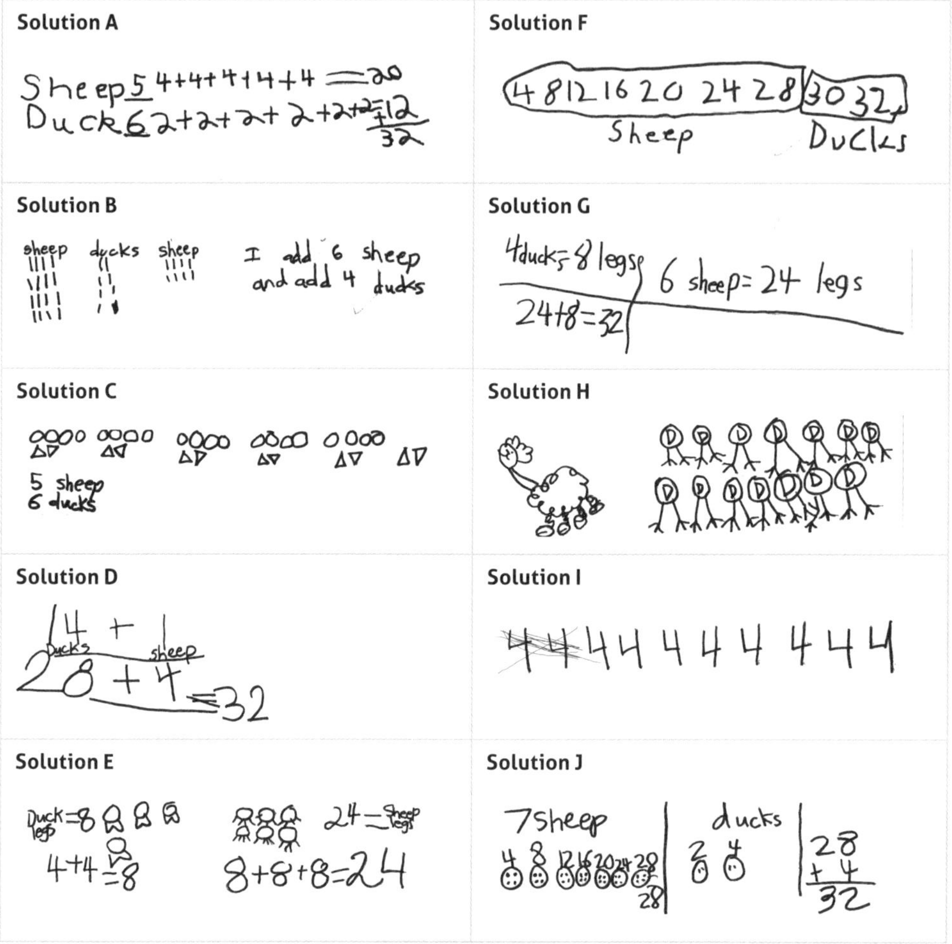

Solution A	Solution F
Sheep 5 4+4+4+4+4 =20 Duck 6 2+2+2+ 2+2+2 = 12 32	4 8 12 16 20 24 28 30 32 Sheep Ducks

Solution B	Solution G
sheep ducks sheep I add 6 sheep |||| || |||| and add 4 ducks	4 ducks= 8 legs 6 sheep= 24 legs 24+8=32

Solution C	Solution H
[groups of sheep and ducks drawings] 5 sheep 6 ducks	

Solution D	Solution I
4 + 1 Ducks sheep 28 + 4 =32	4 4 4 4 4 4 4 4 4 4

Solution E	Solution J
Duck=8 [drawings] [drawings] 24= sheep legs 4+4=8 8+8+8=24	7 sheep 4 8 12 16 20 24 28 ducks 2 4 28 28 +4 32

Source: Adapted from Inside Mathematics, © Noyce Foundation 2007.

Selecting Solutions That Highlight Key Ideas—Analysis

There are nine different combinations of sheep and ducks that would result in a total of 32 legs (e.g., 8 sheep, 16 ducks, or 6 ducks and 5 sheep) and a range of different strategies that students could use to determine a winning combination (e.g., direct modeling, counting, addition). Figure 5.11 provides a summary of the combinations and strategies students used to solve the problem.

The students in your class produced five of the nine combinations of legs that would yield a total of 32. Students used a number of different strategies, including direct modeling of equal groups, skip counting, repeated addition, and number sentences. There are a number of different ways that you could select and sequence the students'

Figure 5.11 • Combinations and strategies used by students

SOLUTION	COMBINATION		STRATEGY
	SHEEP	DUCKS	
A	5	6	Repeated addition, number sentences with twos and fours, adds sheep legs and duck legs, names total number of legs, names number of ducks and sheep
B	6	4	Diagram of six groups of 4 and two groups of 2, total legs not indicated, indicates number of ducks and sheep
C	5	6	Direct modeling, indicates number of sheep and ducks, total legs not indicated
D	1	14	Number sentences with numbers of sheep and ducks and indicates total duck legs and total sheep legs, and total legs
E	6	4	Direct modeling, repeated addition of 4 and 8 instead of twos and fours, indicates total legs contributed by ducks and sheep, does not indicate the number of ducks and sheep or the total number of legs
F	7	2	Skip counted by fours, then switched to twos, doesn't explicitly identify the number of sheep and ducks
G	6	4	Writes 4 ducks = 8 legs where 4×2 is implied and 6 sheep = 24 legs where 6×4 is implied, indicates total number of legs
H	1	14	Direct modeling of 14 ducks and 1 sheep, the number of sheep and ducks or the total number of legs is not provided
I	8	0	Recorded 8 fours, doesn't explicitly identify the number of sheep and ducks, no operation, no total number of legs provided
J	7	2	Direct modeling, skip counts sheep by 4 and ducks by 2, finds total number of legs, shows total number of sheep but not ducks

solutions. The challenge is to decide which subset of the 10 unique solutions will help you accomplish your lesson goals, allow all students access to the discussion, and keep students interested and attentive. A review of the solutions indicates that four students drew a model (Solutions C, E, H, and J), two students made equal group diagrams (Solutions B and J), and one student skip counted (Solution J). The student who produced Solution D indicated the number of sheep and ducks and then jumped to the number of sheep and duck legs. This suggests that the student may have been using multiplicative thinking (e.g., $14 \times 2 = 28$, $1 \times 4 = 4$). In addition, many students used number sentences to show their addition of animals and/or legs (Students A, D, E, G, and J).

In determining a possible sequence, you need to keep in mind what you are trying to accomplish mathematically. Since several groups showed equal groups and many used addition, in order to accomplish your goals, it would be important to show different ways students communicated their reasoning and to make connections between different representations. One possible sequence would be Solutions H, A, D, and J in this order. Solution H shows the direct modeling of a solution without any numbers or words and should be accessible to all students. Solution A shows number sentences with groups of 4 and groups of 2. Following the discussion of Solution A, students could be challenged to write a number sentence for Solution H. Solution D shows the same combination of sheep and ducks as Solution H, but instead of a drawing the student has written number sentences for the total number of sheep and ducks and the total number of legs. Juxtaposing solutions H and D would provide students with the opportunity to connect Student H's model with Student D's number sentences.

While Solutions H, A, and D would be sufficient to accomplish the lesson goals, including Solution J provides an opportunity to make additional connections to another strategy—skip counting. Including this solution would provide an opportunity to discuss this strategy and connect it back to Solutions A and H.

Our point here is not that you should only select three or four solutions to share as we have illustrated in the three examples discussed in this section, but rather that the number of solutions to be shared should be driven by your lesson goals and the time you have available for the discussion. Using this rule of thumb, not all students will be able to share each day. This should not be a concern as long as over time each and every student has the opportunity to share their work and their thinking, as we will discuss in the next section.

Expanding Beyond the Usual Presenters

While selecting solutions to be presented should be done based on the mathematical potential of the solution, a secondary consideration needs to be who will do the presenting. Over time all students need the opportunity to present in front of the class. This is an issue of equity! It is also important for the development of identity and being seen by one's peers as competent. While it is tempting to call on students whom you know you can count on to give a coherent and articulate explanation, students do not improve their skills at presenting and explaining simply by listening to others do it. Further, always calling on the same students sends a clear message regarding who the teacher thinks is capable.

PAUSE AND CONSIDER

Reflect on your practice of identifying presenters. Do you tend to call on the same students repeatedly? What could you do to provide more students the opportunity to improve their ability to explain their thinking and to be seen by the class as mathematically capable?

For example, consider the Cars, Bikes, and Trikes task shown in Figure 5.12. During the discussion of this task, you decide that you want to have a student share the "equal groups" solution, since this solution provides a concrete model for division and clearly shows that 52 is divisible by 2 and 4 but not 3 (see Figure 5.13)—thus answering the first two questions in the task. Several different students have produced this solution. Which student do you select to present? We would argue that you should select the student who has not had an opportunity recently to present his or her work during a whole class discussion. You can prepare for this by reviewing monitoring charts from previous discussions (focusing on the *Who and What* and *Order* columns) and making a short list on a sticky note of students who have not recently been featured prominently in a discussion. This will help you in making decisions about which students to select when there are options. Of course, if none of the students on your list have produced the solution you want to feature, you should select someone else and continue to look for opportunities to involve the students on your list in some way.

Figure 5.12 • Cars, Bikes, and Trikes task

Cars, Bikes, and Trikes

A toy factory makes bicycles, tricycles, and cars. They make only one type of toy every day. One day they make bikes, another day they make tricycles, and the next day they make cars.

1. If the factory used 52 wheels, which toy did they make? Did they make cars, tricycles, or bicycles?

2. Explain why it is possible to have two answers to this problem.

3. Identify two other amounts of wheels that would allow you to make two different toys on the same day.

Source: Task created by the University of Pittsburgh Institute for Learning (2009).

 Download the Task from
resources.corwin.com/5practices-elementary

Figure 5.13 • Equal groups solution to the Cars, Bikes, and Trikes task

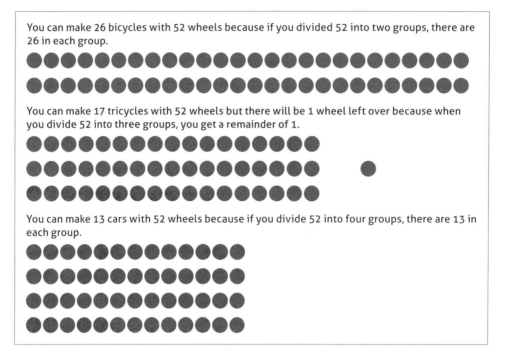

You can make 26 bicycles with 52 wheels because if you divided 52 into two groups, there are 26 in each group.

You can make 17 tricycles with 52 wheels but there will be 1 wheel left over because when you divide 52 into three groups, you get a remainder of 1.

You can make 13 cars with 52 wheels because if you divide 52 into four groups, there are 13 in each group.

Once you have identified students to present, you should let the students know that you want them to share their solution. This will give the students a chance to practice their explanation in the safety of their group before giving it in front of the whole class. While this is particularly important for English Language Learners, it can help all students feel more confident about standing up in front of the class. In addition, a student may feel more comfortable presenting if he or she can do so with a partner. However, in this situation you need to make sure that the partner is not the one doing all the explaining!

In some cases, you may be able to include students whom you would like to involve in the discussion, even if they have not produced the solutions you initially targeted. Consider, for example, what occurred in Mr. Nunez's fourth-grade class. He wanted students to use their place-value understanding and the properties of operations to perform multidigit multiplication. He gave his students the Box of Crayons task shown in Figure 2.12 because he felt it would be accessible to all students and aligned with his lesson goal.

As he monitored students' work on the task, Mr. Nunez noticed that most students solved the problem in one of three ways he had anticipated—repeated addition, distributive property, or by creating an area model—as shown in Figure 5.14. In addition, Alicia, one of the students in the class, drew a base ten model showing four groups of 64 and explained that this would be 24 tens and 16 ones, which was the same as 256. Another student, Jesse, used the standard algorithm for solving the problem (see Figure 5.15).

Figure 5.14 • Strategies used by students in Mr. Nunez's class to solve the Box of Crayons task

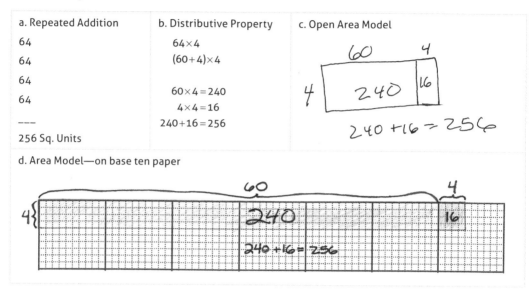

a. Repeated Addition	b. Distributive Property	c. Open Area Model
64	64×4	
64	$(60+4) \times 4$	
64		
64	$60 \times 4 = 240$	
	$4 \times 4 = 16$	
---	$240 + 16 = 256$	
256 Sq. Units		

d. Area Model—on base ten paper

Figure 5.15 • Alicia (left) and Jesse's (right) solutions for the Box of Crayons task

Mr. Nunez decided to begin the discussion by having Alicia explain her drawing. Although a base ten drawing was not a solution he had anticipated students using at this point, he thought it was a good place to start for several reasons. First, Alicia's drawing clearly showed 64 decomposed into tens and ones, four equal groups, tens added to tens and ones added to ones, and recomposing tens and ones to get 256—key components that he wanted students to understand. Second, it allowed him to include Alicia, who often struggled to represent her ideas and was not a frequent presenter. Explaining her solution would serve to build Alicia's confidence and provide all students in the class with entry into the discussion, since this was a model with which they were familiar. Finally, Alicia's drawing could subsequently be connected to the other representations—to repeated addition (as a concrete way to show four groups of 64), to the distributive property (64 decomposed into four groups of 6 tens and four groups of 4 ones), and to the area model on base ten paper (6 tens and 4 ones, 64 square units shown in each of the four rows as the area).

Mr. Nunez decided to end the series of presentations with Jesse's solution, since it would provide an opportunity to connect Jesse's method with the other methods that were presented. Jesse knows a lot of procedures and wants to share them, but Mr. Nunez is cautious about introducing formal methods too soon and waits until students have first had an opportunity to use methods that make sense to them. So this was a chance to acknowledge Jesse and engage the whole class in making connections between different representations.

The point here is that each and every student—students who struggle as well as those who excel—need the opportunity to participate in whole class discussions in substantive ways so that they can be seen by others as mathematically capable and students can see themselves as doers of mathematics. There may be times when you need to alter your initial plan as Mr. Nunez did in order to ensure wider participation. Jansen, Cooper, Vascellaro, and Wandless (2016) describe a strategy for engaging more students in discussion call *rough-draft talk*. At the heart of this strategy is creating a culture of risk taking and inviting students to share initial ideas— rough-draft presentations—before returning to their groups to revise their thinking toward final draft solutions. Rough-draft talk presentations serve to get a range of ideas on the table to stimulate thinking and reduce the threat of being wrong. According to Jansen and her colleagues (2016),

> *If rough-draft talk is valued, brainstormed ideas are welcomed. More students are likely to take risks rather than freeze during challenging tasks. Valuing a wider range of contributions invites greater involvement, in contrast to the same students who participate frequently or not at all.* (p. 304)

Deciding What Work to Share When the Majority of Students Were Not Able to Solve the Task and Your Initial Goal No Longer Seems Obtainable

Your lessons may not always go as planned, despite your best efforts. This may result from the task being too challenging for students, students lacking essential prior knowledge, or because students have pursued solution paths that were not productive. In such cases, continuing with your lesson as planned may ensure that you *cover* the material, but if students are struggling with aspects of the task, it is not clear that they will learn what was intended if you simply forge ahead. At times such as this, you need to readjust your lesson goals to meet students where they are.

This was the situation that Michael McCarthy faced in his lesson on the Table and Chairs Investigation task (see Figure 2.9). Although his students had some prior experience in generating and analyzing patterns, this would be their first experience with a pattern that did not represent a direct variation relationship (i.e., the total number of customers is not a multiple of the figure number). Mr. McCarthy wanted to make sure that his students had lots of opportunities to generalize a wider variety of patterns including those that included a constant.

Mr. McCarthy and his colleagues generated several different solutions to the task as shown in Figure 5.16 (at the top of the next page). While he did not expect his fifth-grade students to express their generalizations algebraically, he did think that students would be able to explain some of these generalizations verbally, using the diagram to show how their description fit with the picture. [Friel and Markworth (2009) describe this as figural reasoning—paying attention to visual cues that can explain and support pattern generalization.]

The majority of students in Mr. McCarthy's class completed the table showing the number of customers who could be seated and recognized the recursive pattern—that the number of seats increased by two every time a table was added. When asked to explain how to figure out the number of customers who could be seated at seven, eight, and nine tables, students extended their tables by adding two to each successive table. As a result, students were not able to describe the pattern beyond "you added two to the number of customers who sat at one less table" and therefore could not predict the number of customers that could be seated at any number of tables. Students were focusing numerically on the amount of the increase in customers (+2) and were not connecting the physical arrangement of tables with the number of customers who could be seated or the figure number. Rather than pursue his original goal of getting to a generalization, Mr. McCarthy decided to focus the discussion on finding different ways to determine the number of customers at a specific number of tables.

Figure 5.16 • The equations and representations that Mr. McCarthy and his colleagues anticipated

EQUATIONS	VISUAL REPRESENTATION	VERBAL DESCRIPTION
$c = 2t + 2$	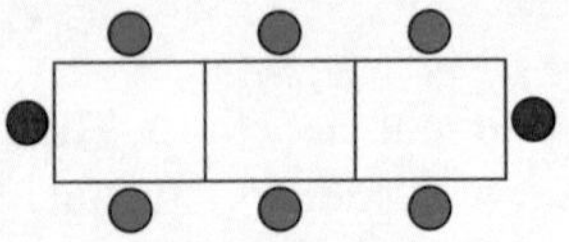	The number of customers on the top and on the bottom is the same as the figure number or number of tables. Then there are always two seats on the end.
$c = 2(t + 1)$	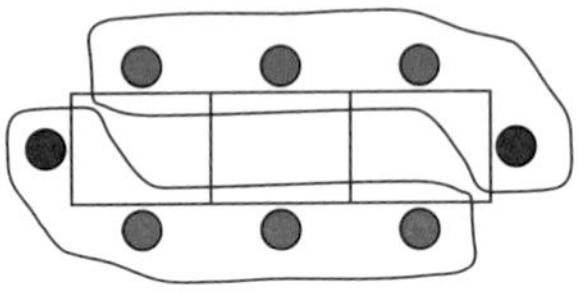	The number of customers on the top plus the one on the right end is the number of tables plus 1. This is the same as the number of customers on the bottom plus the one on the left end.
$c = 4 + 2(t - 1)$	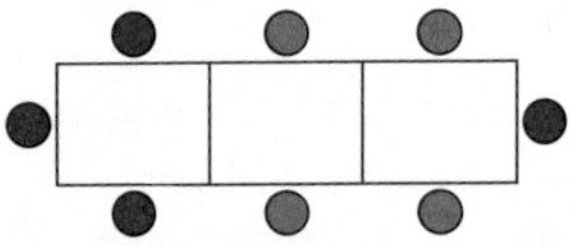	The three customers at the first table plus the one customer at the end table on the right always give you 4. The number of customers sitting at the remaining tables is the number of tables minus 1 on the top and the number of tables minus 1 on the bottom.
$c = 4t - 2(t - 1)$	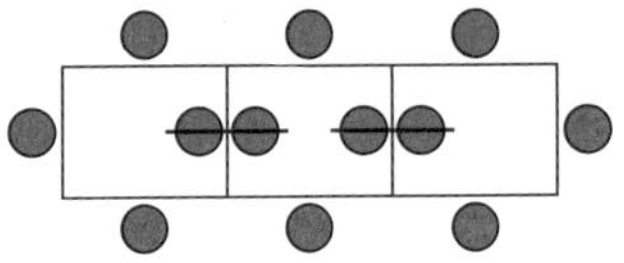	Each table could seat four customers if they were not pushed together. But for every junction between two tables, you lose two seats. The number of times you lose two seats is one less than the number of tables or the figure number.

Note: In each of the equations, *t* is the number of tables and the figure number; *c* is the number of customers.

While he was monitoring students as they worked in groups, Mr. McCarthy noticed that one group had created a model that clearly showed various numbers of tables with people seated appropriately. When he talked with the group about their drawing, they were able to explain that they found the total number of people who could sit at tables in the first six figures using a pattern they had noticed. While the group had not generalized beyond the specific tables they had investigated, Mr. McCarthy decided to invite one of the members of the group, Tylor, to share his drawing (shown in Figure 5.17), which showed the first four figures.

Figure 5.17 • Tylor's drawing of the tables and customers

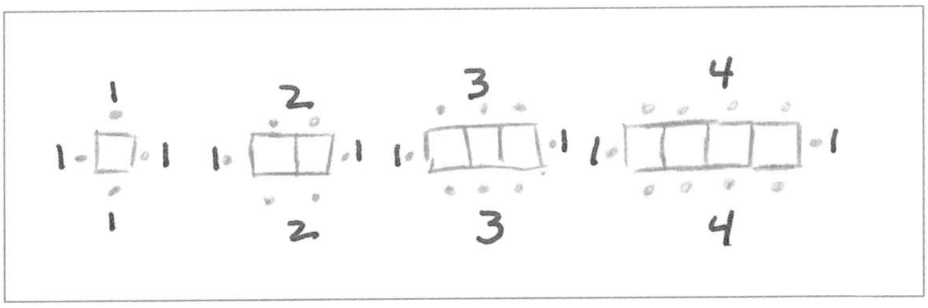

Mr. McCarthy thought that Tylor's work would generate discussion regarding how to predict the number of customers who could sit at any number of tables using his method and, ultimately, stimulate students to consider other ways to connect the number of tables and customers without counting. With this revised agenda for the discussion, Mr. McCarthy felt that he would ultimately reach his goal, but not in one class period as he had initially planned.

If the majority of students are struggling with some aspect of the task, moving forward as planned will leave too many students behind. By determining what students are struggling with and how to help them move beyond the struggle, the class will be better positioned to make progress on the initial lesson goals. The student work selected and sequenced needs to help students gain clarity on the aspects of the task with which they struggled.

Moving Forward When a Key Strategy Is Not Produced by Students

When you engage in the practice of anticipating, you consider the correct and incorrect strategies that students are likely to use in solving a task and how you would respond to the work students produced. This is also the time when you consider which of the strategies that you anticipate students using will be most useful in accomplishing the goals for the lesson. What happens then, if during teaching, you discover that no students used a strategy that you consider essential to discuss in order to meet the lesson goals. What can you do?

In preparing her lesson on the Ms. Tyus's Markers task, Ms. Tyus indicated that she wanted her students to understand the rounding and compensating strategy (i.e., numbers can be rounded up or down to make a multiple of ten before subtracting and that the amount rounded up or down must then be subtracted from or added to the difference to compensate for the amount added to or taken away initially). While the two main problems in the task lent themselves to this strategy (e.g., $69 - 40 = 70 - 40 - 1$), it was not a strategy that students had used up to this point. If this solution was not produced by a student, Ms. Tyus was prepared to introduce it after they had discussed $69 - 40$ on the hundreds chart by saying, "We've already done $69 - 40$ on the hundreds chart. Now let's look at what $70 - 40$ is." She explained that they would then talk about what happened when you started with 70 instead of 69 and what you would have to do to get the answer they had already determined. Her expectation was not for every student in the class to understand and use this strategy, but instead for students to explore the strategy as a means of developing flexible thinking.

As we discuss in Part One, Ms. Tyus did not need to resort to this plan, since a student did use the strategy. Following the class, Ms. Tyus commented, "I was surprised I did have one student actually round up and compensate on their own. It was very shocking. I didn't expect Elsie to do that." She indicated that she would continue to work on this strategy with students.

Ms. Tyus was prepared to introduce the rounding and compensating strategy by linking it to a known strategy and asking students questions. There are several other options you might consider to prepare yourself in the event that a solution you want to discuss is not produced by your students. You might pull a solution from a previous class period or highlight student work you have saved from a previous year. Another option is one that Mrs. Ellis often uses. Although Mrs. Ellis anticipated a wide range of strategies that her fourth-grade students might use to solve the Treat Bags task (see Figure 3.12), she identified a smaller number of strategies—area model, base ten model, and repeated subtraction (Figure 3.13)—that she felt would be critical to share during the end of the class discussion in order to ensure that her students understood what division means and how it could be represented. Mrs. Ellis did not want to leave it to chance that students will produce these during the discussion. She explains:

> Sometimes I write out a strategy ahead of time just in case students don't use a particular strategy that I know is important to the lesson goals. I write it out like a student wrote it. I pull this example out and refer to it and say, "Oh, you know, last year one of my students did this. What do you think about it?"

By preparing critical solutions in advance, or having access to key solutions saved from a previous year or a different class period, you will be prepared to introduce a solution that your students did not produce in class that day into the sequence of solutions presented. Students could be asked to consider whether the solution strategy is viable—Does it work? Will it always work? Asking students to make sense of another student's reasoning is challenging and important work and will give you additional insight into what students truly understand.

Determining How to Sequence Errors, Misconceptions, and/or Incomplete Solutions

You may be most comfortable having students share only work that is both complete and correct so that students have models of good work. Incomplete solutions, however, can provide opportunities for analysis and discussion that completed correct solutions do not. For example, starting with a base ten solution to the Ms. Tyus's Markers task that did not include an equation could provide all students with the opportunity to discuss how to represent the physical model numerically.

PAUSE AND CONSIDER

All three teachers—Ms. Tyus, Mr. Strong, and Ms. Stastny—planned to use incorrect solutions in their whole class discussions. What role do incorrect solutions play in your instruction? Can you think of a situation you have recently encountered where a wrong answer might have served as a learning opportunity for students?

Incorrect solutions can provide an opportunity for students to investigate what is going on and why it does or does not make sense. Finding a correct answer is one thing, but determining why an answer is not correct requires a different level of understanding. In Ms. Tyus's class, for example, having Leah share her incorrect equation for the Ms. Tyus's Markers task (i.e., $6 - 4 = 2$ instead of $60 - 40 = 20$) could provide an opportunity for the class to consider what each number represents in terms of its place value.

Mr. Strong also included an incorrect answer in his whole group discussion. As discussed previously, Group 2 initially wrote the equation for Mr. Strong's Hike as $\frac{1}{3} \div 4 = \frac{1}{12}$ before realizing and correcting their mistake. While no other groups made this error, discussing it in a whole group setting provided an opportunity to ensure that students understood why this did not make sense in the context of the problem.

In addition to the two solutions Ms. Stastny selected for presentation during the whole class discussion around the Lasagna task (see Figure 3.6) as discussed previously, she also planned to begin the discussion by presenting the misconceptions she had observed as she monitored students working in groups.

There is one caution in having students share incorrect work: If you want to share an error that the student has made but is not yet aware of, you need to ensure that the classroom culture is such that wrong answers are seen as opportunities for new learning and that the student will not be ridiculed for being wrong. (We will see this in the case of Leah in Ms. Tyus's class in Chapter 6.) Alternatively, you could introduce an incorrect solution as one you saw in another class and ask students to determine whether or not it is correct and why or why not or simply reproduce it as

Ms. Stastny did. This way, the student who produced it does not have to own it unless they choose to identify themselves as the author.

All incorrect solutions, however, are not worth sharing. If the errors are simply computational in nature, are the result of a misunderstanding of the problem, or are made only by one or two students, you may want to address these individually rather than during the whole group discussion. When several students have made the same error, or one or more students have a major misconception, then it makes sense to share the incorrect solution. Ms. Stastny provides a good example of how to do this. She did not identify a particular presenter but rather put on the table the issue she wanted the class to grapple with. Students could then discuss the issue and hopefully, as a class, conclude that $\frac{2}{4}$ and $\frac{4}{4}$ were not equivalent and why.

Incorrect and incomplete work can be used to enhance a discussion and to press students to make sense of someone else's reasoning. This may not be something you need to do in every discussion, but do not avoid something just because it is wrong! Leah Alcala (not a pseudonym) developed a routine for engaging students in analyzing mistakes. She calls it "My Favorite No." At the heart of this routine is giving students a problem to work on, collecting student responses to the problem, reviewing the solutions, identifying the most interesting wrong answers, and selecting a wrong answer for the class to discuss. The incorrect response selected for discussion shows *some good mathematics* but also some error and is not linked to a particular student. The entire class is then engaged in careful analysis of what is correct, what is incorrect, and why. While Ms. Alcala uses this routine as a warm-up activity prior to the lesson for the day, it could be used as a formative assessment activity at any point in a lesson or as a more general technique for sharing incorrect solutions. [See https://www.teachingchannel.org/videos/class-warm-up-routine for more details on "My Favorite No."]

Conclusion

As we have discussed in this chapter, it is through the practice of selecting and sequencing that you determine what solutions will be shared and the order in which they will be shared. This is important because the solutions that are shared publicly provide the grist for the discussion that is to follow. Hence, the identified solutions *must* have the potential to highlight the mathematical ideas that are targeted in the lesson. The sequence in which solutions are shared must provide students with access to the discussion and achieve a coherent storyline for students to follow. The first solution presented should be one that all students can make sense of regardless of what they themselves have produced, and as additional presenters share their work, there should be a clear sense of a developing story where one solution builds on the next.

The key to successful selecting and sequencing is careful consideration of what you are trying to accomplish in the lesson. The work of Ms. Tyus provides an illustration of a teacher who reflected on what she was trying to accomplish in light of the work students had produced and made a thoughtful determination of what she would feature during the discussion. Her work highlighted how the data she had collected as she monitored students' work on the task served as a resource for decision-making when it was time to select and sequence.

While selecting and sequencing are not without their challenges, as we discussed in Part Two of the chapter, these are challenges you can overcome. The illustrations from the classrooms of Ms. Stastny, Mr. Strong, and Mr. Nunez provide some concrete ideas regarding how to select and sequence solutions in order to limit the number of solutions shared, keep the mathematical ideas central, and ensure that different voices are heard.

The situation in which Mr. McCarthy found himself is a critical one to consider. Lessons do not always go as planned, and it is important to be sure that you are teaching children, not teaching a lesson. What students do during the lesson may cause you to revise your plan. In such cases, you will need to think about how the work students produced can help you achieve your revised goals.

Selecting and Sequencing Student Solutions—Summary

Video Clip 5.1
To hear and see more about selecting and sequencing, watch Video Clip 5.1.

 Videos may also be accessed at
resources.corwin.com/5practices-elementary

In the next chapter, we explore the practice of connecting. Here, we will return to Ms. Tyus's lesson and consider what it takes to engage in this practice and the challenges it presents.

Linking the Five Practices to Your Own Instruction ◄

SELECTING AND SEQUENCING

It is now time to reflect on the lesson you taught following Chapter 4, but this time through the lens of selecting and sequencing.

1. What solutions did you select for presentation during the whole group discussion?

   • Did the selected solutions help you address the mathematical ideas that you had targeted in the lesson? Are there other solutions that might have been more useful in meeting your goal?

   • How many solutions did you have students present? Did all of these contribute to better understanding of the mathematics to be learned? Did you conclude the discussion in the allotted time?

   • Which students were selected as presenters? Did you include any students who are not frequent presenters? Could you have?

2. How did you sequence the solutions?

   • Did the series of presentations add up to something? Was the storyline coherent?

   • Did you include any incomplete or incorrect solutions? Where in the sequence did they fit?

3. Based on your reading of this chapter and a deeper understanding of the practice of selecting and sequencing, would you do anything differently if you were going to teach this lesson again?

4. What lessons have you learned that you will draw on in the next lesson you plan and teach?

" I want to see students making connections when they talk about what they did and what other ones did so they can say, 'Oh, there are other ways I can do it.' "

—TARA TYUS, FIRST-GRADE TEACHER

CHAPTER 6

Connecting Student Solutions

Having selected and sequenced student solutions with the goals of the lesson in mind, you are now ready to conduct a whole class discussion and engage in the last of the five practices, connecting student solutions. While you designed the discussion so that students play a central role as they share their strategies with their peers, you also play an essential role in the discussion. For students to truly learn what is intended, you need to help students see the connections between the solutions that are shared and the goals of the lesson. To do this requires careful facilitation of the discussion on your part.

Smith and Stein (2018) describe connecting in the following way:

> [Connecting involves asking] questions [that] must go beyond merely clarifying and probing what individual students did and how. Instead, they must focus on mathematical meaning and relationships and make links between mathematical ideas and representations. (p. 70)

Facilitating meaningful discussions involves helping students to share their thinking in a way that is understandable to others. You may need to help them recognize where to stand, how loudly to speak, and the importance of explaining both their process and their reasoning (Boaler & Humphreys, 2005; Kazemi & Hintz, 2014). Students who are not presenting may also need your help to understand their roles as they engage in active listening and prepare to ask questions of their peers (Hufferd-Ackles, Fuson, & Sherin, 2015). For example, you may need to model initially how to ask a question, how to disagree, and how to share an alternate idea. Working with students to establish explicit norms for participation can help all students better understand what is expected of them during classroom discussions (Horn, 2012).

The practice of connecting goes even further. Connecting involves helping students relate strategies or ideas to one or more of the lesson goals and see the relationships between different solutions. Your task here is to consider the solution strategies you have selected and the kinds of connections that will be important for students to make. Some of this work will need to take place on the fly, during instruction, as you see how students describe their strategies, and what questions arise from peers. Still, it can be helpful to consider, before the discussion, what connections you anticipate will be critical for students to make and the questions you can ask to help students make these connections.

In this chapter, we first describe key aspects of connecting and illustrate what this practice looks like in an elementary school classroom. We then discuss what aspects of connecting are typically challenging for teachers and provide an opportunity for you to explore connecting in your own teaching practice.

Part One: Unpacking the Practice: Connecting Student Solutions

Connecting student solutions involves relating the ideas that students present to the class, both to the goals of the lesson and to each other. Here we explore each of these components by looking inside Ms. Tyus's classroom. Figure 6.1 highlights the components of this practice along with key questions to guide the process of connecting.

Figure 6.1 • Key questions that support the practice of connecting

WHAT IT TAKES	KEY QUESTIONS
Connecting student work to the goals of the lesson	What questions about the student work will make the mathematics being targeted in the lesson visible?
Connecting different solutions to each other	What questions will help students make connections between the different solution strategies presented?

Connecting Student Work to the Goals of the Lesson

In selecting solution strategies to have students share in class, you purposefully choose student work that contains important mathematical ideas that advance the goals of the lesson. As the discussion unfolds in your classroom, you will want to keep those ideas in mind. While it is possible that students will make these connections in their presentations, this will not always be the case. You want to be prepared to ask questions about the students' work that will make the important mathematics in the lesson visible for the class. In this way, connecting involves creating bridges from what students share to the mathematically significant ideas underlying the lesson (Leatham, Peterson, Stockero, & Van Zoest, 2015). Without seeing these connections, students may walk away from the lesson without clarity about what it was they were supposed to learn.

How can you do this? For each solution shared, you want to keep in mind the key mathematical takeaways for the class. Many times, this will have less to do with *what* a student did and more to do with *why* a student used a particular approach given the task at hand. You may need to draw out these ideas from students by asking them to share why they chose a particular solution path and to explain the reasoning that guided their work.

You will also want to highlight explicit connections between the student work and the goals of the lessons. "How does this approach help us answer the question we are working on?" "Where does this idea fit with what we are trying to figure out?" Students may be applying mathematical ideas that have important connections to the lesson goals and yet be unaware of these connections. Your objective is to help make these connections visible to the presenter and to the class. Boaler and Brodie (2004) describe the importance of using such questions because they target the key concepts in a lesson for students.

Once such ideas have been made public, it is often helpful to give everyone a chance to digest these connections. Using a *turn-and-talk* strategy (Kazemi & Hintz, 2014) can provide needed time for students to consider new information with a partner and reflect on how an idea might fit (or not) with their own approach.

What does engaging students in making connections look like in practice? In Analyzing the Work of Teaching 6.1, you will have an opportunity to see how Ms. Tyus helps her students make connections between the solutions that are presented and her goals for the lesson. We encourage you to view the video clips and consider the questions posed before you read our analyses.

Analyzing the Work of Teaching 6.1

Connecting Student Work to the Goals of the Lesson—Part One

Video Clip 6.1

As you watch Video Clip 6.1, consider Jocelyn's presentation of her solution and the comments from Ms. Tyus and other students in the class. Recall that Ms. Tyus selected Jocelyn's work in order to address Goals 1 and 2 of the lesson. Here again is Jocelyn's written work, which is projected on the board during her presentation.

- What questions does Ms. Tyus ask to connect Jocelyn's presentation to Goals 1 and 2 of the lesson?

- How do students' responses address these goals?

Goal 1: When subtracting two-digit numbers, tens are subtracted from tens and ones are subtracted from ones. If you are subtracting a multiple of ten, then only the number in the tens place changes because there are no ones to subtract.

Goal 2: Decomposing and recomposing numbers in systematic ways can help you solve problems and make relationships among quantities of tens and ones more visible.

 Videos may also be accessed at
resources.corwin.com/5practices-elementary

Connecting Student Work to the Goals of the Lesson, Part One—Analysis

In this video clip, we see Jocelyn, the first presenter, describe her approach to the class. Jocelyn explains her drawing, saying, "I did 6 tens and 9 ones and then I x'd out 4 tens." Jocelyn continues: "Then I still had 2 tens and then I still had my ones, so I counted on." What is it about this solution that Ms. Tyus wanted to make public?

To gain insight into Ms. Tyus's objective, we can look closely at the questions she asks in response to Jocelyn's explanation. After asking Audrey to "explain what Jocelyn did," Ms. Tyus asks a series of more specific questions about Jocelyn's approach: "I'm a little confused. I see 6 and I see 2 and 9 . . . How'd you get 29?" When Laila responds that Jocelyn "counted on," Ms. Tyus then asks, "What does that look like or sound like?"

At this point, it seems that Ms. Tyus's goal is to have students explain in detail the work of decomposing and recomposing that Jocelyn did. Jocelyn clearly states the process of decomposing 69 into 6 tens and 9 ones. She is less specific, however, about the process involved in recomposing the remaining 2 tens and 9 ones, stating, "I counted on." Ms. Tyus's questions "What does [counting on] mean?" and "What does that look like or sound like?" probe this further. As Allison responds "20, 21, 22 . . . ," Ms. Tyus asks for additional clarification concerning why Allison first counts by tens and then by ones. It is this idea that 29 is formed by combining the remaining 2 tens and 9 ones that Ms. Tyus seems to want to be made explicit for the class. And this information is precisely what is essential to achieving Goal 2 of the lesson. While the students do not explicitly discuss Goal 1, it seems implicit in Jocelyn's solution, since she adds on the ones to the remaining tens. To confirm this, Ms. Tyus might have asked why only the value in the tens place changed.

Following Jocelyn's presentation, Ms. Tyus calls on DuJuan to explain his approach, which involves using the hundreds chart to solve the task. In addition to having DuJuan share his strategy with the class, Ms. Tyus's goal is to highlight connections between Jocelyn and DuJuan's solutions. For our purposes, it will be more useful to discuss this solution in the next section when we discuss connecting different solutions. For now, we move on to the third presenter Ms. Tyus calls up to the board, Leah. Recall that Leah's solution was also intended to address Goals 1 and 2. In Analyzing the Work of Teaching 6.2, you will take a close look at how Ms. Tyus connects Leah's solution to the goals of the lesson.

Analyzing the Work of Teaching 6.2

Connecting Student Work to the Goals of the Lesson—Part Two

Video Clip 6.2

As you watch Video Clip 6.2, consider Leah's explanation of how she solved the Ms. Tyus's Markers task, and in particular her description of the equations she uses. The work that Leah produced is shown below.

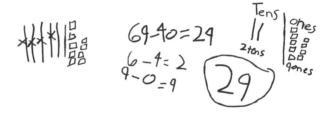

- What questions does Ms. Tyus ask to connect Leah's presentation to Goals 1 and 2 of the lesson?

- How do students' responses address these goals?

Goal 1: When subtracting two-digit numbers, tens are subtracted from tens and ones are subtracted from ones. If you are subtracting a multiple of ten, then only the number in the tens place changes because there are no ones to subtract.

Goal 2: Decomposing and recomposing numbers in systematic ways can help you solve problems and make relationships among quantities of tens and ones more visible.

Videos may also be accessed at
resources.corwin.com/5practices-elementary

Connecting Student Work to the Goals of the Lesson, Part Two—Analysis

In this video clip, Ms. Tyus begins by asking Leah to explain her thinking about the problem. Ms. Tyus again seems focused on making explicit the process of decomposing and recomposing numbers, in this case with a focus on the equations that Leah produced. She asks Leah to "show us your thinking" and in particular to "tell us about your equations."

Leah describes two of her equations. "I know that 6 minus 4 equals 2. And then, 9 minus 0 equals 9." As she continues, Leah explains what the 2 and the 9 mean. She states, "Two is the ten since it went first. And then 9 was the ones since it went last." The idea that the 2 stands for 2 tens, or 20, is at the heart of what students need to know in order to recompose the 20 and 9 to make 29. Thus, Ms. Tyus wants to make sure this is clear to the class. She asks John what Leah means by "the 2 goes first and the 9 goes last" and asks London and Jacey, "What is that? What is that 2 really?" Students respond that the 2 is in the tens place and means 20, but Ms. Tyus does not stop there. In addition, she asks the class if there's a way to rewrite the equation to make that explicit. "What should we do," she asks. Laila responds, "60 minus 40 equals 20."

This is an important moment in the class discussion. On the one hand, Leah's base ten drawing is similar to what most students in the class created, with 4 tens crossed out to represent the 40 markers that were given away. However, Leah's equations, $6 - 4 = 2$ and $9 - 0 = 9$, looked much different from what Ms. Tyus had seen on other students' work. And while Leah seems clear on what the 2 means and that it is "a ten," Ms. Tyus understood that this was an opportunity to engage the class in clarifying how to represent 2 tens in an equation so that *anyone* looking at the equation would understand its meaning. Interestingly, while not shown on the video, after this discussion, DuJuan suggests that Leah add one more equation to her solution and together the class decides to include $20 + 9 = 29$. This appears to further emphasize the idea that students recognize the value of using equations to represent the recomposition of numbers.

After Leah's presentation, Ms. Tyus calls on the final presenter, Elsie, to share her strategy of rounding and compensating. In Analyzing the Work of Teaching 6.3, you will take a close look at how Ms. Tyus attempts to connect Elsie's solution to Goal 3 of her lesson.

Analyzing the Work of Teaching 6.3

Connecting Student Work to the Goals of the Lesson—Part Three

Video Clip 6.3

As you watch Video Clip 6.3, consider the discussion of Elsie's strategy for solving the Ms. Tyus's Markers task and the questions Ms. Tyus asks the class about this approach.

- What questions does Ms. Tyus ask to connect Elsie's presentation to Goal 3 of the lesson?
- How do students' responses address these goals?

Goal 3: Numbers can be rounded up or down to make a multiple of ten before subtracting. The amount rounded up or down must then be subtracted from or added to the difference to compensate for the amount added to or taken away initially.

 Videos may also be accessed at **resources.corwin.com/5practices-elementary**

Connecting Student Work to the Goals of the Lesson, Part Three—Analysis

In this video clip, Ms. Tyus begins by telling the class that Elsie "did something a little different" and then asks Elsie to describe the strategy. Elsie's explanation focuses on the idea that if Anna uses the equation $70 - 40 - 1$, she would get the same answer of 29. "That's why I think that's a good equation for Anna, just for a different way," Elsie says.

Ms. Tyus, however, wants to highlight for the class *why* this approach works. She asks, "Is anybody wondering where she got 70 from?" A number of students respond, "Yes!"

To help the class visualize the strategy, Ms. Tyus asks Elsie to demonstrate the process on the hundreds chart. Leah then explains what Elsie did: "She's at 70 and then she hopped to 30 then she went back to 29." While Ms. Tyus's goal is to focus on the rounding up 1 to 70 and then compensating by subtracting 1 at the end, she first asks about the 4 hops Elsie makes from 70 to 30. She asks the class, "Why would she even hop four times?" In doing so Ms. Tyus encourages students to make the connection between Elsie's strategy and the problem context—that 69 is the number of markers Ms. Tyus started with and 40 is the number that she gave away. Particularly because the number 70 does not appear in the problem at all, Ms. Tyus may have wanted to clarify that the number 40 is directly connected to the task.

Ms. Tyus then returns to her main focus and asks, "But why would she go back 1?" Leah responds that 70 is one more than 69, and Audrey adds that's why "when she got [to] the 30 . . . she went back one." Despite Leah and Audrey's comments, it seems likely that at this point students do not fully grasp Elsie's strategy. Nevertheless, when the class moved on to the second problem in the Ms. Tyus's Markers task (see Figure 2.4 for the full task), several students in addition to Elsie tried to use this approach, including Nancy, Rylee, and Audrey, whose work is shown in Figure 6.2.

Figure 6.2 • Audrey's work showing the use of the rounding and compensating strategy

> 2. Ms. Tyus has 79 neon markers. She gives 30 neon markers to her friend. How many markers does she have left? Make a diagram and write an equation that shows how Anna can solve this problem.
>
> $$79 - 30 = 49 \qquad 80 - 30 - 1 = 49$$

Ms. Tyus later commented, "When we did the second problem, at least a few of them decided to try the rounding up to compensate. So that was good. I think that was successful since they wanted to do it on their own." Thus, while there is not evidence that most students understood the rounding and compensating strategy (one of her goals for the lesson), by introducing the strategy Ms. Tyus believed she had taken an important step in that direction. She continued: "Rounding and compensating is definitely something I want to go back to. With more practice, I believe all students or most students will be able to apply that strategy."

Connecting Different Solutions to Each Other

In addition to connecting students' solutions to the goals of the lesson, it is important to connect students' solutions to each other. Different strategies can open up new opportunities for problem solving and increase students' learning (Schukajlow & Krug, 2014). Doing so can also help build connections for students among mathematics ideas rather than adding to a sense of mathematics as a set of disconnected facts.

You might find it important to help students investigate how various solution methods lead to the same answer, and you may help students examine whether some methods are more efficient than others. This can provide students with valuable information should they be ready to use a more sophisticated strategy in the future (Murata & Fuson, 2006). Alternatively, you might find yourself in a situation where it is necessary to investigate why different approaches lead to incorrect versus correct answers and how to explain those differences.

Another connection you might explore with students is the relationship between more concrete and more abstract solutions. Both types of solutions play an important role in the elementary mathematics classroom. Working with manipulatives and directly modeling situations can support the development of conceptual understanding (Felton-Koestler, 2016). In addition, the ability to move beyond a specific case to a more generalized case has been found to be beneficial for elementary students (Blanton, Brizuela, Gardiner, Sawrey, & Newman-Owens, 2015). Recall our discussion in Chapter 2 of the modified version of the Baking Cookies task and the Tables and Chairs Investigation task. Both tasks asked students to explore several cases and to look for a pattern that could ultimately be used to generalize for any case. Identifying opportunities such as these for students to consider a wider set of problems and look for patterns can help students begin to think algebraically.

It can also be important for students to investigate variations in the representations that are used. At the elementary grades in particular, students should have ongoing opportunities to move among different representations, including drawings, diagrams, words, and symbols (Marshall, Superfine, & Canty, 2010) (refer back to Figure 3.11 for a discussion of different ways to represent a mathematical idea). The idea is that students develop *representational fluency*, that they understand how key features in one representation appear in another representation (Suh, Johnston, Jamieson, & Mills, 2008).

In Analyzing the Work of Teaching 6.4, you will return to the presentations in Ms. Tyus's classroom. At this point the class hears from DuJuan, the third presenter, as he shares how he solved the Ms. Tyus's Markers task.

 # Analyzing the Work of Teaching 6.4

Connecting Different Solutions to Each Other

Video Clip 6.4

As you watch Video Clip 6.4, consider DuJuan's explanation of how he used the hundreds chart to solve the Ms. Tyus's Markers task and listen to Ms. Tyus's comments and questions to the class. The work that DuJuan produced is shown below.

- What connections does Ms. Tyus encourage students to make between DuJuan's solution and other approaches students have taken?

- How do students respond?

 Videos may also be accessed at
resources.corwin.com/5practices-elementary

Connecting Different Solutions to Each Other—Analysis

As with the other presenters, Ms. Tyus first asks DuJuan to share his thinking. Using a large hundreds chart on the board, DuJuan re-creates his solution for the class, noting that he started by identifying 69 and then made 4 vertical hops to represent subtraction of 40. "I x'd 69 and hopped 40 times and I get 29," he says. Ms. Tyus first aims to clarify DuJuan's approach with the class. "What did he do?" she asks. Rylee offers that 69 comes from the number of markers and Leah adds that 40 is the number of markers that were given away.

Next Ms. Tyus asks the class to compare DuJuan's strategy with how Jocelyn solved the problem. She asks, "How do base ten blocks and the hundreds chart—how are they the same?" To give students time to consider this, she tells students to "turn and talk to a partner." After they talked with partners for a few minutes, Ms. Tyus brings the class together to discuss the connection between the strategies. Jacey suggests that "they both subtracted 40." Ms. Tyus asks for more information: "What do you mean? Show me." In particular, the students explain that when DuJuan "was hopping four times," he was subtracting the 40 markers that were given away. Although the students do not explicitly discuss the way in which Jocelyn subtracted 40, it may have been that this was implicitly understood, from her explanation that she "x'd out 4 tens."

Interestingly, one of Ms. Tyus's goals for the lesson (Goal 4) was for students to recognize that multiple representations could be used to solve problems and that these multiple representations could be connected to each other. Thus, in asking students to compare DuJuan and Jocelyn's approaches as she did here, Ms. Tyus was attending to both her lesson goal and the important work of connecting students' solutions to each other.

Tara Tyus's Attention to Key Questions: Connecting

In facilitating the class discussion of the Ms. Tyus's Markers task, Ms. Tyus encouraged students to draw connections between the work that was being discussed and the goals that she had established for the lesson. While she had chosen specific student solutions because they related to the lesson goals, during the discussion, Ms. Tyus asked a variety of questions in order to ensure that those connections were visible for students.

Ms. Tyus also made an effort to highlight for the class the ways that different solutions were related and in particular that it was important to connect features of the problem across different representations. Connecting students' solutions to the goals of the lesson and to each other is critical in order to fully realize the benefits of the five practices. Despite its importance, connecting is not without difficulty. In fact, many teachers tell us this is the most challenging of the practices to accomplish. We now take a look at some specific challenges teachers face as they work to connect students' solutions.

Part Two: Challenges Teachers Face: Connecting Student Responses

The whole group discussion that takes place around the work students share is an opportunity for students to continue to solidify their learning. It is during the discussion that you need to ensure that the key mathematical ideas that you have targeted during the lesson are made public and accessible to the students in your class. The key to a successful discussion is building on the ideas put forth by students without telling students what it is you want them to know. This is not easy. The pressures of time and accountability weigh heavily on teachers, and the temptation to summarize the lesson for students is strong. In this section, we focus on four specific challenges associated with this practice, shown in Figure 6.3, that we have identified from our work with teachers.

Figure 6.3 • Challenges associated with the practice of connecting

CHALLENGE	DESCRIPTION
Keeping the entire class engaged and accountable during individual presentations	Often, the sharing of solutions turns into a *show and tell* or a dialogue between the teacher and the presenter. The rest of the class needs to be held accountable for understanding and making sense of the solutions that are presented.
Ensuring key mathematical ideas are made public and remain the focus	It is possible to have students share and discuss a lot of interesting solutions and never get to the point of the lesson. It is critical that the key mathematical ideas that are being targeted in the lesson are explicitly discussed.
Making sure that you do not take over the discussion and do the explaining	As students are presenting their solutions, the teacher needs to ask questions that engage the presenters and the rest of the class in explaining and making sense of the solutions. There is a temptation for the teacher to take over and tell the students what they need to know. When this happens, opportunities for learning are diminished. Remember whoever is doing the talking is doing the thinking!
Running out of time	Teachers may not have enough time to conduct the whole class discussion the way they had planned it. In such cases it is important to come up with a *Plan B* that provides some closure to the lesson but does not turn into telling.

Keeping the Entire Class Engaged and Accountable During Individual Presentations

It is easy for the student presentations that take place at the end of a lesson to turn into a series of show and tells, where each presenter explains what he or she did and the rest of the class is silent. Having some students sit passively, while other students explain, however, is not sufficient to ensure learning. The teacher needs to make certain that the entire class is engaged in and accountable for what is being presented. According to Michaels, O'Conner, Hall, and Resnick (2013),

> When classroom talk is accountable to the learning community, students listen to one another, not just obediently keeping quiet until it is their turn to take the floor, but attending carefully so that they

can use and build on one another's ideas. Students and teachers paraphrase and expand upon one another's contributions. If speakers aren't sure they understood what someone else said, they make an effort to clarify. They disagree respectfully, challenging a claim, not the person who made it. Students move the argument forward, sometimes with the teacher's help, sometimes on their own. (pp. 2–3)

So what exactly can you do to hold students accountable? In Figure 6.4, we have identified a set of moves that teachers can make to hold students accountable for attending to the discussion.

Figure 6.4 • Talk moves intended to hold students accountable for participation in a discussion

TEACHER MOVES	PURPOSE	EXAMPLES	SOURCE
Adding on: Prompting students for further participation	To invite additional contributions to the discussion in order to engage more students or to gain a deeper understanding of an idea	• Would someone like to add on to what she just said? • Can you say more about how you figured that out?	Chapin, O'Connor, & Anderson (2009, pp. 13–16)
Reasoning: Asking students to compare their own reasoning to someone else's reasoning	To allow students to engage with and make sense of their peer's ways of thinking that may be different from their own	• Do you agree or disagree? Why? • How is what he said the same as or different from how you thought about it?	
Repeating: Having a student repeat what another student has said in her own words	To give students another version of a contribution and to ensure that students are engaged in listening to their peers	• Can someone repeat what he just said in their own words?	
Revoicing: Repeating what a student has said and then checking with the student to make sure you have accurately captured their idea	To clarify what a student has said or to amplify an important idea	• So, you are saying . . . • So, here is what I heard you say . . .	
Waiting: Giving students time to think about the question that has been posed before asking for a response	To ensure that all students have an opportunity to think about the question posed and to provide a student who has been called on time to gather his or her thoughts	• Take a minute to think about this. • I am going to wait until I see more hands. • Take your time . . . we will wait.	

TEACHER MOVES	PURPOSE	EXAMPLES	SOURCE
Revise: Allowing students to revise their initial thinking based on new insights	To make it clear to students that changing one's mind based on new information is how learning occurs and that this is valued	• Would anyone like to revise his or her thinking? • Has anyone's thinking changed? Why?	Kazemi & Hintz (2014, p. 21)
Turn and talk: Allowing time for students to discuss an idea that has been presented with a partner or small group	To give students time to think about a question that has been posed rather than be expected to answer immediately and to clarify and share ideas with a small number of peers before doing so publically	• Take two minutes and turn and talk to your table group about . . .	
Challenging: Redirecting a question raised back to students or using students' contributions for further investigation	To turn the responsibility for reasoning and sense-making back to students and develop shared understandings in the classroom	• That's a good question. What do you think about what she just said?	Michaels, O'Conner, Hall, & Resnick (2013, p. 22)
Marking: Noting a valuable contribution that was made to the discussion	To highlight a contribution that is directly relevant to what the teacher is trying to accomplish in the lesson	• Did everyone hear what she just said? She . . . • That's an important point.	
Recapping: Summarizing key points made in the discussion by several students	To make public in a concise and coherent way what can be concluded at a particular point	• So in looking across the presentations, here is what I am hearing . . . • Here is what we have discovered . . .	

(Continued)

Figure 6.4 • (Continued)

TEACHER MOVES	PURPOSE	EXAMPLES	SOURCE
Inviting: Asking a student to contribute in the discussion	To make diverse points of view available for public discussion	• _____, would you share what you and your group came up with? • _____, you have a puzzled look on your face. What are you thinking? • _____, your strategy was not the same as this one. What did you do differently?	Herbel-Eisenmann, Cirillo, Steele, Otten, & Johnson (2017, pp. liv–lvii)
Probing: Following up on what an individual student has explained or produced	To make a student's thinking process more transparent to others, to elicit additional justification for why he took a particular action	• Can you explain how you got . . . ? • How do you know that? • Why does that work?	

[See Appendix D for a summary of each of the identified sources. Although we have associated particular authors with specific moves, you will find that many of the moves are addressed in each of the resources.]

In Analyzing the Work of Teaching 6.5, you will analyze the discussion that took place in Ms. Stastny's class as students tried to determine which fractions and related diagrams fulfilled the conditions stated in the problem.

Analyzing the Work of Teaching 6.5

Holding Students Accountable

Video Clip 6.5

In Video Clip 6.5, students in Ms. Stastny's class are discussing the three diagrams shown below and trying to determine which ones fit the conditions stated in the problem and why. Many students had the fractions $\frac{1}{2}$ and $\frac{2}{4}$ and the related diagrams to show Tanesha and David's portions, respectively.

As you watch the video clip, consider the following questions:

1. What does Ms. Stastny do to help her students engage in the discussion of the three representations? What talk moves (see Figure 6.4) does she use?

2. What evidence is there that students **are** making sense of the presented ideas?

 Videos may also be accessed at
resources.corwin.com/5practices-elementary

Holding Students Accountable—Analysis

Ms. Stastny wanted students to see that while $\frac{1}{2}$ and $\frac{2}{4}$ were equivalent, they did not meet the conditions stated in the problem—that Tanesha ate two pieces while David ate four pieces and they both ate the same amount. She wanted students to see instead that $\frac{2}{4}$ and $\frac{4}{8}$ were equivalent to each other and gave Tanesha and David both the correct number of pieces and the same amount of lasagna. In addition, she wanted students to see that equivalence could be determined by the fact that the fraction $\frac{2}{4}$ was doubled to get $\frac{4}{8}$ and that the areas represented by the two fractions were the same.

While Ms. Stastny could have selected a student to present the incorrect solution—that $\frac{1}{2}$ and $\frac{2}{4}$ represented the portions of lasagna that Tanesha and David ate, respectively—she decided not to do so and instead presented it herself. As we said in Chapter 5, she made this decision because students had actually changed their answer during their small group discussions and had "either erased it or crossed it out and so it wasn't very legible on their paper." We would argue that not attributing ownership of this solution to an individual held all students accountable for making sense of the three models. No one took the floor to explain what they did and why, so the burden of explaining fell to the entire class. The first question posed by Ms. Stastny, "So $\frac{1}{2}$ and $\frac{2}{4}$. Who can talk about this one for me?" was an open invitation to the entire class to make sense of the models.

Throughout the discussion, Ms. Stastny used several different talk moves to engage students and hold them accountable for making sense of the ideas being discussed. She used repeating, adding on, inviting, and turn and talk to promote broad participation in the discussion and to ensure that important ideas were made public and elaborated on by different students. Over the course of the discussion, ten different students (of the 20 in the class) made contributions to the whole group discussion. The following transcript segment (see Video Clip 6.5, 01:57:00–04:20:00) highlights specific talk moves that occurred during a portion of the discussion shown in the video clip.

1	Olivia:	Okay, so she [Tanesha] ate her two pieces. If I had this one [referring to $\frac{2}{4}$ and
2		the related model], how could I have David's? What would his lasagna look
3		like? Vinny?
4	Vinny:	Four-eighths.
5	Olivia:	Four-eighths? Why do you say four-eighths? **(probing)**
6	Vinny:	Because I disagree with one-half because it said he had four.
7	Olivia:	So he had four pieces, okay, so you're saying it should be four-eighths? Can
8		somebody say more about that? Who can add on to that—agree, disagree,
9		whatever? Demetrius? **(adding on, revoicing, reasoning)**
10	Demetrius:	On the two-fourths one if you were going to try to make it David's, you
11		would have to add two more and then it would be four-fourths.
12	Olivia:	So just looking at these two models [for $\frac{2}{4}$ and $\frac{4}{8}$]. Talking about these
13		two models, does this work? For Tanesha and David? Amy?
14	Amy:	It does.
15	Olivia:	Okay, tell me more. **(probing)**
16	Amy:	Because those add two actual lines to two-fourths and it's the same as
17		four-eighths.
18	Olivia:	Can you come point to what you just said? **(probing)**
19		So you just said, I added two more lines. Will you go point to the lines that
20		were added?
21	Amy:	This one and this one.
22	Olivia:	Okay, so Amy just told us that these two lines were added, so what did I just
23		do? Anasimon? **(adding on)**
24	Anasimon:	You just kept on dividing them up.
25	Olivia:	Okay, so I divided the pieces into smaller pieces? Can anybody say more on
26		that? Sara? **(revoicing, adding on)**
27	Sara:	You splitted [sic] them so it could be equal.
28	Olivia:	I did split them so that equal amounts were shaded. Is that what you're
29		saying? **(revoicing)**
30	Sara:	Mm-hmm. [affirmative]
31	Olivia:	Okay, so equal amounts are shaded. I have two pieces and four pieces. Okay.
32		Can anybody add on to that? Demetrius? **(adding on)**
33	Demetrius:	So when you added on two lines in the middle, it just made the
34		denominator bigger.
35	Olivia:	Okay, so it made my denominator bigger. Did it make my pieces bigger or
36		smaller? **(revoicing)**
37	Demetrius:	Smaller.
38	Olivia:	Okay.
39	Demetrius:	Since you added that many lines, so it would get smaller.
40	Olivia:	Okay, so if I had more lines, I have my smaller pieces so I divided it or I cut
41		each piece in half, okay? How are these two equivalent? I want y'all to turn
42		and talk with your group real quick. How are these two equivalent? **(turn and**
43		**talk and reasoning)**
44	Olivia:	Alright, who can tell me? What did your group decide? How are these two
45		fractions equivalent? Abdulla. **(inviting and reasoning)**
46	Abdulla:	So the two-fourths, if you just put two lines in each of two squares, it's going
		to be the same thing as four-eighths. It's like double.

In particular, Ms. Stastny used "adding on" throughout the discussion to encourage students to participate. By asking some variant of "Who can say more?" she continued to invite students to contribute their ideas to the discussion . . . and they did. All of her requests for students to "say more" resulted in students doing just that. Clearly Ms. Stastny had established a culture where there was an expectation for students to listen to what their peers were saying and to contribute their own thinking to the ongoing discussion.

In the transcript (and in the entire video clip) you will also note that Ms. Stastny does a lot of revoicing. Revoicing allows her to amplify an important idea. By repeating something a student has said, the other students have an opportunity to hear it again. Revoicing also gives the teacher a chance to add an important detail to a student's explanation. In line 27, Sara says, "You splitted [sic] them so it could be equal." Ms. Stastny revoices Sara's explanation as "I did split them so that equal amounts were shaded. Is that what you're saying?" (line 28). By adding the fact that the equal amounts were shaded, she brings students back to the diagram and the fact that equal areas indicated equivalence. Finally, she checks in with Sara to make sure she has accurately captured her idea.

Now that we have examined what the teacher did (as shown in Video Clip 6.5), we need to consider whether the teacher's actions served the purpose for which they were intended. That is, did students come to understand that $\frac{2}{4}$ and $\frac{4}{8}$ was a valid solution to the task because they were equivalent, representing the same amount of lasagna, and they gave Tanesha and David the specified number of pieces? We would argue that the discussion brought to light several key ideas:

1. $\frac{1}{2}$ and $\frac{2}{4}$ are equivalent. Anasimon states, "If you make the two-fourth[s] into one-half, it's going to be the same. You just broke [it] up into more pieces." Lap goes on to say, "I think it's equal because if you double one-half, it equals two-fourths."

2. Tanesha's portion of the lasagna could be represented by the model of $\frac{2}{4}$. Through the contributions of Selvia, Amy, and Sara, it was established that Tanesha could have eaten two of the four pieces and that this was $\frac{1}{2}$ of the lasagna, which was $\frac{2}{4}$.

3. David's portion of the lasagna could be represented by the model of $\frac{4}{8}$. Vinny first identifies $\frac{4}{8}$ as David's portion because David ate four pieces. After a bit of confusion as others tried to elaborate on Vinny's statement, Amy explains that $\frac{2}{4}$ is equal to $\frac{4}{8}$: "Because those add two actual lines to two-fourths and it's the same as four-eighths."

4. $\frac{2}{4}$ and $\frac{4}{8}$ are equivalent but the size of the pieces in $\frac{4}{8}$ are smaller than the size of the pieces in $\frac{2}{4}$. Several students weigh in on this idea (Anasimon, Sara, Demetrius, Abdulla, and Edgardo), establishing that when you double the fraction $\frac{2}{4}$ to get $\frac{4}{8}$, you double the number of pieces, the denominator in $\frac{4}{8}$ is bigger but the pieces are smaller, and you split the pieces in $\frac{2}{4}$ to get $\frac{4}{8}$.

5. The areas shaded in the models of $\frac{2}{4}$ and $\frac{4}{8}$ are equal. Lap explains, "Because two-fourths, there's just two pieces shaded, but on four-eighths there is four pieces shaded but because they just put two lines to make it eight parts." Demetrius goes on to explain, "If you add these two lines, you, the size would be different because these squares are smaller. These four squares are smaller than these two squares. But if you take these lines away, they would be the same."

While it is impossible to say whether each of the 20 students in the class came away with the targeted understanding, it is clear that ideas were made public and articulated by several students over the course of the discussion. While not all of the students in the class participated in the discussion, they all had access to the ideas being discussed. Hatano and Inagaki (1991) argue that silent participants can learn from discussions:

> Silent members may be actively participating. They can learn much by observing the ongoing discussion or debate carefully. This is often characterized as a vicarious process, but it is more than that. In a sense, these students are all trying to find an agent, someone who really speaks for them. A good agent or vocal participant can articulate what a silent member has been trying without success to say. (p. 346)

In looking at the discussion that took place in Ms. Stastny's class, we see the teacher using several different moves to actively engage students in making sense of the three models and we hear students who were coming to understand key ideas of equivalence. The critical point here is that the entire class is being held accountable for expressing their ideas clearly and for listening closely to and thinking deeply about the mathematics being discussed.

Ensuring That Key Mathematical Ideas Are Made Public and Remain the Focus

Productive discussions are ones that clearly and explicitly target the mathematical ideas that you want students to learn as a result of engaging in the lesson. Having selected students to present their solutions—even solutions of the highest quality—is not sufficient to ensure that students will learn what is intended. Students need assistance in drawing connections among methods and in tying specific solutions to key mathematical concepts (Smith & Stein, 2018).

Consider, for example, a teacher who is teaching a lesson featuring the Treat Bags task discussed in Chapter 3 and shown again in Figure 6.5. As a result of engaging in the lesson, she wants her fifth graders to understand that

1. In division $(a \div b)$ you are trying to find how many iterations of b are contained in a; and

2. Division can be represented in different ways and the different representations can be connected.

Figure 6.5 • Treat Bags task

Treat Bags

Julia's mother made 153 cookies for her birthday party. Julia's job is to put them into treat bags for each of her 12 friends who are coming to her party. How many cookies will be in each bag if all her friends get the same number of cookies? How many cookies will be left over?

---

 online resources   Download the Task from
resources.corwin.com/5practices-elementary

Imagine that during the lesson students produced the solutions shown in Figure 3.13. Although all the solutions shown are correct, getting the correct answer is not equivalent to understanding the targeted ideas. In fact, no combination of these solutions is going to make the lesson goals transparent on their own. For example, although students may be able to draw or build a base ten model that depicts the situation, this does not imply that they understand why it is a division problem or that they could connect their base ten model to an area model or to repeated multiplication. By asking questions about the base ten drawing (e.g., Why did you draw 12 treat bags? How did you decide how much went in each bag? What did the number in each bag tell you? How is your model the same as or different from the area?), students can reflect on their work and make connections that may have not been clear to them. The point is that student solutions do not make the mathematics to be learned transparent. You need to identify the solutions that have the potential to address the lesson goals, and then you must ask specific questions of students that will help them make connections to the concepts you have targeted.

TEACHING TAKEAWAY

Correct solutions alone are not enough. Teachers must ask questions in order to help students make connections to the targeted mathematical ideas.

What occurred in Mr. Strong's class provides a context for exploring this idea further. As we first discussed in Chapter 3, as a result of engaging in the Mr. Strong's Hike task, Mr. Strong wanted his students to understand that

1. To divide a whole number by a fraction (e.g., $4 \div \frac{1}{3}$) means to determine how many iterations of the fraction ($\frac{1}{3}$) fit inside the whole number (4).

2. The quotient of a whole number divided by a fraction can be found by multiplying (e.g., $4 \div \frac{1}{3} = 4 \times 3$) because you are determining how many iterations of the fraction there are in 1 unit of the dividend and then multiplying the number of iterations in 1 unit by the total number of units in the dividend (e.g., there are three $\frac{1}{3}$s in 1 mile so the number of $\frac{1}{3}$s in 4 miles is 4×3).

3. When dividing by a number less than 1, the quotient will be greater than the dividend because you are making groups of an amount less than 1.

In Analyzing the Work of Teaching 6.6, you will analyze a portion of the discussion that took place at the end of class and determine which ideas were made public and how.

Analyzing the Work of Teaching 6.6

Making Key Ideas Public

Video Clip 6.6

In Video Clip 6.6, three different ideas are discussed.

- First, Ester explains why the equation $\frac{1}{3} \div 4 = \frac{1}{12}$ is not correct and this leads into a discussion regarding whether the order of the numbers ($\frac{1}{3} \div 12$ versus $12 \div \frac{1}{3}$) matters.

CONTINUED

CONTINUED FROM PREVIOUS PAGE

- Three students in the class—Markel, Joaquin, and Zane—describe what happens to the quotient when you multiply by a fraction.

- Rutland and Joaquin explain their generalization—the number of total drinks you take is the number of miles hiked times the number of times you stop each mile.

As you watch the clip, consider the following questions:

1. What mathematical ideas are being targeted in each of these presentations?

2. What does Mr. Strong do to highlight the mathematics he wants students to learn?

 Videos may also be accessed at resources.corwin.com/5practices-elementary

Making Key Ideas Public—Analysis

As we discussed in Chapter 5, Mr. Strong decided to begin the discussion with the number lines produced by Group 1 (Zane, Henry, Kamaria, and Aidyn) and Group 3 (Connie, Jackson, Zalijah, and Jahnisa) as shown in Figure 5.6. The groups had labeled their segments of one-third differently and Mr. Strong thought this was an important point to discuss. This discussion of these two number lines made salient that 4 miles was divided into segments of $\frac{1}{3}$ and that the quotient (12) was the number of $\frac{1}{3}$s in 4 miles. Students explained that since there were 3 one-thirds (drinks) in 1 mile, you need to multiply 3 by 4 to determine the number of one-thirds (or drinks) in 4 miles. This initial discussion addressed Goals 1 and 2, both of which would be explored in the subsequent presentations.

Following the discussion of the number lines, Mr. Strong asks Ester to explain the equation, which had not been previously discussed. Ester began by explaining that her group had initially written $\frac{1}{3} \div 4$ before realizing that this not only did not give the correct solution but, more importantly, did not represent what was happening in the problem. As Ester explains, "We're not dividing one-third 'cause this shows that this is the dividend. But it's not what we're dividing. We're actually dividing the miles, so we change it up to this because four is what we're dividing." Connie then repeats what Ester said "The bottom one was wrong because in the bottom one, she's saying that they're dividing one-third into four but in the actual problem, we're dividing four into thirds." The class agrees that order matters, and Ester concludes, "When we divided the miles, we knew that every one-third mile, you stop to take a drink and that happens three times in each mile." Ester's presentation resurfaced the meaning of division and what they were trying to find when they divided 4 by $\frac{1}{3}$.

Mr. Strong next invites Markel, Joaquin, and Zane to describe what happens to the quotient when you multiply by a fraction. Markel begins by stating that "it gets bigger" and later adds "than the dividend started as." Joaquin adds, "If you divide by your fraction, your quotient gets bigger. If you divide by a whole number, then it gets smaller because it's the other way around in multiplication." Zane sums things up: "So, when you're dividing the four into thirds, you're gonna have a lot more pieces because they're smaller than the whole mile. But if you're gonna divide it by a whole mile, there are gonna be less pieces 'cause they're a lot larger." The contributions of the three members of the group made salient Goal 3—when dividing by a number less than 1, the quotient will be greater than the dividend because you are making groups of an amount less than 1.

Finally, Mr. Strong invites Rutland and Joaquin to discuss the generalization they had made. Rutland begins, "You can figure out how many times he stops each mile by multiplying the number of miles by how many times he stops each mile. So, it doesn't matter what number of miles or how many times he stops." Rutland's explanation is not quite right—instead of saying it is the number of stops for each mile (shaded above), he actually meant *for any number of miles*. Joaquin jumps in with an example: "You have 256 miles and then 7 is your fraction, then you just multiply the number of miles by the fraction." Joaquin's example does not clear things up completely, since he refers to 7 as a fraction when in fact he means $\frac{1}{7}$, where 7 tells you how many stops you make each mile. This eventually gets cleared up through Mr. Strong's questioning. The generalization provided another opportunity to explore Goal 2—the quotient of a whole number divided by a fraction can be found by multiplying because you are determining how many iterations of the fraction there are in 1 unit of the dividend, which means you need to multiply the number of iterations in 1 unit by the total number of units in the dividend.

What did Mr. Strong do to highlight the mathematics to be learned? First and foremost, Mr. Strong carefully selected students to present the ideas that were at the heart of the lesson. This was more than just having students explain the posters they had made. Given the similarities across posters in terms of the representations used, this could have resulted in considerable repetition. Instead, Mr. Strong identified specific things for each of the presenters to talk about in order to ensure that the key ideas would be made public.

While the student presenters explained what they had determined, Mr. Strong asked questions or invited other students to contribute in order to help bring clarity to their explanations. Since the three presentations featured in the video occurred within the last seven minutes of class, each was a bit rushed. Given more time, Mr. Strong might have invited more students to weigh in on the ideas being discussed in order to ensure that students had a firm grasp of the ideas. But the discussion did surface the key ideas he was targeting, thus laying the groundwork for future lessons where the ideas could be explored in more detail.

The key takeaway from the discussion in Mr. Strong's class is that he did not leave it to chance that the ideas he wanted students to grapple with would surface or that hearing only one explanation of an idea would be sufficient to ensure that students were making sense of it. By carefully selecting the work that would be presented, he was able to draw students' attention to specific aspects of the work.

Making Sure That You Do Not Take Over the Discussion and Do the Explaining

As a teacher, you know what it is you want students to learn from a lesson, and you may at times feel that the most expedient way to communicate this to students is to simply tell them what you want them to know. It is not clear, however, what students learn and retain when they simply listen to the teacher explain. Steven Reinhart (2000), an experienced teacher, said it best:

> *When I was in front of the class demonstrating and explaining, I was learning a great deal, but many of my students were not! Eventually, I concluded that if my students were to ever really learn mathematics, they would have to do the explaining, and I, the listening. My definition of a good teacher has since changed from "one who explains things so well that students understand" to "one who gets students to explain things so well that they can be understood."* (p. 478)

 PAUSE AND CONSIDER

Think of a time when you found yourself doing all the explaining at the end of a lesson. What do you think students learned when this occurred? How do you know? What might you have done differently that would have provided more insight into what students understood about the ideas you were targeting?

Let us return to the example from Ms. Stastny's class that we explored in Analyzing the Work of Teaching 6.5. Instead of asking students to discuss the three models representing $\frac{1}{2}$, $\frac{2}{4}$, and $\frac{4}{8}$, she could have just started the discussion by pointing out the errors that students made and explaining why they were incorrect. While more efficient, it would have provided her with no idea what students were thinking or how (or if) they were making sense of the situation. Through her use of talk moves, she learned what students understood, identified what they were struggling with, and gave all students the opportunity to make sense of the situation and key ideas related to equivalence.

In the case of Mr. Strong, he could have just stopped after the two groups had presented their number lines and summed up the key ideas he wanted to learn. This would have been much faster and less *messy* than the discussion that took place.

Both Ms. Stastny and Mr. Strong view classroom discussions as critical to student learning and resisted the urge to step in and take over the discussion. Reinhart (2000) echoes this sentiment:

> Good discussions take time; at first, I was uncomfortable in taking so much time to discuss a single question or problem. The urge to simply tell my students and move on for the sake of expedience was considerable. Eventually, I began to see the value in what I now refer to as a "less is more" philosophy. I now believe that all students learn more when I pose a high-quality problem and give them the necessary time to investigate, process their thoughts, and reflect on and defend their findings. (p. 480)

Running Out of Time

As Reinhart states in the quote above, good discussions take time. So can you facilitate a good discussion when you may only have 45 minutes for the entire class? Here are a few suggestions that might help. First, you can extend the lesson over two days. For example, you might plan to do a lesson featuring the Sheep and Ducks task (see Figure 5.9) as a two-day lesson. On day one, you could introduce the task and have students work in groups on the task. At the end of the first day, you could collect the work. You could then review the work prior to day two and determine which responses (see Figure 5.10) you wanted to have shared, who would share them, and in what order they would be presented. Then on day two, you could conduct the whole class discussion. This approach has several advantages. It gives you time to review the work and make thoughtful decisions regarding selecting and sequencing. It also gives you time to conduct the discussion without feeling rushed. This, however, is a solution that needs to be used judiciously since every lesson cannot take two days!

Another thing to consider is limiting the time students have to work on a task in groups. Some of the teachers with whom we have worked have set timers so that groups know exactly how much time they have and how much is remaining at any point. This will hold students accountable for moving along in their work and keep you aware of how much time has passed. You can always extend the time if students have not made sufficient progress.

It is also important to keep in mind that when monitoring student work, your goal is to help students make progress on the task, not to ensure that each and every student has a correct answer before beginning the discussion. Rather the goal is to make sure that students are positioned so that they can make sense of the discussion. As Cartier and her colleagues (Cartier, Smith, Stein, & Ross, 2013) noted:

> The teacher's goal when intervening in a small group is not to make sure that, by the end of the work session, all students have produced a complete and correct response. Rather it is to support students' fledgling efforts to make sense of the task before them and to make sure that students are working in a productive direction. Later in the lesson, students will have the opportunity to compare their work with what other students have produced and to participate in a class-wide discussion that clarifies the thinking behind and the features of a good explanation for whatever task on which they are working. (p. 88)

Ms. Stastny's class provides a good example of this. Not all students came to the whole class discussion with a model that accurately depicted the situation. When Ms. Stastny visited small groups, she challenged them to reflect on what they had done and to consider whether it made sense in terms of the task. We saw this in her interactions with Selvia, Anasimon, Vinny, and Johanna. Selvia and Anasimon had two different models. Anasimon's showed $\frac{2}{6}$ and $\frac{4}{12}$, while Selvia's showed $\frac{2}{6}$ and $\frac{4}{6}$. Ms. Stastny asked the group to examine the model showing $\frac{2}{6}$ and $\frac{4}{6}$ and determine whether it showed that Tanesha and David ate the same amount (see Analyzing the Work of Teaching 4.5).

TEACHING TAKEAWAY

All students do not have to have a correct answer or need to have completed the entire task in order to participate in and benefit from the whole class discussion.

Ms. Stastny did not check in with the group again prior to the whole class discussion. During the discussion, she asked Anasimon to present her model of $\frac{2}{6}$ and $\frac{4}{12}$. Selvia, who originally had $\frac{4}{6}$, explained why it should be $\frac{4}{12}$. She said, "I doubled 6 to get 12, and if you double the 2, that would get you to 4. And if you actually split the 6 into 6 more pieces, you would get the 12." This shows that between the time Ms. Stastny left the group and the time Anasimon presented her model, Selvia had come to understand what she had not previously understood.

Despite your best efforts, you may still run out of time. This is what happened to Mr. Strong. In Analyzing the Work of Teaching 6.6, we indicated that Mr. Strong did not have enough time left in class to thoroughly discuss the ideas presented by Ester (why the equation is $4 \div \frac{1}{3}$, not $\frac{1}{3} \div 4$), Markel, Joaquin, and Zane (what happens to the quotient when the divisor is a fraction), and Rutland and Joaquin (how you can generalize to find the number of drinks given the number of miles and the distance between stops).

So what should Mr. Strong do as a follow-up to this lesson? Since students all seemed to be able to write the equations $4 \div \frac{1}{3}$ and 4×3, he might want to focus explicitly on why the division equation becomes a multiplication equation. Toward this end, he might want to use a problem such as the one shown in Figure 6.6.

Figure 6.6 • An example of a problem that could be used by Mr. Strong

Jesse has 5 pizzas. He claims that each of his friends will eat $\frac{1}{4}$ of a pizza. How many friends will get pizza?

1. Draw a diagram and explain how many friends can be invited if each will receive $\frac{1}{4}$ of a pizza.

2. If Jesse has 5 pizzas and decides to give each friend $\frac{1}{8}$ of a pizza, how many friends can he invite for a $\frac{1}{8}$ serving of pizza each?

3. If Jesse has 5 pizzas and decides to give each friend $\frac{1}{2}$ of a pizza, how many friends can he invite for a $\frac{1}{2}$ serving of pizza each?

4. How can you figure out the number of times any unit fraction goes into a whole number?

 Download the example problem from
resources.corwin.com/5practices-elementary

This problem pushes students to generalize beyond the specific problem in the way that Rutland and Joaquin described. This would give the other students in the class the opportunity not just to solve problems but to grapple with the big ideas. At some point Mr. Strong might want to push for the most generalized version of the problem—finding the number of servings you could make given any number of pizzas when each friend gets the same fractional amount.

Another idea Mr. Strong might want to follow up on is to ask students to solve a series of tasks in which a fraction is divided by a whole number. They can consider how much would be in a serving if they had $\frac{1}{2}$ of a pizza and were going to share it among five friends. This would allow them to explore the difference between $5 \div \frac{1}{2}$ and $\frac{1}{2} \div 5$.

The key point here is that you cannot assume that just because the ideas were made public, everyone understands them. If students do not have sufficient time to make sense of the ideas themselves and provide some indication that they understand—either through their verbal contributions or their written work—they need the opportunity to revisit the ideas in another context.

Conclusion

The practices that we have discussed in the previous chapters—setting goals, selecting tasks, anticipating, monitoring, selecting, and sequencing—are intended to prepare you to orchestrate a productive discussion. The discussion is the culmination of all your work in carefully planning the lesson and in closely attending to what students do and say as they work on a task. It is in the discussion that connections are made and the mathematical ideas that you target in the lesson are made public.

The work of students, when purposefully and carefully selected and sequenced, becomes the basis for the classroom discussion. The discussions orchestrated by Tara Tyus, Olivia Stastny, and Andrew Strong illustrated this point. Each teacher positioned students as authors of mathematical ideas and allowed them to explain what they did and why. Through careful questioning the teachers were able to help students clarify their explanations and to engage the entire class in making sense of the presenter's work. In this way, all students were held accountable for making sense of the presenter's work and the mathematical ideas that were at the heart of the lesson.

As we noted, orchestrating a discussion can be challenging. Perhaps the biggest obstacle to overcome is yourself—resisting the temptation to tell students what you want them to know and take over the thinking. As noted in *Principles and Standards for School Mathematics* (NCTM, 2000) nearly two decades ago, "teachers must decide . . . how to support students without taking over the process of thinking for them and thus eliminating the challenge" (p. 19). The challenges we have identified highlight some of the pitfalls you may encounter as you engage students in whole class discussion. We hope that the ways in which Mr. Strong and Ms. Stastny handled these challenges will help you as you continue to orchestrate discussions in your own classroom.

In the next chapter, we address questions about why you should consider using the five practices model and how you can get started in making these practices a component of your instructional toolkit.

Connecting Student Responses—Summary

Video Clip 6.7

To hear and see more about connecting student responses, watch Video Clip 6.7.

 Videos may also be accessed at
resources.corwin.com/5practices-elementary

Linking the Five Practices to Your Own Instruction

CONNECTING

It is now time to reflect on the lesson you taught following Chapter 4, but this time through the lens of connecting student responses.

1. What connections were made between student responses and the lesson goals?

2. What connections were made between different student responses?

3. To what extent were the mathematical ideas that were targeted in the lesson made public?

4. What did you do to ensure that all students in the class were participating in and accountable for making sense of the ideas being presented?

5. Based on your reading of this chapter and a deeper understanding of the process of connecting, would you do anything differently if you were going to teach this lesson again?

6. What have you learned from this chapter that you will draw on in the next lesson you plan and teach?

“ What I found valuable about the five practices is that I choose a high-level task for my students and plan, plan, plan. The biggest part of doing the five practices for me is the planning, the anticipating, and figuring out what the student might do so I'm prepared to advance them in their learning. ”

—OLIVIA STASTNY, THIRD-GRADE TEACHER

CHAPTER 7

Looking Back and Looking Ahead

In Chapters 2 to 6, we explored each of the five practices for orchestrating productive mathematics discussions, identifying the components of each practice and the related challenges. The lessons taught by Olivia Stastny, Andrew Strong, and Tara Tyus brought the five practices to life and provided a rich context for analyzing teaching and learning in real urban classrooms.

At this point, you may be feeling overwhelmed. You may be starting to wonder if you can really do this and if it is really worth the effort. If so, you are not alone. What we are asking you to do takes a considerable amount of time to *get good at it*, and it may require rethinking current practices. The three Metro Nashville teachers had similar feelings. They offer the following advice:

> *It's not going to be perfect. Not every lesson is perfect. You might not get to everything. Let it flow, just definitely plan out your phases and what you want to do. Pre-planning is very important and the more you do it, the better you'll get at it. You'll make those connections and your students will love and enjoy mathematics.*
>
> —*Tara Tyus*

The more you do it, the more you try it and practice it, the more innate it becomes in your teaching. It's not the easiest thing to do, so you've got to practice it. If you have those steps in mind, those ideas, those approaches in mind and you practice them, they become the way you teach.

—Andrew Strong

Don't be afraid to try this way because it is different. Let your kids take control of their own learning and you just kind of step back and let them. The biggest advice is just to plan!

—Olivia Stastny

In the remainder of this chapter, we address three questions: Why should you consider using the five practices model? How can you get started in making these practices a component of your instructional toolkit? How often should you engage your students in discussions around high-level tasks? Answers to these questions may relieve some of your anxiety and provide a pathway for moving forward with the five practices.

Why Use the Five Practices Model

Discussions around high-level mathematical tasks, such as those discussed in Chapters 2 to 6, are the primary means through which students develop an understanding of mathematics. Research shows that learning outcomes are the greatest when students have consistent opportunities to engage with high-level tasks (Boaler & Staples, 2008; Stein & Lane, 1996; Stigler & Hiebert, 2004). High-level tasks, however, are the most difficult to implement in ways that maintain the demands of the task (Stein, Grover, & Henningsen, 1996). When the cognitive demands of a task are not maintained during a lesson, opportunities for students' thinking and problem solving are lost, and students are often left to apply a rule or procedure with limited effort. (For example, see "The Case of Mr. Stevenson and the Band Concert Task" in Huinker & Bill, 2017, or "The Case of Fran Gorman and Kevin Cooper" in Stein, Smith, Henningsen, & Silver, 2009.)

The five practices model is intended to help teachers maintain the cognitive demands of a high-level task during a lesson by focusing on thoughtful and thorough planning prior to the lesson. By limiting the number of decisions that you need to make during the lesson, you are better prepared to support students by asking questions rather than telling them what to do. As Smith and Stein (2018) note,

Simply put, the five practices can equip teachers in supporting students' work on challenging tasks without lowering the demands of the task. In particular, by anticipating what students are likely to do when solving the task (including not being able to get started)

and the questions that can be asked to assess and advance their understanding, the teacher is in a much better position to provide scaffolds that support students' engagement and learning without taking over the thinking for them. (p. 131)

Each of our three featured teachers was successful in maintaining the demands of the high-level task they selected, and we would argue, this was due in large measure to their use of the five practices. Each of the teachers had a clear goal for what the lesson should accomplish, selected a high-level task that was aligned with the goal, and anticipated what students would do and how to respond. As a result, the teachers were prepared to interact with students in ways that supported students' work on the tasks, without doing too much of the thinking for them, and kept them moving toward the goal. For example, when Mr. Strong interacted with Lucian, Jasper, Ester, and Markel as they worked on the Mr. Strong's Hike task (Analyzing the Work of Teaching 4.4), he could have accepted the students' answer (Mr. Strong stopped to drink 12 times because $3 \times 4 = 12$) and explained how multiplying by 3 was the same as dividing by $\frac{1}{3}$. Instead, he pressed students to explain why there was a fraction in the original problem but no fraction in their equation. He asked, "Where did the fraction go in here?" When Mr. Strong returned to the group later in the class (Analyzing the Work of Teaching 4.6), he found that they had made some progress and had now written an additional equation: $4 \div \frac{1}{3}$. He pressed them to connect multiplying by 3 and dividing by $\frac{1}{3}$. Mr. Strong asked, "If you're saying both of these [equations] will get me the same answer, where's the three in here [referring to $4 \div \frac{1}{3} = 12$]?"

While it may have been more expedient for Mr. Strong to simply explain to students the relationship he wanted to see (that 3 was the number of one-thirds in 1 mile), this would have taken the opportunity for thinking and learning away from the students. It is not clear that the teacher's explanation—an explanation over which they had no ownership—would have contributed to their understanding. Through his actions, Mr. Strong was able to maintain the demands of the task and maximize students' opportunity to learn.

In addition to promoting learning, discussions around high-level tasks can also promote access and equity. According to the National Council of Teachers of Mathematics (2014), providing access and equity requires teaching that "ensures that all students have opportunities to engage successfully in the mathematics classroom and learn challenging mathematics" (p. 68). Using high-level tasks that have multiple entry points, allow for the use of different representations, and can be solved in different ways is the first step in giving each and every student access to meaningful mathematics. According to Boaler and Staples (2008), "When there are many ways to be successful, many more students are successful" (p. 16).

....
TEACHING TAKEAWAY
Using the five practices model helps teachers enact high-level tasks without lowering the demands of the task.

Engaging students in discussions featuring their work on a high-level task is the next step in achieving access and equity. Discussions provide the opportunity to honor student thinking, position students as authors of mathematical ideas, and acknowledge contributions to understanding the task and its solution. Sorto and Bower (2017) describe the ways in which discourse can advance access and equity:

> Productive discourse provides opportunities for students to contribute and to understand, through discussion, mathematical concepts and strategies. Students also are offered access to the problem and its understanding while being supported by fellow students. As the teacher creates an environment of safe intellectual contributions, there is a sense of high expectations and accountability for everyone in the classroom. Students' participation and reasoning is always validated to the extent that it contributes to the approach to successfully solving the problem. (p. 68)

Take, for example, the discussion that took place in Ms. Tyus's class. By inviting Elsie to present her rounding and compensating solution (Analyzing the Work of Teaching 6.3)—a solution that no one else in the class had produced—she was honoring Elsie's thinking and positioning her as an author of important mathematical work. Through Elsie's discussion of her solution, all of the students in the class were offered access to a different way of conceptualizing the situation and solving the task. Students were held accountable for making sense of the solution. Ms. Tyus posed questions to the class (e.g., Who can say what she said? Is anybody wondering where she got 70 from? Why would she go back one?) and expected students to answer these questions.

TEACHING
TAKEAWAY

Using the five practices model helps teachers provide each and every student with access to high-quality mathematics.

The discussion in Ms. Tyus's class provided each and every student with access to challenging mathematics and with the opportunity to extend their understanding of the problem.

Discussions around high-level tasks can also support the development of students' identities as mathematical doers. Aguirre, Mayfield-Ingram, and Martin (2013) define *mathematical identities* as "the dispositions and deeply held beliefs that students develop about their ability to participate and perform effectively in mathematical contexts and to use mathematics in powerful ways across the contexts of their lives" (p. 14).

So how do you help students develop positive mathematical identities? Aguirre and colleagues (2013) identify a set of equity-based teaching practices that help build students' positive identities. At the heart of these practices is engaging students in high-cognitive-demand tasks that offer multiple entry points, supporting students in justifying their solutions, promoting persistence, and positioning students as sources of expertise.

Consider, for example, Ms. Tyus's decisions regarding who would present and in what order. She explains her decision to have Jocelyn go first:

I called on Jocelyn because I haven't called on her in a while and I really want there to be some equity in the classroom. So I decided to call her up so she could explain her math thinking. And she was able to have the base ten blocks and show an equation.

By having Jocelyn present the strategy that most students in the class had produced, Ms. Tyus gave Jocelyn an opportunity to demonstrate competence and gave the entire class access to the discussion.

In looking across all three classrooms, we see the teachers—Ms. Tyus, Ms. Stastny, and Mr. Strong—positioning students as sources of expertise. While not all students presented, several students in each class had the opportunity to share their solutions. In addition, many other students had the opportunity to have their voices heard during the discussion.

We would argue that the five practices lessons developed and enacted by Olivia Stastny, Andrew Strong, and Tara Tyus supported students' learning of meaningful mathematics, provided access and equity for each and every student, and in so doing, helped students develop identities as competent and capable of doing mathematics.

> **TEACHING TAKEAWAY**
> Using the five practices model helps teachers develop students' positive identities.

Getting Started With the Five Practices

Whether you are a newcomer to the five practices or someone who was using them prior to reading this book, practice and reflection will help you either begin or continue your journey to orchestrating productive mathematics discussions in your classroom. The key to making progress on this challenging work is to collaborate with and learn from other teachers. Ms. Stastny sums it up:

You have to collaborate with other people to see all of the different strategies because sometimes you miss them but somebody that you work with will see it and so actually collaborating and planning together is critical.

In the sections that follow, we provide some guidance on how to get started with or continue your work on the five practices.

Plan Lessons Collaboratively

Plan lessons with colleagues. While planning with teachers in your school or district may be optimal since you are working in the same context, given the technologies now available, your collaborators could live in another city, state, or country!

The three lessons that we featured in this book—Lasagna, Mr. Strong's Hike, Ms. Tyus's Markers—were planned collaboratively using the lesson-planning template shown in Appendix E and the monitoring chart shown in Appendix B. Working on the lessons in collaboration with colleagues provides teachers with access to a broader set of ideas regarding what can be learned from engaging in a task, the ways in which students could respond to the task, questions that will assess and advance student learning, and the solutions that will be most useful in ensuring that the mathematical ideas that are targeted in the lesson are made public. Such detailed collaborative lesson planning shares many of the characteristics of lesson study, a professional development approach that originated in Japan (Lewis, Perry, & Hurd, 2004).

The lesson-planning template supports the discussion by providing a set of questions that focus on key aspects of the lesson. While many lesson-planning tools focus on what the teacher is going to do during the lesson, the lesson-planning template shifts the focus to what students are going to do and how the teacher is going to support them. As Smith, Bill, and Hughes (2008) explain, "The goal is to move beyond the structural components often associated with lesson planning to a deeper consideration of how to advance students' mathematical understanding during the lesson" (p. 137).

While the five practices model addresses many of the key aspects of planning (shown in gray shading on the lesson-planning template in Appendix E), there are other aspects of planning that should also be considered, such as the prior knowledge that students will draw on in solving the task; the tools, resources, and materials that will be provided to students; how the task will be launched; what homework will be assigned that will extend the learning; and what you will take as evidence that students understand the ideas you have targeted. These additional questions help ensure that students have what they need to engage with the task and that the teacher is clear on what will count as evidence of learning.

You can find completed planning documents—lesson plans and monitoring charts—for each of the three lessons we have featured in this book at resources.corwin.com/5practices-elementary. You and your colleagues may find it helpful to review these plans in light of what you have learned about instruction in these classrooms and consider ways in which you think the planning supported teaching and learning. [See Huinker and Bill (2017) and Smith and Stein (2018) for additional examples of lesson plans created with the lesson-planning template.]

If taking on the entire lesson-planning template initially seems overwhelming, you can begin by focusing on a subset of the practices. While the five practices when taken together are greater than the sum of their parts—there is synergy in doing all of the practices—you could begin by focusing on setting goals, selecting tasks, and anticipating responses and questions. Engaging in these three practices as a first step will prepare you to support students by giving you clarity regarding what you are trying to accomplish, a task that will give students something challenging to work on, and questions to help students make progress. Once you are comfortable with the practices that can be done in advance, you can begin to add others to your repertoire.

Observe and Debrief Lessons

Engage in observations and analysis of teaching with one or more colleagues. The point of the observation is not to see if you can find evidence that the teacher used the five practices but rather to see if you can find evidence that students learned mathematics. The following questions could structure your observation and debriefing of the lesson:

- What are students doing and saying? Who are students talking with?
- Who is asking questions? What questions are being asked?
- Who is offering explanations? What counts as an explanation?
- What evidence is there of learning?

In a live observation of a five practices lesson, each observer could be given a copy of the completed monitoring tool to use to collect data on what students are doing and saying during the lesson. The annotated monitoring charts produced by observers can then be used to support an evidence-based discussion on what students were doing and saying during the lesson and the extent to which students appeared to learn what was intended.

Reflect on Your Lesson

Reflect on your lesson in close proximity to the completion of your lesson. At the end of each lesson, it is important for you to ask yourself whether you accomplished what you set out to do and what you take as evidence that students learned (or are in the process of learning) what was intended. While it is easy to feel satisfied with a lesson if there were no major disruptions and students were engaged with the task, this does not necessarily imply that students learned what was intended. It is important to press yourself to find evidence to support your beliefs about what occurred. A video recording of the class discussion, student work from the lesson, your completed monitoring chart, and/or an exit ticket given at the end of class are a few sources of data that can inform your reflection on student learning.

If you cannot find evidence that students learned what was intended, you need to decide your next steps. Reflection is only worth doing if you are willing to do something different as a result of what you learned. This may mean doing something different the next day, and/or it might mean changing some aspect of your instruction.

As we discussed in Chapter 6, in her reflection following the lesson, Ms. Tyus acknowledged that even though one of her lesson goals was for students to understand the strategy of rounding and compensating, this was something she would need to continue to work on since only one student used the strategy on the first problem and a few others tried it on the second problem. She explained,

> When we did the second problem, at least a few of them decided to try the rounding up to compensate. So that was good. I think that was successful since they wanted to do it on their own. Rounding and compensating is definitely something I want to go back to. With more practice, I believe all students or most students will be able to apply that strategy.

Through her reflection, Ms. Tyus was able to identify what she was going to do next to move the class forward. The honest appraisal of where students are in their thinking and understanding is key to ensure that each and every student learns mathematics with understanding.

Video Clubs

Start a video club at your school. Video clubs are opportunities for groups of teachers to come together to view and discuss videos of one another's teaching. These clubs could meet before or after school, during a designated shared planning period, or during a meeting of a professional learning community.

The purpose of video clubs is to help teachers learn to notice and make sense of significant events that occur in their classrooms and the classrooms of their colleagues (Sherin & Linsenmeier, 2011). Learning to notice through the use of video helps teachers learn where to focus their attention in the moment as events unfold in their classrooms. According to Sherin and Dyer (2017),

> Working with video can help shift how teachers make sense of what they notice. The reasons underlying student thinking are often complex and not easily observable on first glance. Video provides space for teachers to consider intricacies of student thinking in ways that are not always possible during the moment of instruction. (pp. 51, 53)

However, simply looking at any video, without guidance, does not guarantee that teachers will attend to aspects of instruction that matter most. Sherin and Linsenmeier (2011) provide a set of guidelines for using video, which support the development of teachers' professional vision (i.e., the ability to make sense of significant classroom events):

- Attend to the evidence: Focus on what did take place, not on what might have been.
- Attend to the details: Focus on specific aspects of classroom events (e.g., student thinking).
- Attend to what's typical: Focus on examples of everyday practice, not on exemplars. (p. 41)

It is also critical to capture video that will provide interesting fodder for discussion. If you and your colleagues are working on the five practices, you may find it particularly helpful to focus on capturing what happens during monitoring when the teacher interacts with students as they work on a task or on students' presentations when the teacher helps students make connections between strategies and to the mathematical ideas targeted in the lesson.

Sherin and Dyer (2017) provide suggestions on how to best capture video in your own classroom. These guidelines can help you consider where and when to video record so that you capture interesting interactions, where to place the video recorder, the value of annotation tools, and the lens through which your colleagues will view your video.

Using video recordings in this way can make it possible to *get inside* classrooms that would otherwise be impossible to visit, to collaborate with teachers near and far, to expand your professional networks, and to further develop your ability to notice and attend to classroom events.

Organize a Book Study

Organize a book study with colleagues either face-to-face or virtually around this book. Set up a regular meeting (weekly, biweekly, monthly) during which time you and your colleagues near or far can work through the chapters in this book together, discussing the Pause and Consider questions, the Analyzing the Work of Teaching activities, and the Linking the Five Practices to Your Own Instruction assignments. Through discussion of each chapter you can share your insights and reactions, personal experiences, and challenges and determine next steps.

Explore Additional Resources

Explore resources outside of this book that may give you additional tools to enact the practices. For example, in Chapter 6, we identify several resources that provide additional insights for holding students accountable during whole class discussions. In addition, throughout the book we have identified references that will provide more insight on particular topics.

 PAUSE AND CONSIDER

What will you do to get started? Who will be your collaborators?

Frequency and Timing of Use of the Five Practices Model

Two questions you may be asking at this point are "How often do I need to engage my students in a discussion using the five practices to support my work?" and "Is this something I should be doing every day?" While you do not have to engage students in discussions around challenging tasks every day, we do know from research that students need regular opportunities to engage in high-level thinking and reasoning—hence, once a unit, once a month, or once a quarter is not sufficient.

We recommend that you work toward engaging students in a whole class discussion around a *doing-mathematics* task once a week. To start, it is often productive to partner with one or more colleagues (face-to-face or virtually) and collaboratively plan lessons, even taking turns leading the planning effort. By collaborating with others, you will share the responsibility for creating lesson plans and at the same time benefit from a broader set of ideas about a specific lesson. Over time, you will compile a set of lesson plans that you can continue to refine and use in subsequent years. As your library of lessons grows, you can continue to add to it, increasing the number of lessons and relatedly the frequency with which you engage students in such discussions.

In addition to frequency, it is important to decide when working on a doing-mathematics task will be most beneficial to students. If you give such a task after you have taught a procedure that could be used to solve the task, you are likely to see many students doing what has been taught. When this occurs, there is limited opportunity for students to think and reason, and you will learn little about what students understand about mathematics. By contrast, by engaging students in solving a doing-mathematics task before they have learned specific procedures, they will have the opportunity to actually learn through their engagement in the task. In the process, you will learn how students are making sense of the situation and what it is they understand.

So what happens on days when you are not engaging students in a whole class discussion around a doing-mathematics task? Students will also need time to engage in other activities such as making sense of procedures and developing procedural fluency (for examples of what this might look like, see Huinker & Bill, 2017). While such activities may not require the same level of planning or discussion, we encourage you to look for ways to elicit and support student thinking regardless of the level and kind of activity in which you engage your students.

Conclusion

Making the five practices a central component of your instructional toolkit will not happen overnight. It is a personal journey that will take time and effort. As with any journey, taking someone along with you can enhance the experience by providing a sounding board when you need one as well as having someone with whom to share the joys and tribulations.

We encourage you to keep a journal throughout your journey, documenting the challenges you have faced, noting how you are dealing with them, and describing your personal victories. There may be times when you want to tweet about something you have discovered, write a blog about a victory or challenge, or post a request for assistance through an established network. Extending your professional network can provide you with additional insights and support.

Keep documentation from your completed lessons! This includes lesson plans, completed monitoring charts, photos or scanned images of student work, and exit tickets. These artifacts will provide evidence to support your reflection on the lesson immediately following the lesson, but they will also be useful when you are ready to teach the lesson again. You can begin your planning of a previously taught lesson by reviewing what occurred in previous implementations of the lesson—what went well, what did not, what should change, and what should remain the same. Rather than start planning from scratch each time, you can build on your prior work and gradually improve your lessons (and your teaching) over time. Through this cycle of planning, teaching, reflecting, and revising, you will build a storehouse of good lessons to which you can continue to add.

The best advice we can give you is *do not give up*! As a teacher commented,

> *Investing time and effort into learning/implementing the five practices is far from easy and has taken me a while (and I still have a long way to go) but is well worth the investment. Using them has created "magical moments" where students are engaged and truly learning from one another, discovering mathematics, and gaining insight into the mathematical process of discovery, connections, revision, etc. It truly shifts the responsibility and workload onto the students, allowing the teacher to become a facilitator and empower students to take responsibility for their learning. In [this] day and age, the five practices become an incredibly powerful tool to push students toward problem solving and critical thinking.* (Smith & Stein, 2018, p. 131)

Resources

National Council of Teachers of Mathematics:

> **Activities with Rigor and Coherence (ARCs):** Sequences of lessons (K–12) that address a specific mathematical topic and support the implementation of the eight effective mathematics teaching practices (NCTM, 2014) and the five practices for orchestrating productive discussions (Smith & Stein, 2018).
>
> http://www.nctm.org/ARCs/
>
> **Illuminations:** Lessons and activities (K–12) that are aligned with NCTM's *Principles and Standards for School Mathematics* (2000) and the National Governors Association Center for Best Practices & Council of Chief State School Officers' *Common Core State Standards for School Mathematics* (2010).
>
> http://illuminations.nctm.org/
>
> **Problems of the Week:** Tasks per grade band (K–2, 3–5, 6–8) and content strand (algebra, geometry, trigonometry, and calculus) plus solution strategies, rubrics, and teaching suggestions.
>
> http://www.nctm.org/Classroom-Resources/CRCC/Math-Forum-Problems-of-the-Week-Resources/

Inside Mathematics: A K–12 resource for educators that includes video lessons, problems of the month, performance assessment tasks, and a range of resources.

> http://www.insidemathematics.org/

Mathalicious: Real-world lessons, aligned to *Common Core State Standards*, designed to build proficiency in mathematical practices and build conceptual understanding; some lessons are free but access to all resources requires membership and a fee.

> http://www.mathalicious.com

Robert Kaplinsky's Lessons: Lessons for K–8, Algebra 1, Algebra 2, and geometry built around visual images and general questions that are intended to engage students in further exploration.

> http://robertkaplinsky.com/lessons/

Institute for Learning: Set of eight related lessons on decimal operations for Grade 5. Lesson guides include tasks, goals, anticipated solutions, assessing and advancing questions, and questions to ask during the whole class discussion in order to ensure that the key math ideas in a lesson are made salient.

> https://ifl.pitt.edu

APPENDIX B Monitoring Chart

Strategy	Assessing Questions	Advancing Questions	Who and What	Order

online resources

Download the Monitoring Chart from resources.corwin.com/5practices-elementary

APPENDIX C Ms. Tyus's Monitoring Chart

Solution Strategy	Assessing Questions	Advancing Questions	Who and What	Order
Solution A. Decompose and Recompose With Base Ten Blocks Student decomposes 69 using base ten blocks and then removes 4 tens. Student recomposes the 2 tens and 9 ones. Student writes 69 − 40 = 60 − 40 = 20 20 + 9 = 29	• Tell me about your thinking. • How do the blocks show what happened with the markers? • What does the 69 represent? The 40? • Why did you add 9 to 20?	• (If no equation) What equation could you use to represent your model of the task? • (If there is an equation) Can you show how the parts of your model connect to your equation? *Jacey 69 − 9 = 60 − 40 = 20*	*Jocelyn working on* *69 − 40* *69 − 40 = 29* *Landon, Eyosias, Emiliano, Allison, Oreo, Rylee, Laila, John, Devione* *69 + 40 = 29* *Markiya, Nancy*	*✱Most popular* *1st − Jocelyn share*
Solution B. Count Back by Tens on a Hundreds Chart Student starts at 69 on a hundreds chart, then jumps to 59, 49, 39, 29. Student writes 69 − 40 = 69 − 10 = 59 59 − 10 = 49 49 − 10 = 39 39 − 10 = 29	• Show me how you used the hundreds chart to explore the task. • How did you know how many jumps to make? • What does each jump represent? • What does the 69 represent? What does 59 represent? • How did you know which way to move on the hundreds chart?	• How could you use the hundreds chart to check your answer? • How could you use the hundreds chart to show that the difference between 69 and 29 is 40?	*DuJuan started at 69 and hopped 4 times to 29*	*2nd − DuJuan* *(compare with base 10)*

		Didn't see	
Solution C. Count Back by Tens on an Open Number Line Student draws a number line and labels the point 69. The student then makes 4 jumps back and marks 10 above each, stopping at 29. Student writes $69 - 40 = 29$	• Show me how you used the number line to explore the task. • Can you show me how you counted? • How did you know how many jumps to make? • Why did you go backward on the number line? • What does the "10" you wrote represent? • When you subtracted 40 from 69, why did only the tens place change?	• (If no equation) What equation could you use to represent your model for solving the task? • (If there is an equation) How is each part of your equation represented in your model?	
Solution D. Round and Compensate Student adds 1 to 69 to get 70. Student models 70 with base ten blocks or a base ten drawing and then removes 4 tens and has 3 tens left. Student then subtracts 1 from 30 to compensate for the 1 added initially. Student writes $69 - 40 =$ $69 + 1 = 70$ $70 - 40 = 30$ $30 - 1 = 29$	• Tell me about your thinking. • Why did you add 1 to 69? What does 70 represent? • I thought we had 69 markers. What does 70 mean? • Why did you subtract 1 from 30? What does this say about the number of markers Ms. Tyus gave away?	• What would be different about your strategy if Ms. Tyus started with 68 markers? • Would this strategy work on another problem? Try the next problem and see if you can use this strategy. • (If no model) Can you create a physical model or drawing that explains why this strategy works?	*Elsie 70-40-1 using 100s chart* *4th - Elsie*

Solution Strategy	Assessing Questions	Advancing Questions	*Who and What*	*Order*
Solution E. Subtract Tens, Then Subtract Ones Instead of Add Ones Student decomposes 69 and then subtracts 40. Student incorrectly subtracts 9 from the remaining 20 rather than recomposing 20 + 9. Student writes 69 − 40 = 60 − 40 = 20 20 − 9 = 11	• Tell me about your thinking. • What does the 69 represent? The 40? • What does the 9 represent? • Why did you take 9 away from 20?	• Can you show how your equations and model connect? • Where does 60 − 40 connect to the situation? Where does 20 − 9 connect to the situation?	*Didn't see*	
Solution F. Round Up, Subtract, and Then Add One Instead of Subtract One Student adds 1 to 69 to get 70. Student models 70 with base ten blocks or a base ten drawing and then removes 4 tens and has 3 tens left. Student then incorrectly adds 1 to 30. Student writes 69 − 40 = 69 + 1 = 70 70 − 40 = 30 30 + 1 = 31	• Tell me about your thinking. • Why did you add 1 to 69? What does 70 represent? • Why did you add 1 to 30? What does it mean about the number of markers Ms. Tyus gave away?	• Can you use your base ten model or drawing to show how many markers Ms. Tyus has at each step? • When we look at 70 − 40, is that going to be more or less than 69 − 40 and why?	*Didn't see*	

Students cannot get started.	• What is the problem asking you to find? • How many markers did you start with? • How many markers did Ms. Tyus give away to her friend?	• Can you draw a picture or use your base ten blocks to show what happened in the problem?	
			3rd – Leah
Other Problem #1 Audrey – models with lines Ethan – draws 69 circles Leah $69 - 40 = 29$ $6 - 4 = 2$ $9 - 0 = 9$ Problem #2 $79 - 9 = 70$ $70 - 30 = 40$ Jacey, Markiya, John	$79 - 30 = 49$ DuJuan, Jocelyn, Ethan, Eyosias, Emiliano, Landon, Oreo, Laila, Allison	$80 - 30 - 1 = 49$ Elsie, Nancy, Rylee, Audrey	

Chapin, S. H., O'Connor, C., & Anderson, N. C. (2009). *Classroom discussions: Using math talk to help students learn* (2nd ed.). Sausalito, CA: Math Solutions.

In this book, the authors describe five talk moves that they have found effective in supporting students' mathematical thinking and learning: revoicing, asking students to restate someone else's reasoning, asking students to apply their own reasoning to someone else's reasoning, prompting students for further participation, and using wait time. (See Smith & Stein, 2018, for an illustration of these moves in the context of a lesson.)

Herbel-Eisenmann, B., Cirillo, M., Steele, M. D., Otten, S., & Johnson, K. R. (2017). *Mathematics discourse in secondary classrooms: A practice-based resource for professional learning.* Sausalito, CA: Math Solutions.

This resource includes a set of discourse moves and tools that provide support for teachers to begin to change discourse practices in their classrooms. The videos and cases provide powerful images of discussion-based learning in middle and high school classrooms.

Kazemi, E., & Hintz, A. (2014). *Intentional talk: How to structure and lead productive mathematical discussions.* Portsmouth, NH: Stenhouse.

In this book, the authors provide a set of principles and a collection of tools that will help you in facilitating productive classroom discussions. The classroom vignettes provide images of productive talk in elementary classrooms.

Michaels, S., O'Conner, M. C., Hall, M. W., & Resnick, L. B. (2013). *Accountable Talk™ sourcebook: For classroom conversations that work.* Pittsburgh, PA: Institute for Learning, University of Pittsburgh.

This resource provides an overview of the three components of accountable talk—accountability to the community, accountability to rigorous thinking, and accountability to accurate knowledge—and a set of talk moves associated with each component. (Free download available at http://iflpartner.pitt.edu/index.php/educator_resources/accountable_talk)

Learning Goals (Residue)	Evidence
What understandings will students take away from this lesson?	What will students say, do, or produce that will provide evidence of their understandings?

Task	Instructional Support—Tools, Resources, Materials
What is the main activity that students will be working on in this lesson?	What tools or resources will be made available to give students entry to—and help them reason through—the activity?

Prior Knowledge	Task Launch
What prior knowledge and experience will students draw on in their work on this task? **Essential Questions** What are the essential questions that I want students to be able to answer over the course of the lesson?	How will you introduce and set up the task to ensure that students understand the task and can begin productive work, without diminishing the cognitive demand of the task?

Anticipated Solutions and Instructional Supports

What are the various ways that students might complete the activity? Be sure to include incorrect, correct, and incomplete solutions.

What questions might you ask students that will support their exploration of the activity and *bridge* between *what they did* and *what you want them to learn*? These questions should *assess* what a student currently knows and *advance* him or her toward the goals of the lesson. Be sure to consider questions that you will ask students who cannot get started as well as students who finish quickly.

Use the monitoring chart to provide the details related to Anticipated Solutions and Instructional Supports.

Sharing and Discussing the Task

Selecting and Sequencing	Connecting Responses
Which solutions do you want students to share during the lesson? In what order? Why?	What specific questions will you ask so that students— • make sense of the mathematical ideas that you want them to learn? • make connections among the different strategies/solutions that are presented?

Homework/Assessment

What will you ask students to do that will allow you to determine what they learned and what they understand?

Connections to the five practices are noted by the gray shading.

References

Aguirre, J., Herbel-Eisenmann, B., Celedon-Pattichis, S., Civil, M., Wilkerson, T., Stephan, M., Pape, S., & Clements, D. H. (2017). Equity within mathematics education research as a political act: Moving from choice to intentional collective professional responsibility. *Journal for Research in Mathematics Education*, *48*(2), 124–147.

Aguirre, J., Mayfield-Ingram, K., & Martin, D. (2013). *The impact of identity in K–8 mathematics: Rethinking equity-based practices.* Reston, VA: National Council of Teachers of Mathematics.

Arbaugh, F., Smith, M. S., Boyle, J. D., Stylianides, G. J., & Steele, M. D. (2018). *We reason and we prove: Putting critical skills at the heart of your mathematics teaching.* Thousand Oaks, CA: Corwin.

Ball, D. L., Lubienski, S. T., & Mewborn, D. S. (2001). Research on teaching mathematics: The unsolved problem of teachers' mathematical knowledge. *Handbook of Research on Teaching*, *4*, 433–456.

Blanton, M., Brizuela, B. M., Gardiner, A. M., Sawrey, K., & Newman-Owens, A. (2015). A learning trajectory in 6-year-olds' thinking about generalizing functional relationships. *Journal for Research in Mathematics Education*, *46*(5), 511–558.

Blanton, M. L., & Kaput, J. J. (2003). Developing elementary teachers' "algebra eyes and ears." *Teaching Children Mathematics*, *10*(2), 70–77.

Boaler, J., & Brodie, K. (2004). The importance, nature, and impact of teacher questions. In D. E. McDougall & J. A. Ross (Eds.), *Proceedings of the twenty-sixth annual meeting of the North American Chapter of the International Group for the Psychology of Mathematics Education* (Vol. 2, pp. 774–790). Toronto: Ontario Institute for Studies in Education at the University of Toronto.

Boaler, J., & Humphreys, C. (2005). *Connecting mathematical ideas: Middle school video cases to support teaching and learning.* Portsmouth, NH: Heinemann.

Boaler, J., & Staples, M. (2008). Creating mathematical futures through an equitable teaching approach: The case of Railside School. *Teachers College Record*, *110*(3), 608–645.

Boston, M. D., & Wilhelm, A. G. (2017). Middle school mathematics instruction in instructionally focused urban districts. *Urban Education*, *52*(7), 829–861.

Boyle, J. D., & Kaiser, S. B. (2017). Collaborative planning as a process. *Mathematics Teaching in the Middle School*, *22*(7), 407–411.

Burns, M. (2015, September 9). Using children's literature to teach math. Retrieved from http://www.marilynburnsmathblog.com/using-childrens-literature-to-teach-math/

Cartier, J. L., Smith, M. S., Stein, M. K., & Ross, D. K. (2013). *Practices for orchestrating productive science discussions.* Reston, VA: National Council of Teachers of Mathematics.

Chapin, S. H., O'Connor, C. & Anderson, N. C. (2009). *Classroom discussions: Using math talk to help students learn, Grades K–6.* Sausalito, CA: Math Solutions.

Driscoll, M. J. (1999). *Fostering algebraic thinking: A guide for teachers, Grades 6–10*. Portsmouth, NH: Heinemann.

Falkner, K., Levi, L., & Carpenter, T. (1999). Children's understanding of equality: A foundation for algebra. *Teaching Children Mathematics, 6*, 232–236.

Felton-Koestler, M. (2016). Common Core confusion about modeling. *Teaching Children Mathematics, 23*(5), 269–272.

Franke, M. L., Webb, N. M., Chan, A. G., Ing, M., Freund, D., & Battey, D. (2009). Teacher questioning to elicit students' mathematical thinking in elementary school classrooms. *Journal of Teacher Education, 60*(4), 380–392.

Friel, S. N., & Markworth, K. A. (2009). A framework for analyzing geometric pattern tasks. *Mathematics Teaching in the Middle School, 15*(1), 24–33.

Hatano, G., & Inagaki, K. (1991). Sharing cognition through collective comprehension activity. In L. B. Resnick, J. M. Levine, & S. D. Teasley (Eds.), *Perspectives on socially shared cognition* (pp. 331–348). Washington, DC: American Psychological Association.

Herbel-Eisenmann, B., Cirillo, M., Steele, M. D., Otten, S., & Johnson, K. R. (2017). *Mathematics discourse in secondary classrooms: A practice-based resource for professional learning*. Sausalito, CA: Math Solutions.

Hiebert, J., Ballimore, R., & Stigler, J. W. (2003). The new heroes of teaching. *Education Week, 23*(10), 42, 56.

Hiebert, J., Morris, A. K., Berk, D., & Jansen, A. (2007). Preparing teachers to learn from teaching. *Journal of Teacher Education, 58*(1), 47–61.

Hiebert, J., & Wearne, D. (1993). Instructional tasks, classroom discourse, and students' learning in second-grade arithmetic. *American Educational Research Journal, 30*(2), 393–425.

Horn, I. S. (2012). *Strength in numbers: Collaborative learning in secondary mathematics*. Reston, VA: National Council of Teachers of Mathematics.

Horn, I. S. (2017). *Motivated: Designing mathematics classrooms where students want to join*. Portsmouth, NH: Heinemann.

Hufferd-Ackles, K., Fuson, K. C., & Sherin, M. G. (2015). The math-talk learning community: Looking back and looking ahead. In E. A. Silver & P. A. Kenney (Eds.), *Lessons learned from research: Vol. 1. Useful and useable research related to core mathematical practices* (pp. 125–134). Reston, VA: National Council of Teachers of Mathematics.

Huinker, D., & Bill, V. (2017). *Taking action: Implementing effective mathematics teaching practices K–Grade 5*. Reston, VA: National Council of Teachers of Mathematics.

Hung, M. (2015). Talking circles promote equitable discourse. *Mathematics Teacher, 109*(4), 256–260.

Hunt, J., & Stein, M. K. (forthcoming). Constructing goals for student learning through conversation. *Mathematics Teaching in the Middle School*.

Imm, K. L., Stylianou, D. A., & Chae, N. (2008). Student representations at the center: Promoting classroom equity. *Mathematics Teaching in the Middle School, 13*(8), 458–463.

Jackson, K. J., Shahan, E. C., Gibbons, L. K., & Cobb, P. A. (2012). Launching complex tasks. *Mathematics Teaching in the Middle School, 18*(1), 24–29.

Jacobs, V. R., & Philipp, R. A. (2010). Supporting children's problem solving. *Teaching Children Mathematics, 17*(2), 98–105.

Jansen, A., Cooper, B., Vascellaro, S., & Wandless, P. (2017). Rough-draft talk in mathematics classrooms. *Mathematics Teaching in the Middle School, 22*(5), 304–307.

Jilk, L. M. (2016). Supporting teacher noticing of students' mathematical strengths. *Mathematics Teacher Educator, 4*(2), 188–199.

Kazemi, E., Gibbons, L. K., Lomax, K., & Franke, M. L. (2016). Listening to and learning from student thinking. *Teaching Children Mathematics, 23*(3), 182–190.

Kazemi, E., & Hintz, A. (2014). *Intentional talk: How to structure and lead productive mathematical discussions.* Portsmouth, NH: Stenhouse.

Lambert, R., & Stylianou, D. A. (2013). Posing cognitively demanding tasks to all students. *Mathematics Teaching in the Middle School, 18*(8), 500–506.

Lampert, M., & Graziani, F. (2009). Instructional activities as a tool for teachers' and teacher educators' learning. *The Elementary School Journal, 109*(5), 491–509.

Leatham, K. R., Peterson, B. E., Stockero, S. L., & Van Zoest, L. R. (2015). Conceptualizing mathematically significant pedagogical opportunities to build on student thinking. *Journal for Research in Mathematics Education, 46*(1), 88–124.

Leavy, A., Hourigan, M., & McMahon, Á. (2013). Early understanding of equality. *Teaching Children Mathematics, 20*(4), 246–252.

Lewis, C., Perry, R., & Hurd, J. (2004). A deeper look at lesson study. *Educational Leadership, 61*(5), 18.

Louie, N. L. (2017). The culture of exclusion in mathematics education and its persistence in equity-oriented teaching. *Journal for Research in Mathematics Education, 48*(5), 488–519.

Marshall, A. M., Superfine, A. C., & Canty, R. S. (2010). Star students make connections. *Teaching Children Mathematics, 17*(1), 39–47.

Martin, D. B., Gholson, M. L., & Leonard, J. (2010). Mathematics as gatekeeper: Power and privilege in the production of knowledge. *Journal of Urban Mathematics Education, 3*(2), 12–24.

Michaels, S., O'Conner, M. C., Hall, M. W., & Resnick, L. B. (2013). *Accountable Talk™ sourcebook: For classroom conversations that work.* Pittsburgh, PA: Institute for Learning, University of Pittsburgh.

Mills, V. L. (2014). Mathematical goals: The alpha and omega of effective practice. *NCSM Summer Newletter, 44*(4), 2–3.

Monroe, E. E., Young, T. A., Fuentes, D. S., & Dial, O. H. (2018). *Deepening students' mathematical understanding with children's literature*. Reston, VA: National Council of Teachers of Mathematics.

Murata, A., & Fuson, K. (2006). Teaching as assisting individual constructive paths within an interdependent class learning zone: Japanese first graders learning to add using 10. *Journal for Research in Mathematics Education, 37*(5), 421–456.

Nasir, N. S., McKinney de Royston, M., O'Connor, K., & Wischnia, S. (2017). Knowing about racial stereotypes versus believing them. *Urban Education, 52*(4), 491–524.

National Council of Teachers of Mathematics. (2000). *Principles and standards for school mathematics*. Reston, VA: Author.

National Council of Teachers of Mathematics. (2014). *Principles to actions: Ensuring mathematical success for all*. Reston, VA: Author.

National Governors Association Center for Best Practices & Council of Chief State School Officers. (2010). *Common core state standards for mathematics*. Washington, DC: Author.

Polya, G. (2014). *How to solve it: A new aspect of mathematical method*. Princeton, NJ: Princeton University Press.

Reinhart, S. C. (2000). Never say anything a kid can say. *Mathematics Teaching in the Middle School, 5*(8), 478–483.

Santagata, R., & Bray, W. (2016). Professional development processes that promote teacher change: The case of a video-based program focused on leveraging students' mathematical errors. *Professional Development in Education, 42*(4), 547–568.

Schukajlow, S., & Krug, A. (2014). Do multiple solutions matter? Prompting multiple solutions, interest, competence, and autonomy. *Journal for Research in Mathematics Education, 45*(4), 497–533.

Senk, S. L., & Thompson, D. R. (Eds.). (2003). *Standards-based school mathematics curricula: What are they? What do students learn?* Mahwah, NJ: Lawrence Erlbaum Associates.

Shah, N. (2017). Race, ideology, and academic ability: A relational analysis of racial narratives in mathematics. *Teachers College Record, 119*(7), 1–42.

Sherin, M. G., & Dyer, E. B. (2017). Teacher self-captured video: Learning to see. *Phi Delta Kappan, 98*(7), 49–54.

Sherin, M. G., & Linsenmeier, K. A. (2011). Pause, rewind, reflect: Video clubs throw open the classroom doors. *The Learning Professional, 32*(5), 38.

Sherin, M. G., & van Es, E. A. (2009). Effects of video club participation on teachers' professional vision. *Journal of Teacher Education, 60*(1), 20–37.

Slobodkina, E. (1940). *Caps for sale: A tale of a peddler, some monkeys and their monkey business*. New York, NY: W. R. Scott.

Smith, M. S. (2001). *Practice-based professional development for teachers of mathematics*. Reston, VA: National Council of Teachers of Mathematics.

Smith, M., Bill, V., & Hughes, E. (2008). Thinking through a lesson protocol: A key for successfully implementing high-level tasks. *Mathematics Teaching in the Middle School*, *14*(3), 132–138.

Smith, M. S., & Sherin, M. G. (2019). *The five practices in practice: Successfully orchestrating mathematics discussions in your middle school classroom*. Thousand Oaks, CA: Corwin.

Smith, M. S., Steele, M. D., & Raith, M. L. (2017). *Taking action: Implementing effective mathematics teaching practices in Grades 6–8*. Reston, VA: National Council of Teachers of Mathematics.

Smith, M. S., & Stein, M. K. (1998). Selecting and creating mathematical tasks: From research to practice. *Mathematics Teaching in the Middle School*, *3*(5), 344–350.

Smith, M. S., & Stein, M. K. (2011). *5 practices for orchestrating productive mathematics discussions*. Reston, VA: National Council of Teachers of Mathematics.

Smith, M. S., & Stein, M. K. (2018). *5 practices for orchestrating productive mathematics discussions* (2nd ed.). Reston, VA: National Council of Teachers of Mathematics.

Sorto, M. A., & Bower, R. S. G. (2017). Quality of instruction in linguistically diverse classrooms: It matters! In A. Fernandes, S. Crespo, & M. Civil (Eds.), *Access & equity: Promoting high-quality mathematics* (pp. 27–40). Reston, VA: National Council of Teachers of Mathematics.

Stein, M. K., Grover, B. W., & Henningsen, M. (1996). Building student capacity for mathematical thinking and reasoning: An analysis of mathematical tasks used in reform classrooms. *American Educational Research Journal*, *33*(2), 455–488.

Stein, M. K., & Lane, S. (1996). Instructional tasks and the development of student capacity to think and reason: An analysis of the relationship between teaching and learning in a reform mathematics project. *Educational Research and Evaluation*, *2*(1), 50–80.

Stein, M. K., Smith, M. S., Henningsen, M., & Silver, E. A. (2009). *Implementing standards-based mathematics instruction: A casebook for professional development* (2nd ed.). New York, NY: Teachers College Press.

Stigler, J. W., & Hiebert, J. (2004). Improving mathematics teaching. *Educational Leadership*, *61*(5), 12–17.

Suh, J. M., Johnston, C., Jamieson, S., & Mills, M. (2008). Promoting decimal number sense and representational fluency. *Mathematics Teaching in the Middle School*, *14*(1), 44–50.

Turner, E. E., & Celedón-Pattichis, S. (2011). Mathematical problem solving among Latina/o kindergartners: An analysis of opportunities to learn. *Journal of Latinos and Education*, *10*(2), 146–169.

Warshauer, H. K. (2015). Productive struggle in middle school mathematics classrooms. *Journal of Mathematics Teacher Education*, *17*(4), 375–399.

Zbiek, R., & Shimizu, J. (2005). Multiple solutions: More paths to an end or more opportunities to learn mathematics. *Mathematics Teacher*, *99*(4), 279–287.

Index

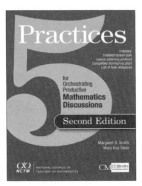
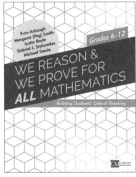
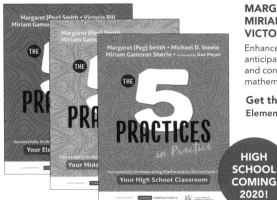

ALL students should have the opportunity to be successful in mathematics!

Trusted experts in mathematics education offer clear and practical guidance to help students move from surface to deep mathematical understanding, from procedural to conceptual learning, and from rote memorization to true comprehension. Through books, videos, consulting, and online tools, we offer a truly blended learning experience that helps you demystify mathematics for students.

JOHN HATTIE, DOUGLAS FISHER, NANCY FREY, LINDA M. GOJAK, SARA DELANO MOORE, WILLIAM MELLMAN

The what, when, and how of teaching practices that evidence shows work best for student learning in mathematics.

Grades K–12

JOHN ALMARODE, DOUGLAS FISHER, JOSEPH ASSOF, SARA DELANO MOORE, KATERI THUNDER, JOHN HATTIE, NANCY FREY

In this sequel to the best-selling *Visible Learning for Mathematics*, these grade-banded companions show Visible Learning strategies in action in Grades K–2, 3–5, 6–8, and high school mathematics classrooms.

Grades K–2, 3–5, 6–8, and High School

BETH MCCORD KOBETT, RUTH HARBIN MILES, LOIS A. WILLIAMS

Plan math lessons that enhance the purpose, rigor, and coherence of state standards and address the unique learning needs of your individual students.

Grades K–2, 3–5, and 6–8

JOHN SANGIOVANNI, JENNIFER ROSE NOVAK

Armed with hundreds of standards-aligned mathematics tasks and analysis of student work, this series helps you identify misconceptions, fill in common learning gaps, and decide your next instructional moves.

Grades K–2, 3–5, and 6–8

A SAGE Publishing Company

Helping educators make the greatest impact

CORWIN HAS ONE MISSION: to enhance education through intentional professional learning.

We build long-term relationships with our authors, educators, clients, and associations who partner with us to develop and continuously improve the best evidence-based practices that establish and support lifelong learning.

The National Council of Teachers of Mathematics supports and advocates for the highest-quality mathematics teaching and learning for each and every student.